Despite the waves of re-engineering, there is still a gap ⟨...⟩ offered by information technology and the progress of business transformation. New forms of information technology offer an increasing variety of network-based applications that range from groupware to electronic commerce, but its applications lack a sound understanding of the link between organisational processes, information and technology. This book provides a new set of concepts and methods to design new forms of business organisations around the latest network infrastructures. Professor Ciborra uses the principles of institutional economics to propose reforms of the relationships with suppliers, customers, strategic partners, and internal work organisation, based on a different mix of three basic organisational forms: teams, markets and hierarchies. Information technology can indeed be harnessed to shape businesses and markets so as to increase the transparency of markets, the agility of hierarchies, and the effectiveness and quality of working life of teams.

Teams, markets and systems

Teams, markets and systems

Business innovation and information technology

Claudio U. Ciborra
Università di Bologna, Italy
Theseus Institute, France

CAMBRIDGE
UNIVERSITY PRESS

PUBLISHED BY THE PRESS SYNDICATE OF THE UNIVERSITY OF CAMBRIDGE
The Pitt Building, Trumpington Street, Cambridge CB2 1RP, United Kingdom

CAMBRIDGE UNIVERSITY PRESS
The Edinburgh Building, Cambridge CB2 2RU, United Kingdom
40 West 20th Street, New York, NY 10011-4211, USA
10 Stamford Road, Oakleigh, Melbourne 3166, Australia

First published 1993
Reprinted 1995
First paperback edition published 1996

Printed in the United Kingdom at the University Press, Cambridge

Typeset in Times 10/12 pt

*A catalogue record for this book is available from
the British Library*

Library of Congress cataloguing in publication data

Ciborra, Claudio.
Teams, markets and systems:
business innovation and information technology / Claudio U. Ciborra.
      p.   cm.
Includes bibliographical references and index.
ISBN 0 521 40463 0
1. Information systems. 2. Technological innovations – Economic aspects.
3. Work groups. 4. Organizational change. 5. Transaction costs. I. Title.
HD31.C532   1992
302.3'5 – dc20   92–23172   CIP

ISBN 0 521 40463 0 hardback
ISBN 0 521 57465 X paperback

SE

Contents

Preface to the paperback edition

Since the conception of this book re-engineering has come, developed and is leaving amidst dismalness and disillusion. It has been the predictable trajectory of business innovation approaches and methodologies that are not able to capitalise at least on a minimum theory of organisations. The teams & markets framework, based on a broad understanding of the transaction-cost theory, pays due consideration to the theory of the firm, as the minimal basis to put forward, and to prescribe, rational designs for reforming organisations and their information systems. The great contributions of the Noble Prizewinners R. Coase (see Coase (1937)) and O. E. Williamson (1975; 1985) have provided us with contractual and informational explanations of why firms exist and are shaped the way they are. Any systems design or re-engineering methodology that does not base itself on an effective understanding of the links between processes, people and information is condemned to fail: the transaction-cost approach provides such an understanding, and this book was written to extend the original paradigm to the domain of information technology.

In this new edition, a few local changed have been introduced, especially in the technology sections, where the future tense of the verbs has been shifted to the present tense. The diffusion of innovations such as Internet, World Wide Web, Netscape, Intranets and Java is supporting the idea that the information system of any organisation should be regarded as 'the network of information flows needed to create, set up, control and maintain the organisation's constituent contracts' (Ciborra (1981)).

But besides updating text and bibliography, and correcting a few mistakes, this new Preface offers an opportunity to review, albeit cursorily, where we stand with the ideas and approaches set forth in the book. We split our update, considering both the reinforcement and support of the framework, and its emerging critiques. Both areas continue to provide exciting research and application questions.

On the constructive side, we can identify progress in teamwork and groupware diffusion; in electronic commerce models and technologies; and, more in general, progress in our ideas about organisational reconfiguration and recombination.

A 'deconstructivist' perspective emphasises instead the limited scope of a pure efficiency view of organisations; the limits to learning that hamper the implementation of effective designs of processes and systems; and finally, the gaps of a narrowly rational view of organisational behaviour, and organisations in general. We explore each direction, pointing to the links with the ideas as originally presented in the book, new relevant literature and an emerging research agenda.

The teams & markets approach suggests that information technology can be used to enable the design of organisations based on a new mix of teams arrangements and market-like mechanisms, replacing existing hierarchies. The advantage of the new mix is given simultaneously by a higher level of efficiency, more flexibility and opportunities for a better quality of working life. This unique approach avoids the narrow focus on efficiency of re-engineering (not supported by any robust theory of economic organisation); or the utopian preference for more democratic, computer-based organisations, which lacks a sound understanding of the economics of co-operation. Moreover, the teams & markets approach provides a language and a set of concepts to understand and to be more specific about the growing importance of the practice of building 'virtual organisations' and telework, as pointed out in the Introduction.

Recent developments in technology and organisation design reinforce these trends. Consider, first, teams and relevant IT support. The diffusion of successful software for collaborative work, such as Lotus Notes, and, more in general, the design of information systems built on open architectures and operating environment such as Intranets, multiply the opportunities for implementing information systems that facilitate teamwork in a variety of organisational settings. A number of small and large firms are exploiting such new opportunities. The very case described in chapter 11 (groupware for the flight crew) has indeed taken off, after a period of latency, as a bundle of network services available to the flight crews of British Airways using a global network service provider: the new system is called Charon. Progress on electronic markets has been equally impressive. To date, the French Minitel (see chapter 9) is probably still the largest electronic market on the globe (though limited to one country), but Internet and Netscape, and the growth of EDI, are showing the true potential for global electronic markets. The millions of Internet users and the smaller but growing base of Web sites and Web users are establishing a platform that anticipates the more sophisticated services of the future information superhighways. On such markets electronic, multimedia catalogues are already available, and, though still in the prototyping stage, intelligent software agents help operators to search, select and filter market offers. Information superhighways will sustain the trend towards 'virtual value chains' connecting customers, suppliers and new intermediaries (see chapters 5 and 6; Benjamin and Wigand (1995)).

More in general, the trends in industrial restructuring that bring about new mixes of teams and markets can be identified in many contemporary exercises of reconfiguring business processes (see chapter 9); for example, one can mention the growing importance of outsourcing (which in our language can be analysed as a transaction-cost-driven make-or-buy choice); or, the introduction of team-based work organisation in the latest manufacturing plants (such as Fiat's new Melfi plant in Southern Italy, where high levels of production automation are combined with semi-autonomous work groups (see chapter 2 and Ciborra, Patriotta and Erlichen (1995))). Similar trends, in different organisational contexts, can be found in R&D where large multinationals, for example in the pharmaceutical industry, are introducing international teams alongside a redesign of the workflow for new product development.

Finally, the underlying common theme emerging out of the continuous recombination and restructuring of organisations, coupled with the growing diffusion of groupware and Internet, is that of knowledge management, as correctly predicted by P. Strassmann a few years ago (see the Introduction). In particular, the powerful navigation tools available over networks and distributed databases envisage the opportunity for building IS as veritable 'corporate memories', i.e. common repositories of organisational knowledge (Stein and Zwass (1995); Ackerman and Malone (1990)). This sort of development would allow for a further widening of the scope for recombining teams & markets arrangements in substitution for the hierarchy and, at the limit, would enhance the diffusion of organisational forms that are ephemeral, temporary, improvised and revisable (Lanzara (1983); Weick (1993a); Ciborra (1996a)). These new organisations can become platforms for yet faster recombinations of resources, i.e. more powerful engines of economic growth (Romer (1990)).

To be sure, a new Preface is not only an occasion for celebration, but also one for critical reflection on the theoretical and practical limitations of the teams & markets approach (see especially chapters 1 and 11). In fact, an exercise of 'deconstruction' of the original framework points out dilemmas in implementation and theoretical impasses.

Consider, first, the diffusion of teamwork accompanied by groupware. Ciborra (1996b) concludes an empirical study of more than fifteen applications of groupware in large organisations worldwide by stating that beyond the contrasts between managerial or critical discourses, we do not know what groupware is in large organisations today: that is, the essence and the meaning of the development and use of this technology in complex organisational contexts escapes us. Note that the word groupware includes two distinct elements: a socio-organisational one: the 'group', a collective way of working, collaboration, the intimacy of staying together and sharing; and a technical one, the 'ware', the artefact and the tool. Groupware connects the two worlds, the one of human, collective endeavour, and the artificial one of the artefact. So much for the etymology. But, are these two worlds actually connected in the organisations adopting the groupware systems? Not always.

Even within the same company, in some cases the groupware applications become the backbone of collective work, while in other cases the link is problematic or nonexistent. Success or failure seems to be path-dependent, and the path is uniquely traced by looking at the interplay in time of several independent factors. Beyond the reach and scope of a sound theoretical understanding of organisations and systems, it seems that the actual implementation of groupware can be better described as 'hosting'. Because of the almost ubiquitous presence of substitutes, and the highly informal and idiosyncratic 'chemistry' of groupworking, it takes courage and a great deal of adaptation for an organisation to adopt, or to host, the new, strange technology. To be sure, groupware is relatively easy to use (at least more so than traditional IS). But empirical evidence seems to show that also the reverse is true; that is: groupware applications can degenerate into traditional IS; groups in the bureaucratic organisation may have legitimate reasons not to share knowledge through the system, for example for fear of being controlled; or they may lack the economic incentives to feed the system, and so on. Thus, adoption of groupware is far from being straightforward and automatic (Grudin (1988)). When organisation members look at the new application as a powerful artefact for communicating, most of them would agree that it is a superior artefact, compared with the traditional IS they have at their disposal. But, just looking at a hammer and its qualities, like shape, weight and balance, is something different from 'hammering' in a fluently natural and effective way. In many cases, the shift from groupware as a package or an infrastructure to 'group-waring' is quite difficult, or even seems to prove to be impossible. Intellectual hospitality may turn then into practical indifference, or even hostility towards the strange, new technology.

Heidegger (1977) described the essence of the 'moderne Technik' as highly ambiguous. Far from being just a docile tool that can be harnessed by mankind, technology imposes its own structure ('Gestell') over people and nature, exploiting them in ways that potentially are out of human control. And the two dimensions cannot be separated. Technology can unveil the essence of being human, but at the same time its frantic and mindless deployment represents the danger of hiding and hindering the freedom of being human. In brief, the cases collected in our empirical research (Ciborra (1996b)) seem to indicate that groupware in modern organisations is ambiguous. On the one hand, systems like videoconferencing enable improved ways of communicating, especially for geographically dispersed teams in R&D; or, software like Lotus Notes allows an extremely open way to share, store and access information, by remaining open to whatever reconfiguration the organisation adopting it needs to implement. On the other hand, users are wary of availing themselves of the transparency brought in by the new tool: they fear the possibility of being subjected to hierarchical control enhanced by the system; thus, they do not use public 'work in progress' files, because they are afraid that managers could peek into them. Or, applications designed to support communicating are perceived as a means for headquarters to centralise the distribution of information to the affiliates. In other instances, the opportunities offered by the applications to share knowledge for the benefit of the user community are simply ignored by the individual, who finds no incentives, and perhaps only disadvantages, in sharing his/her knowledge; or, subgroups in the organisation may use public information available through the system to play opportunistic games in project management. Systems conceived to enhance conviviality and collaboration sometimes generate (unexpectedly) subtle forms of hostility, not extremely severe or open, but sufficient to slow down the innovation and undermine its potential.

Only when care, absorbed coping with the task, the workflow and the supporting technology are allowed to unfold do the more or less overt forms of fear and resistance recede, as successful applications seem to show. To be sure, it must be noted that if the technology were totally 'disambiguated' and flat in delivering its impacts and consequences, that is, once any reason for fear and hostility be eradicated, 'hosting' the technology would amount for the organisation to a purely formal behaviour. Hospitality, to be of any value, feeds upon the strangeness of the person or object hosted. Otherwise, it is just passive, detached and formal adaptation. Indeed, the latter is the world where technologies are just objects, knowledge is data, work is business process, and actors are emotionless executors who risk nothing and have to adapt to changes rationally planned for them. It is the 'de-worlded' world of business re-engineering models, where designers, consultants and managers juggle around boxes and flows, to come up with the solution that the rationality criteria of the moment legitimise: lean production; just-in-time; computer-supported workflows; and so on. The intricacies and uncertainties of hospitality, hostility and ambiguity are ruled out of such a de-worlded world of abstract organisations, but so is the 'organisingness' of everyday life populated by real people and not abstract decision-makers. It is precisely such 'organisingness' that is the necessary and effective component that makes the groupware applications tick and work. 'Organisingness' is made of absorbed coping, care, being there amidst ambiguity, intimacy, performing hospitality as well as tamed hostility towards what the new is disclosing. Research in this field appears more and more to be an essential complement to any form of modelling of organisations and systems.

A further critique to the whole orientation to efficiency pursued by the transaction theory and the need for a fresher approach, and possibly a new language, is advocated by Normann and Ramirez (1995). Their framework, which goes beyond the notion of value chain seen as a sequence of transactions between separable organisational units, focalises on the processes of value creation through co-production among different organisations. The firm is not just a 'ring' in the value chain, but rather the centre of a complex web or 'value constellation', through which goods and services are produced to improve the customer's value-adding processes. Alliances, and complex relationships for sharing knowledge and production activities, enrich the relationships between organisations. The notion of transaction, and its costs, appears to be too narrowly conceived: its economising seems to be more focused on the job of 'saving' value, rather than on the mission of creating a new one. To wit, any transaction can be looked at as a complex social relationship that carries informational 'codings'. These can multiply the possibilities of deploying the same transaction for many different purposes to add value. Strategic applications of information technology have shown all this to be feasible and successful (see chapters 9 and 11).

The study of co-production and value constellation can also illustrate how by using IT in transacting one can generate knowledge (codings) to create new value. This goes beyond the process of knowledge management and leads to that of innovation and knowledge creation as the true source of competitive advantage (Nonaka and Takeuchi (1995)). From this perspective the application of the transaction-costs theory to the analysis and design of electronic markets appears to be limited, if carried out *sensu strictu*. The need for a broader perspective, also advocated through the case study of chapter 11, is still urgent, and the contributions by authors like Nonaka, Takeuchi, Normann and Ramirez help us in this new fascinating research and application domain. Again, while transaction-costs theory can provide a solid foundation, but needs to be integrated and possibly surpassed, re-engineering models are mute on such developments, and can hardly be utilised even as suggestive design ideas.

In chapter 1 a model of 'adaptive rationality' is presented which, through the notion of formative context as a background condition for human action, puts forward the hypothesis of a dual structure of knowledge. Reference to this kind of cognitive structure of the human agent, specifically the organisational man, can be used to shed a critical light on the transaction-costs theory (Ciborra (1989; 1990; 1991)). The model of adaptive rationality attempts to explain change and transformation, under what circumstances it takes place and under what conditions.

Now, one can say that while transaction-costs economics is preoccupied, in both descriptive and prescriptive terms, with the efficiency differentials of alternative organisational forms, it assumes implicitly that a shift from one form to another can be obtained in a frictionless fashion, based on the rational choice of the actors: if circumstances require it, and agents are aware of the need to change, they will do so, knowing that inertia will be fatal under competitive market conditions. The industrial landscape shows instead that adaptability occurs unevenly, and lack of information on the necessity to change explains failure to adapt only in part. Many times, instead, organisations know they have to change, but they fail to do so (Argyris and Schon (1996)). Defensive routines, power games, inertial behaviour of various sorts, are the causes of 'transition costs'. One could put forward the critique that *transaction*-costs economics largely assumes *transition* costs to be zero, that is, it lacks a systematic treatment of organisational inertia. Now, both Ciborra (1989) and more recently Scarborough (1995) and Ghoshal and Moran (1996) suggest that this does not happen by chance, but is rooted in the very basic assumptions on which Williamson's version of Institutional Economics is based, in particular the notion of *opportunism*. Ghoshal and Moran indicate that Williamson fails to distinguish between opportunism as an attitude and as a behaviour: in other words, is opportunism an inclination or just the characterisation of a situation-dependent economic action? In the first case, opportunism would be a constant human trait: a scenario that Williamson seems to reject – see for example Williamson (1985). Or is it an attitude that depends upon the situation, and can vary and evolve, and thus can be modified by the agents' learning? On the latter scenario Williamson is silent, and his theory, especially when interpreted normatively, seems to lean towards the former conception. Relatedly, Ciborra (1989) explores a further issue: is the opportunist organisational man a 'wanton', able to react immediately to incoming signals, adjusting his preferences and calculating both legal and illicit means to achieve his goals, or shouldn't we admit that, more in line with human nature as we know it (Knight (1921)), he is influenced, because of the dual knowledge structure, by cognitive and behavioural processes of weakness of will, self-deception and inner conflicts that may hamper adaptive decision-making? What if the design of organisations carried out following the principles of transaction-costs economics, in particular the tenet according to which control mechanisms should be set up to keep in check the hazards of opportunism, actually reinforces such inner conflicts and self-deception impeding an individual's learning, to engage in new behaviour when circumstances require it? What if opportunism is just another face of defensive, anti-learning behaviour (Ciborra (1989)), and organisational control mechanisms, designed to curb it, end up reinforcing such self-defensive routines, so that transaction-costs economics ends up being 'bad for practice' (Ghoshal and Moran (1996)) at least for organisations and individual that have to change? Efficient survival of the organisational *status quo* would be granted by the transaction-costs economising, but flexibility in the face of environmental turbulence would be an open design issue. The challenge for transaction-costs theory is then to show that it is able to escape the traditional way of visualising economic problems, such as 'how capitalism administers existing structures, whereas the relevant problem is how (capitalism) creates and destroys them' (Schumpeter (1950)). As a research theme I submit that the role of opportunism should be put in perspective, and challenged at the cognitive and behavioural levels. The study of hybrid forms of organisations, such as alliances, which seem to contradict in part the prescription of transaction-costs economics, suggests that sometimes organisations struggle with issues that are not focused on efficiency, but deal with limited learning. In order to defy limits to organisational learning, firms have to engage in actions and implementations of designs that, for example, may run counter to the principles of keeping in check strategic behaviour. In other words, in turbulent environments breaking the organisational defensive routines requires organisations to engage in actions that may appear to be at odds with efficiency-driven concerns to control opportunism (Ciborra (1991)).

A final point in the deconstruction of the transaction-costs approach deals with the breakdown of (part of) the rationalistic assumptions embedded in its neoclassical economics roots. In chapter 9 the idea is put forward that so-called strategic applications of information technology are largely the outcome of tinkering and *bricolage* during systems development and use. As a consequence, the design and strategic information systems ought to be based on those 'grassroots' practices, largely improvised and local, that surround the development and use of systems. The resource-based view of strategy (Barney (1986); Amit and Schoemaker (1993)) values such idiosyncratic problem-solving and learning processes that lead from the use of standard resources (the computer hardware and software) to the constitution of unique organisational assets (Andreu and Ciborra (forthcoming)). I submit that the role for improvisation and bricolage is much broader in organisations (Brown and Duguid (1991)): it punctuates the functioning of markets (see chapter 1); emergency situations (Lanzara (1983)) and daily life in hierarchies (Weick (1993a)) and teams (Weick (1993b)). Then, a research hypothesis can be put forward (see Ciborra (1995) according to which there is much more intuition, instinct and background experience, even in carefully planned actions, than it meets the eye when analysing (limitedly) rational decision-making).

Contrary to the assumptions present in Simon (1976) and Williamson

(1975), the deep nature of decision-making would appear to be one of improvisation. Routines and programmable decisions, and the institutions which host them, would be more 'on the edge' (Unger (1987)), than is admitted by mainstream management and IS literature (Winograd and Flores (1986); Suchman (1987)). In other words, a small Copernican revolution shall be envisaged. What appears as an extemporaneous process, improvisation, without known causes and relationships, is indeed grounded into deep-seated human experience (see chapter 1), while what is usually presented by mainstream management and systems models as goal-oriented, rational and planned looks makeshift, artificial and de-rooted. The only chance for such models to have an impact on the actual workflow is for them to be constantly 'worked at' by competent members, who by 'fiddling around' and tinkering fill the frequent gaps between the artificial models and the unfolding circumstances of work. Again, it turns out that research, and theory development, on these mundane activities, i.e. on the phenomenology of everyday life in organisations, needs to complement any rational theory of organisations, such as the one found in the teams & markets framework. We conclude here, for the time being, our short itinerary of construction and deconstruction of the framework. The list put forward of its strengths and weaknesses is far from being complete, still it reveals fruitful research paths ahead.

References

Ackerman, M. S. and Malone, T. W. 1990. Answer garden: a tool for growing organizational memory. *Proceedings of the ACM Conference on Office Information Systems*, 31–9.

Amit, R. and Schoemaker, P. J. H. 1993. Strategic assets and organizational rents, *Strategic Management Journal*, 14, 33–46.

Andreu, R. and Ciborra, C. U. forthcoming. Organizational learning and core capabilities development: the role of IT, *Journal of Strategic Information Systems* (in press).

Argyris, C. and Schon, D. A. 1996. *Organizational learning II*, Reading, Mass.: Addison Wesley.

Benjamin, R. and Wigand, R. 1995. Electronic markets and virtual value chains on the information superhighway, *Sloan Management Review*, Winter, 62–72.

Ciborra, C. U. 1989. Transitions vs transactions: The nature of the firm's change, Theseus Institute, Sophia Antipolis, working paper.

Ciborra, C. U. 1990. X-efficiency, transaction costs and organizational change, in K. Weiermair and M. Perlman (eds.), *Studies in Economic Rationality*, Ann Arbor: The University of Michigan Press.

Ciborra, C. U. 1995. A theory of information systems based on the notion of improvisation, presented at the American Academy of Management Meeting, Vancouver, August.

Ciborra, C. U. 1996a. A platform for surprises, *Organization Science*, 7 (2), 103–18.

Ciborra, C. U. (ed.) 1996b. *Teamwork and Groupware in Large Organizations. The Subtleties of Innovation*, Chichester: Wiley.

Ciborra, C. U., Patriotta, G. and Erlicher, L. 1995. Disassembling frames on the assembly line: the theory and practice of the new division of learning in advanced manufacturing, in W. J. Orlikowski, G. Walsham, M. R. Jones and J. I. DeGross (eds.), *Information Technology and Changes in Organizational Work*, London: Chapman & Hall.

Ghoshal, S. and Moran, P. 1996. Bad for practice: a critique of the transaction cost theory, *Academy of Management Review*, 21 (1), 13–47.

Grudin, J. 1988. Why CSCW applications fail: problems in the design and evaluation of organizational interfaces, *Proceedings of CSCW Conference*, September, Portland, OR: 85–93.

Heidegger, M. 1977. *The Question Concerning Technology* (translated by W. Lovitt), New York: Harper & Row, 1977.

Lanzara, G. C. 1983. Ephemeral organizations in extreme environments: emergence, strategy, extinction, *Journal of Management Studies*, 20, 71–95.

Nonaka, I. and Takeuchi, H. 1995. *The Knowledge Creating Company*, New York: Oxford University Press.

Normann, R. and Ramirez, R. 1995. *Designing Interactive Strategy. From Value Chain to Value Constellation*. Chichester: Wiley.

Romer, P. M. 1990. Endogenous technical change, *Journal of Political Economy*, 98 (5), 71–102.

Scarbrough, H. 1995. Blackboxes, hostages and prisoners: organizing technical knowledge for innovation, *Organization Studies*, 16 (16), 991–1019.

Stein, E. W. and Zwass, V. 1995. Actualizing organizational memory with information systems, *Information Systems Research*, 6 (1), 85–117.

Weick, K. E. 1993a. Organization redesign as improvisation, in G. P. Huber and W. H. Glick (eds.), *Organizational Change and Redesign*, New York: Oxford University Press.

Weick, K. E. 1993b. The collapse of sensemaking in organizations: the Mann Gulch disaster, *Administrative Science Quarterly*, 38 (4), 628–52.

Acknowledgements

This book is the fruit of a long learning and research itinerary that started more than ten years ago. Along the road many people, colleagues, teachers and friends have helped me by drawing my attention to key issues, focusing ideas and developing new perspectives. I would like to take the opportunity to thank at least the most relevant ones. Federico Butera and Adriano De Maio in Milan, Enid Mumford in the United Kingdom, and Louis Davis at UCLA helped me to understand the socio-technical systems. William Ouchi at UCLA introduced me to the transaction-costs approach. Paul Strassmann, Philip Stone and Charles Jonscher in the United States, and the Scandinavian universities of Aarhus and Oslo encouraged me to pursue the application of the approach to the information-systems field. In particular, Kristen Nygaard, Lars Mathiassen, Finn Kensing and the researchers of the Norwegian Computing Centre were immensely supportive.

How to present a new theory of information systems was especially the result of my teaching at the Universities of Calabria, Trento, New York and the Theseus Institute. Among the students who helped me in developing materials on which parts of the book are based, I should mention Roberto Palmieri, Stefano Scarpa and Muriel Caristan.

The collaboration with American colleagues also contributed to the writing of papers that form the background material for some chapters of the book: Margi Olson, Tora Bikson, Chris Argyris, Cynthia Beath and Charles Wiseman.

The theory outlined here, however, would not have credibility if it had been deprived of practical applications. Jean-Yves Gresser at the Banque de France and the entire flight crew at British Airways have my gratitude in this respect, in particular Captain Steve Proffitt. Finally, I would like to thank Piercarlo Maggiolini, Bob Howard, Leslie Schneider, Giovanfrancesco Lanzara and Shoshana Zuboff, who have coached me throughout this decade, always very benevolent towards my clumsy efforts, and Ian Benson and Eva Kandler, without whom this book would not have seen the light of day. Patrick McCartan and Jenny Potts at the Press have enthusiastically co-operated in defining and finalising the editing of the book. Adele, and my brothers Bruno and Carlo have provided over the years a constant background support. Finally, an apology to the many friends to whom I could not give the attention and devotion they deserved since I was distracted by too much reading and writing.

Introduction

An illuminating experiment

In 1987 members of the Institute for Research on Interactive Systems of the Rand Corporation, based in Santa Monica in California, carried out a year-long experiment to assess to what extent computer technology could have an impact on retirers' lives. Two groups were created, each of which consisted of retirers and working employees close to retirement, chosen at random from the Department of Water and Power, one of the largest employers in the Greater Los Angeles area. Identical tasks were assigned to both groups. Each group was to prepare a report for the Department of Water and Power about problems associated with transition to retirement. One group was provided with networked personal computers (PCs), modems and software ranging from communications, spreadsheets, data analysis and wordprocessing packages. The other, the 'control group', had no computers at their disposal and could only rely on a traditional infrastructure such as meeting rooms, phone service and 'snail' mail.

Throughout the year, Rand researchers followed closely the activities of the two groups by means of questionnaires, analysis of work progress, monitoring of the pattern of message traffic and usage of the various media, and examined quantity and quality of interactions between group members. Control of the experiment also included disguised-participant observation: researchers masquerading as technical and organisational 'consultants' were put at the service of the two groups at their own request.

This research design provided one of the best opportunities to evaluate over a certain length of time the evolution of the impact of network technologies on group performance and organisation.

Both groups produced the expected reports, but the differences in the process that led to their production were staggering: namely, the researchers suggest that 'the computer's communications advantages were dramatic' (Hahm and Bikson, 1988) in many surprising ways. First, gains in efficiency could be observed because of the reduction of the constraints that

1

accompany conventional group work through the use of electronic mail (e-mail); for example, distance from the workplace was negatively correlated to the degree of participation for the members of the 'non-electronic' group, while it was not statistically associated in the 'electronic' group. Second, patterns of participation differed sharply. It should be borne in mind that each task force was composed of an equal number of people who were retired and those close to retirement. In the non-electronic group, distance barriers prevailed over time availability of retirers and caused their lower involvement, if not marginalisation. At the opposite end of the scale, with the help of e-mail, the retirers in the electronic group had far higher participation rates than employees in either group by the end of the experimental period (Bikson *et al.*, 1991), for they had more time to learn about computers than their working counterparts, and they were not constrained in accessing the computer during free time *only*. As a matter of fact, the involvement of managers was stifled by the irony of the participating offices allowing employees to use the PCs only during free hours: the inhibitions of the traditional organisation of the workplace overrode the advantage of the managers to be able to communicate in the workplace, to solve problems and become acquainted with the network usage (Hahm and Bikson, 1988).

Session records of the time spent by users on a specific program show that e-mail and wordprocessing were the most used packages, followed by spreadsheets as the preferred means for data displays. In fact, the most used programs after the e-mail are labelled generically 'other software', indicating programs that were not included in the experimental bundle: users thus learned quickly to use the PC to suit their own needs, also beyond the scope of the training provided by the Rand technical staff.

But even more important than learning and using the software tools to accomplish the task assigned are the subtle impacts of familiarity with the tools on the minds and work-oriented behaviour of the members of the electronic group. For example, the group became interested in surveys because of the availability of databases. In view of this they decided to give an innovative tack to the execution of their task by including a survey of the common problems faced by retired people. The task force analysed the data through the database package that was available, though this was not planned or required by the experimental setting. The monthly use of the database exceeded that of the spreadsheet by the end of the period.

The matrix – akin to the appearance of a spreadsheet screen – had in turn another interesting effect on the minds and organisation of the members of the electronic task force. It suggested a new form for their internal organisation. Namely, both groups started to work by adopting a similar form of work organisation based on the functional hierarchy: various subgroups were established to carry out the work for preparing parts of the final report, and co-ordinators were created at various hierarchical levels. Thus, the final product was decomposed functionally, and this suggested a model for the work organisation. However, the electronic group was able to implement a radical change, switching to a matrix organisation, with members playing overlapping roles or having dual responsibilities: the e-mail provided those additional channels of communication that were needed to support the surplus in information exchanges required by the new organisation.

To be sure, in moving towards a higher complexity of organisation, the electronic group assumed a self-organising, 'dissipative' structure (Prigogine and Stengers, 1984) and needed further sources of inputs to support such a move along the scale of organisational complexity. These inputs were provided by the technical and organisational specialists (the disguised Rand researchers): the group used them intensively to solve the problems they encountered in carrying out their own survey, analysing the data and implementing the new matrix organisation.

At the end of the experiment, the electronic group requested that Rand assist its acquisition of the network, and transformed itself into a volunteer service group.

The experiment shows in a nutshell and in a scientifically controlled way the potential effects or impacts of network technologies as detailed below:

The efficiency effect: The infrastructure allows barriers in time and space to be overcome, and the surplus in communication and information-processing needs to be taken over.

The content effect: The systems offer programs to process information more effectively; thus they provide scope for carrying out new tasks, such as a survey, in an improved way.

The socialisation effect: By providing more opportunities for reciprocal exchange, the network allows the scope and depth of teamwork and, more generally, group activities, to be enlarged.

The learning effect: Group members are engaged in a number of learning processes because of the technology. They must be trained in the use of the tool; they learn by using both the tools assigned to them and those they can get from different sources (tinkering or *bricolage*); they learn to learn, that is, they are able to learn about the setting they are immersed in, and to reproduce it (initially objects of surveys, the members of the electronic task force become proposers of a survey where they assume the role of the researchers).

The transformation effect: The interaction between the task force and the systems leads to new ways of thinking about the world and the way to intervene in it; this course of events brings about a radical change in work organisation, and results in the dismissal of the hierarchical organisation probably considered at the outset as the 'natural' way to go about the task assigned.

Are all these important effects associated with information technology in general, and with network-based systems in particular? More importantly, can they be actively looked for, designed and enacted in business and public organisations in a viable and not merely utopian way?

This book tries to provide a positive answer to these questions, by exploring models of organisations, conceptions of the technology and concrete methods of system design and development. The ground to be explored is for the most part untrodden, and is very different from the perspective of current thinking in the field of Management Information Systems (MIS). While these assume almost naturally the ubiquitous role of the hierarchy and so design systems accordingly (the famous pyramidal models of the organisation and its information system), this book takes another tack.

First, it adopts the comparative perspective on economic organisations derived by the recent contribution of institutional economics. According to such a view, hierarchies are just one possible set of arrangements for establishing relationships of production, exchange and division of labour. The hierarchy is probably not the most diffuse: both within and between hierarchies one can find countless examples of other organisational arrangements, such as teams and markets.

Second, present economic circumstances require organisations to be flexible and to adjust incrementally or change radically their boundaries between hierarchy, team and market arrangements due to continuous make or buy decisions, introduction of production work groups or creation of alliances and joint ventures (Rubin, 1990). The book suggests ways to unfreeze hierarchies according to circumstances, and to introduce teams and markets as required, using computer-based systems, while not clashing with their hierarchy-reinforcing effects, a fact noted by many researchers (Scott Morton, 1991).

Third, alternative development strategies are devised and systems-design methodologies are put forward as enabling tools for implementing and managing the new designs.

In the background, theoretical models and a language, that of the transaction-cost approach, are also provided to design systems and organisations from the new perspective, at all levels, strategic and operational, in both the private and public sectors.

We will focus on teams and markets as economically sound building blocks for constructing alternatives to hierarchies as circumstances dictate, and on the 'mediating' effects of information technology as a platform for enhancing the efficiency, content, socialisation, learning and transformation effects that the Rand researchers were able to isolate so crisply in the retirers experiment. The application of a teams and markets strategy to redesigning organisations is spelled out in the final part of the Introduction.

But first, we need to look at the wider context in more detail, that is, at those developments in the economy and in the technology that make such a new approach desirable, if not urgent and necessary. The trends listed here are in fact hardly disputable today, and they are becoming part of a common awareness that something has to change in our conception of the technology and the way we design through it new business and public organisations. This awareness has yet to generate a different framework for grasping information systems in a novel organisational context, and even more importantly, new ways to go about the construction of economically viable alternatives.

The technology and organisation scenario

We can divide the major trends that are relevant to connoting the changing role of information technology (IT) in organisations into two broad classes: technical and organisational.

Technical change

1 *Components and systems:* The increase in the processing power, the miniaturisation of components and their price reduction place on a desk a workstation with the capacity of a mainframe built some years ago. At the beginning of the 1980s, when outlining a scenario on the evolution of information technology for the Xerox corporation, Benjamin (1982) suggested that in 1990 a processing power of 4.5 mips, equivalent to an IBM 3033 or 18 IBM 360, would be able to be purchased for the equivalent of 2–8 white-collar salaries, while in the 1970s the same computer power required the equivalent of 210 white-collar salaries. Similarly, while a dumb terminal (a teletype) represented in 1970 almost a half of the annual salary of a professional, in 1990 a workstation based on a 32-bit microprocessor would cost less than one-tenth of a professional's salary.

Some of these forecasts contained in Benjamin's scenario, regarded only a few years ago as very ambitious, have been outdone in real terms. Actual costs are one-third of those expected and in the year 2000 they will be one-tenth of the 1990 cost (Benjamin, 1992). As a consequence, organisations will face 'radically different trade-offs over time among processing power, human effort, and dollars with which to best meet the organisation's objectives' (Scott Morton, 1991).

2 *Technologies:* The integration of computers and telecommunications is unfolding both within firms and local area networks and between firms with remote geographic networks, both private and public. The decrease in the price of components and the higher data-transfer capacity of the means of communication, specifically fibre optics, extend on an unprecedented scale the concept of distributed processing: the network links between powerful workstations form the alternative to the conventional idea of one big centralised data-processing system.

To be sure, this gives rise to new problems, such as connectivity, communication standards and software necessary for managing complex networks. Furthermore, wideband networks allow the transmission of voice and image as well as data, leading to the integrated processing of these three forms of communication and to the convergence of data processing, telecommunications and media. As for the contents and the user interface, these developments take us from traditional printouts or green and black screens to hypertexts delivered on multimedia workstations. The recent explosion of the Internet/World Wide Web sums up all these phenomena.

3 In the *application environment* another revolution is taking place: we are moving from a highly centralised, simplified hierarchical architecture of different data-processing (d.p.) routines linked to a centralised database to a composite set of applications which span an archipelago of systems and technologies that can support both centralised and decentralised business organisations (McKenney and McFarlan, 1982).

Inside the telecommunication network that connects the different data-processing resources of a number of firms, the number of bits carrying electronic mail, voice messages and images is overtaking the stream of bits related to the pure processing of data and number crunching. The variety of applications of office automation systems such as EDI (Electronic Data Interchange), POS (Point of Sale) or, more generally, those applications related to strategic information systems, play a role that transcends that of centralised data processing.

At the periphery, end-user computing puts powerful application packages in the hands of users, including some techniques and programs originating from artificial intelligence (AI), such as expert systems, and other systems for decision support. Prototyping languages are enabling the end user to develop by himself/herself, or with the help of specialist staff, advanced applications tailored to his/her needs.

With the distribution of data-processing resources, a client-server architecture of information systems is emerging which is more complex than the simplified systems mimicking the hierarchy of the firm. To be sure, this entails new problems: such as the need to provide users, specialists, the various units of the firm and different companies with common criteria to navigate in this more complex and challenging technological archipelago. This development triggers the effort to create centralised policies, standards and architectural criteria, on the one hand, and to promote further the spread of end-user computing, on the other.

4 In addition, dramatic changes are taking place in the *development and construction* of the new information systems. By saying this, we do not refer only to CASE (Computer Aided Software Engineering) tools, that is, tools which can help the automation of software production or to the growing role that data communications are playing in system development. Rather, one should think about the growing complexity of systems and applications that spark off the rethinking and maybe the re-invention of our conventional ways of conceiving and managing projects.

Specifically, concerns and practices can be identified that go beyond the automation trend represented by CASE tools, and some mechanistic, hierarchical models developed in the software-engineering domain, of which the system life cycle concept and the waterfall model are typical examples. We are moving to more fluid approaches, where there is greater room for the application and development of prototypes, mixed design teams, the acknowledgement of the contractual nature of systems developed and the understanding of system development as a process of organisational learning and change.

5 All this has repercussions on the general *conception of the technology*, its role and possible application in the business environment and in society. That is, from the conception of the computer, hardware and software, we are moving to the conception of *information technology*, which comprehends aspects of data processing and data communication. But two other developments are also noteworthy in this respect: one is generated by AI and its emphasis on the cognitive processes related to systems; the other is the convergence of media with information technology.

Strassmann has summarised the necessary reconception of IT as follows: if early on the central problem was one of implementation of information technology by constructing distributed processing systems, the challenge is to build a management information system conceived as a system for sharing knowledge based on a network of advanced workstations. Such an information system constitutes the method on which basis people can organise their internal and external communications, where the communication process is very much linked to the processes of knowledge sharing and organisational learning rather than to the pure technical idea of data transmission (Strassmann, 1990).

The concept of the computer itself is being replaced by the one of *media*, to the extent that the computer is becoming a communication medium that integrates all the functions of new and traditional systems such as television, telephone, telex, fax, video telephone and data processing. The computer is evolving into a system that fosters links both in physical terms, channelling and processing bit streams that are at the same time voice, image and data, and also in cognitive and social terms, linking ideas, minds and people.

In today's scenario people perceive their information environment within organisations as a system of multimedia objects; on any workstation people have simultaneous access to messages, each one of a different type, but all of them integrated on the same screen. The use of video images will be very important for management. Printout data are useful for analyses and to justify certain results on the basis of a rational procedure, as well as courses of action and decision outcomes, but in order to instil a team spirit, to motivate individuals as members of a team, communication through images and through what Peter Keen (1991) calls the repersonalisation of leadership, thanks to the new media, represents rhetorical devices which are much more effective than a printout. Thus, new management information systems based on new architectures such as the Intranet are not only heavily network based, but include media as tools for management.

As far as user-machine interaction is concerned, if information and knowledge are processed by multimedia workstations, the objects which appear on the screens are an integrated set of text, data, voice and image organised into hypertexts. The electronic document is multi-dimensional and has a complex structure made up of composite objects. In general, these complex documents or hypertexts provide the users with a set of linkages between ideas, media and objects, and these sets of linkages suggest to the user different degrees of freedom in composing new and more complex messages conceived as maps of ideas.

One of the consequences is, as Strassmann points out, the reduction of the distance between the author of a document and the user or reader of that document.

Industrial change

The technological changes are not occurring in an organisational vacuum, that is, the organisational settings – markets and firms – are far from being stable or neutral. Rather, they are torn by different economic, organisational and social forces which in the end amplify the drive towards complexity and decentralisation of systems (Antonelli, 1988). These pro-cesses which are affecting the economic, social and organisational scenario can be described briefly by pointing to some key phenomena (Keen, 1991).

1 First, the *growing globalisation of firms* not only brings about increased communications and the purchase of network equipment but also puts in doubt the traditional ways of coping with growth. In fact, the growth of a firm on the basis of the principle of economies of scale has always implied, organisationally speaking, new hierarchical levels. That is, administrative overheads, more control routines and procedures, a leadership style strictly impersonal and bureaucratic and management information systems that are hierarchically shaped and centralised. This growth path has led to various pathologies which have not been solved by traditional MIS. On the contrary, depersonalisation of leadership, decrease in team spirit, middle-management crises, tensions between the periphery and the headquarters, all these phenomena have set limits to the advantages of economies of scale.

The new information technologies provide a solution to some of these pathologies, not by trying to reinforce or by filling the gaps of existing hierarchies but by applying organisational-design strategies, such as expanding economies of scope, fostering flexible specialisation and splitting the hierarchy into autonomous units connected through networks. Across the network, leadership can be sustained by the use of video communication; decision making can be decentralised in federations of small networked firms and finally knowledge sharing at all levels can be enhanced by relying on multimedia workstations, synchronous communications and systems to support teamwork such as groupware.

2 Second, the very *concept of industry* is breaking down. The traditional ways for firms to gather information about other industries or sectors or the environment in which they operate are being challenged by the continuous redefinition of industries due to different factors, such as de- or reregulation. Think, for example, of how the telecommunication industry has been redefined in the United States to include the Bell system, the cable televisions and the information-technology vendors, too. Airline companies are increasingly changing into software houses and service firms, providing reservation services, or distribution companies that are being transformed into financial services.

This reconfiguration of business puts in doubt the role of information systems developed in a 'closed perspective' – that is, one that assumes that the firm is a closed system operating in a totally static environment where change takes place only gradually. On the other hand, all this reinforces the conception of pluralist, distributed information systems with plenty of duplication and redundancy to face and absorb environmental variety. The PC and the VSAT (Very Small Aperture Terminals) revolutions reconcile redundancy of computing resources with organisational efficiency and flexibility.

3 The *speeding-up of economic processes:* Within a firm and within the networks of firms, what seems to matter is the flexibility and adaptive capability in the face of environmental discontinuities. Businesses are being increasingly reconfigured. Technologies are continuously unveiling solutions that seek application. Product lifecycles have shortened while research and development (R&D) expenses are becoming more and more voluminous. In such a turbulent context, a firm's information system cannot be just a replica of the hierarchy with all its rigidities and constraints, but must actively support the sharing of knowledge at all levels in an organisation and between different organisations; it must stimulate reflection and the acknowledgement of changes, rather than the execution of routines or the centralisation of information flows for control purposes.

4 *Strategic alliances:* These organisational phenomena, very much linked to those above, emphasize the span of information systems across the firm's boundaries. A growing number of firms, even those competing with each other, are joining and teaming up around common pre-competitive R&D projects, unifying their forces into joint ventures, establishing links such as licensing and franchising and getting involved in global strategic alliances. This redesign of firms' boundaries requires higher connectivity between different information systems, the extension of networks and protocols to an inter-firm environment and underlies the importance of systems such as EDI and groupware applications (Ciborra, 1991; De Michelis, 1989).

5 *Industrial districts:* There is a growing awareness that there are alternatives to mass production and large bureaucracies as the best ways to run a business. The industrial districts of modern Europe provide an example of the alternative to mass production based on flexible specialisation (Piore and Sabel, 1984). The industrial districts in France, Italy, Denmark and Germany are characterised by networks of numerous small, technologically advanced and internationally competitive firms (Best, 1990), which are often involved at various stages in the production of similar products. A characteristic feature of the district is that it has to be looked at as a social, economic and political whole (Piore and Sabel, 1984; Pyke, Beccatini and Sengenberger, 1990). The flexibility of the industrial district stems precisely from the not purely economic transactions that build up the network of relationships between member firms. Designing an information system for an industrial district cannot boil down, then, to EDI or other more conventional interorganisational information systems. Rather, the design

should take into account the new, subtle dimensions of networking across social and political as well as economic spheres of action.

All these processes represent a set of organisational and strategic thrusts that will influence the deployment of information technology as a tool for flexible and negotiated co-ordination (Stone, 1980). Also they justify the study of the technologies, their design and their impact in a new perspective that does not separate the organisational aspects from data processing and multimedia communication.

To be sure, today each of the developments we have listed is already penetrating the information-systems area of any firm. But, what is left still untouched is our conception of the role of information systems (Walton, 1989). The current framework for understanding MIS is still based on Herbert Simon's concept – that is, centred on the notion of the computer as a support for decision making. In practice, however, what has been happening is a series of applications that, almost by chance, have revealed themselves as something completely different from the idea of computers as a support to decision making.

This volume sets out a new paradigm that can help us to understand all the technological and organisational developments mentioned above and help designers and managers to try out new applications in a more systematic way.

The paradigm put forward for understanding information systems is based on a promising way of analysing and designing organisations and the communications processes occurring within and between them. The alternative perspective is based mainly on the economics of transaction costs (Coase, 1937; Williamson, 1975).

The distinctive advantage of the transaction-cost approach resides essentially in that it considers economic organisations as networks of exchanges. This allows us to highlight the following themes. Firstly, the analysis of the economic efficiency of the matching of information technology and organisational structures. Secondly, the network of transactions between individuals and organisational units is a useful concept for analysing and designing telematic, office automation and EDI applications and new systems to support workgroups (Ciborra, 1987c). And finally, it allows us to consider the contractual nature of the use of information in an organisation where there is only a partial congruence of goals and interests among its members.

Applying teams and markets

The transformation of the hierarchy through the use of teams and markets is something that takes place every day in your organisation. Consider the following examples. An association of small firms wants to co-ordinate better the exchanges between its member companies and decides to set up a network to streamline some transactions, and in general to improve communications and co-ordination. Where a price system obtains, the network improves the market and inserts some elements of teamwork. No hierarchical planning is deployed to achieve the same objectives. Something similar may happen when alliances are set up between competitors. Instead of vertical integration, that is, a hierarchy, a mix of teams and markets is employed to arrange co-ordination between the members of the alliance. The information system to support the alliance cannot be a vertical one, but one that supports simultaneously market transactions and collaborative work.

Telework is another phenomenon (Olson, 1983): here the office bureaucracy is dismantled in favour of people working at home, often through a different employment contract: market constraints replace a hierarchy. But can the new workers communicate with each other through the network? If the answer is yes, this can be an instance of electronic teamwork.

Or consider manufacturing. In conventional product development, production engineers have to wait until the design engineer has finished before they can begin planning how to manufacture a part. New approaches prescribe a shift from this type of serial development to parallel development, or simultaneous engineering, in which design and production engineers at the company and at its suppliers work jointly from beginning to end. Where a pure arm's length or a hierarchical relationship obtains between different firms or departments, simultaneous engineering fosters the deployment of cross-functional or cross-firm teams. Networks, distributed Computer Aided Design (CAD) and simulation tools can support the communication and design tasks between engineers throughout the development and production phases (Ciborra, 1992).

Though in different contexts, these examples show the same trend: deconstructing the hierarchy and replacing it by a different mix of organisational forms, before applying automation. But how can this be done in practice?

The book suggests a series of tactics, since the process of organisational change is contractual and complex in nature, and cannot be planned in advance, and since one of the features of new technologies is to be open, a sort of platform for surprises. In any event, the economic perspective adopted in this book points to the following sequence.

First, unfreeze the hierarchy by creating a market for certain subsets of transactions. This can take place in a variety of ways depending upon specific circumstances: a decision to buy rather than make; the deregulation of public universal services; the disinvestment from certain businesses; vertical disintegration; the establishment of alliances that open up the organisation; change in the employment contract of the workforce; and so on.

Second, support the new market electronically. This technological move can also take place in different ways. It can be an EDI system; a videotex network; a telework system; electronic commerce through the Web; a strategic information system to link suppliers to link suppliers and customers; or a groupware application to manage an alliance. The important aspect is that people find it attractive to use the new electronic market, because it provides them with positive externalities: they meet others (interdependence effect); they get access to standardised services more cheaply; they save on co-ordination costs; they can obtain more customised, prompt services.

At this point, there is a design choice: either the new electronic market successfully replaces the bureaucracy, since information technology has been able to standardise sufficiently the production of services and the co-ordination of the activities, or the pure move to a market, though supported by the technology, is not enough, because tasks are complex, cannot be fully standardised and a certain degree of *ad hoc* integration is still required in order for the work units to stay flexible and effective. The market may not be the best means to achieve such an integration, and the system we have set up may lead to failures that require the reinstatement of the hierarchy. But the same technology platform can help us to refreeze the organisation on an equilibrium different from the hierarchical one. That is to say, we can introduce team elements among the members of the newly created market, for example by providing ubiquitous, structured e-mail and bulletin boards. Note that, as will be explained in Part I of the book, the hierarchy is applied to meet two different types of gaps or failures: that of the market (often generated by asymmetric information and the small number of bargaining agents) and that of teams (caused by the large size). Here we envisage the application of information technology to fill *simultaneously* the two gaps that would otherwise undermine the validity of the teams and markets mix: that is, information asymmetries of imperfect markets, and co-ordination and control problems of large teams.

Implementing the teams and markets strategy unfolds, then, like a dance: first step, unfreeze the hierarchy and liberate individual behaviour and entrepreneurship through the more effective incentives of a price system. Next, refreeze the organisation, introducing teams elements where required by the nature, complex and uncertain, of tasks and products, or by emerging needs of collaboration and socialisation. The aim of the whole exercise is to increase at the same time efficiency and teamwork in organisations. Information technology plays a crucial role in allowing the teams and markets dance to be sustained. Only information systems must be designed according to a new perspective. The notion of mediating technology put forward in Part I may, I hope, suggest to the technical specialists the development of new architectures to reach such an aim.

The book is divided into three parts. The first contains the foundations of the teams and markets approach. As a basis for the models of organisation and their information systems, the first chapter discusses four models of rationality, that is, four ways to portray the decision-making behaviour of the economic agent and the reasons why information is used and produced in organisations. Often in models of information systems assumptions about the agents' behaviour are made implicitly and this does not help us to appreciate in what real organisational setting a given model can be applied effectively. The first chapter should help the reader to see the scope of the model of strategic rationality employed in the rest of the book and the main methodology presented, that of transaction-costs analysis.

The second chapter introduces the notion of teams, one of the two building blocks of our design perspective. The structural and economic aspects of team arrangements are analysed, starting from the results of the socio-technical approach to work-group design. The cognitive aspects of teams are also briefly discussed. The 'economic team' effect is introduced to help us to appreciate the economic forces that condition the life of real teams, and that have often been neglected by organisation theorists.

In the third chapter, a reconceptualization of information technology is pursued by discovering new dimensions of the concept of 'mediating technology' originally introduced by the sociologist J. D. Thompson (1967). Information technology is regarded as belonging to those means that affect socio-economic exchanges through the extension of linkages, standardisation of interactions and mediation of exchanges. The chapter addresses the issue of how to connote and classify the various dimensions of information technology according to the new criterion of 'mediation'.

The next two chapters are dedicated to exploring the organisational impacts of information technology on teams and markets respectively. In chapter 4 it is shown that there are different types of team, stretching on a continuum that goes from pure hierarchical arrangements to markets. Information technology, especially groupware, can support a variety of forms and also be harnessed to foster the shift from one form to another. A case is analysed in more detail to show the deeper cognitive and transformational effects of groupware on team organisation. In the fifth chapter, markets and systems that support electronic markets are discussed. The economics of information provides us with a systematic analysis of the various reasons why markets fail as a co-ordination and control mechanism, when information cannot travel seamlessly. This sets the stage for understanding the role of information technology as mediating market transactions. Various types of strategic information systems link organisations, suppliers and customers, improving the functioning of existing markets and creating new ones. The chapter explores different types of electronic markets and analyses the essential steps to build them at the micro and macro level.

The second part of the book is concerned with design, specifically with a framework for carrying out in a systematic way the setting-up of a different architecture of organisational forms, using markets, hierarchies and teams as the building blocks and information technology as a support medium. In chapter 6 the framework of the transaction-costs approach is introduced extensively, and both a static and a dynamic analysis are carried out of the fit between different forms of technical systems and organisational structures. Chapter 7 adds the economic evaluation of information systems from two main perspectives: decision making and transaction costs.

Chapters 8 and 9 tackle the issues of systems development, always in a team and markets perspective. That is, it may not be sufficient to have the right theory to build computer-supported markets and teams if one is not able to manage the process of construction. These chapters explore two axes of intervention: the first is the negotiation of organisational change when introducing the new technology; the other deals with the important aspects of how to 'play Lego', how to tinker in practice with different organisational forms at hand. Teams and markets, we submit, is the outcome of a vision, a systematic analysis, but also of negotiations and tinkering.

Specifically, chapter 8 looks at the contractual processes that are relevant in managing systems development, and using the economic perspective compares different governance structures for managing the process efficiently. The next chapter deals with the issue of how new applications are created, in particular the so-called strategic information systems. The economic analysis suggests that current strategic applications provide only a temporary advantage, and tactics that generate new applications must be looked for in other models of organisation, closer to the learning model introduced in the first chapter.

The third part introduces applications. Chapter 10 contains a case of how new systems have been deployed to modify radically the functioning of a financial market, that of government bonds in the United States. The introduction of teams supported by electronic mail in the flight-crew area of a major European airline is the subject of chapter 11. This is the key case for understanding the whole philosophy of the book. A lagging bureaucracy has to be changed: information technology can support a different mix of teams and markets arrangements able to address the multiple failures of the existing bureaucracy.

The last chapter is dedicated to the exploration, always in an economic perspective, of the possibilities and limitations of applying computers and networks in the public administration. The notion of political exchange is introduced to complement that of economic transaction, in order to allow for a comparative assessment of various forms of economic and political organisations in governing the socio-economic processes that take place on the territory. The scope of information technology in the public sector is clarified significantly thanks to such an institutional comparison.

The Conclusion contains a recapitulation of the main points of the teams-markets approach.

PART I   Foundations

1 Cognitive models of man, organisation and information

Introduction

Any form of design activity guided by a methodology requires the adoption of one or more models of the designed artifact that can be used to test and validate the design itself. The design of computer-based information systems needs to make reference to models of organisation, in which the ways information is processed by people and systems are highlighted. For example, current models in data processing and software engineering focus on the information-processing function, that is, they provide descriptions of information flow, storage and retrieval. The designer, who applies them, constructs a system design based on the flow of electronic data and storage in databases; he or she will validate the design by inventing hypothetical test cases and by simulating the behaviour of the system in handling each test case (Newman, 1980). In general, it has been shown that a sound model of the organisational setting object of computerisation can be an effective guide to a good design, and save costs during implementation and maintenance (Couger, Colter and Knapp, 1982).

Our exploration of the ways information technology can support a different mix of organisational forms, that is, teams and markets instead of hierarchies, needs to make explicit the most important models embedded in computer-supported organisations. In order to avoid the failures of the past (Huber, 1984), our investigation should not be limited to the modelling of the individual manager's cognitive styles in sensing, formulating and solving problems, lest collective, *organisational* issues related to the sharing of information and the implications they pose for individual information processing may go undetected to a great extent. The models we are going to consider contain hypotheses on how people in different types of organisations produce, use and communicate information related to executing tasks, sharing work, co-operating, co-ordinating, solving problems and managing conflict.

The term 'information' employed here covers a wide spectrum of

19

phenomena, ranging from data to knowledge. *Data* record signs and observations in or on a medium. The context of data is generally simple, widely accepted and unambiguous, so that the evidence of the sign or data can hardly be disputed. *Information* shapes the meaning of data in relation to a specific context of action or speech. Data can be exchanged if at both ends of the communication the same simple and standardised context holds. Also, information can be shared only if at both ends the same understanding of the relevant context obtains, and if the actors of the information exchange can make sense of the signs received and transmitted by making reference to similar contexts of interpretation. *Knowledge* describes the capability of an individual or an organisation to relate complex structures of information to new contexts of action. Thus, for example, a city map contains data (signs) on street names and location. Such a map can be the information system of a taxi driver, in the sense that it contains the information he or she needs to find a particular street. But the knowledge of the taxi driver is more than the information contained in the city map: it is his or her ability to take the customer to the final destination given specific and complex circumstances, such as point of departure, traffic conditions, time of day, current roadworks, choice of alternative routes available and so on (Greiner and Metes, 1992). Knowledge is composed of means–ends chains retrievable for action. It is based on experience, know-how, theories, rules of thumb and procedures for carrying out validity tests. Knowledge, as defined here, is interwoven with practice and is situated (Suchman, 1987); therefore, it can be shared less easily than data or information. In order to turn knowledge into information and information into data, one has to make explicit what has hitherto been tacit in the competence of those having the knowledge and in the situation where such knowledge was put to work (Dahlbom and Mathiassen, 1991).

In organisations knowledge is applied according to the principle of *rationality*; that is, an organisational action relies on knowledge to select appropriate means to reach designated ends (Thompson, 1967). The function of knowledge in an organisational action, for example a decision or a transaction, is to determine which consequences follow upon which of the alternative strategies available at the moment: it thus helps to shape expectations of future consequences, and simulate them, the expectations being based upon known empirical relationships and information about the existing situation (Simon, 1976).

This chapter examines four different ways of looking at rational processes of production, communication and accumulation of knowledge and information in organisations. The four models examined are the following: unlimited rationality and fully accessible knowledge; limited rationality and tacit knowledge; strategic rationality and opportunistic information; and adaptive rationality and limited learning. Such models will be referred to frequently in the remainder of the book, for they establish the context in which to appreciate and design the various classes of effects of information technology on efficiency, task content, socialisation, learning and transformation.

The models include multiple perspectives for studying organisations that stem from various disciplines: computer science, management science, administrative theory, anthropology, philosophy and economics. It is our belief that richer and more effective models must depart from the current information flow and procedural models of business activities that tend to neglect important details of everyday organisational life. On the other hand, we must highlight and appreciate the limitations inherent in the models put forward (Markus and Robey, 1988). This is made easier if we isolate, though in a schematic way, the basic hypotheses on which each of them is based.

Unlimited rationality and fully accessible knowledge

Though largely criticised in the fields of organisation theory and economics, this first representation of individual and organisational cognitive processes is still the prevailing one in many current models and methods for information-systems design and business re-engineering.

According to this view, individual and organisational knowledge is *fully accessible* to an expert analyst, and structured methods have been put forward to capture and include it in formalised (computerised) routines. Specific instances of this perspective can be found in the models of neoclassical economics, scientific management and formal administrative theory. In the perfect market each agent has full access to information about the price and quality of the product or service when engaging in a transaction: thanks to a full standardisation of transactions and commodities, each agent operating in a perfect market has the same information on the basis of which he or she can make a decision (Hirschleifer, 1980). Scientific management (Taylor, 1911) assumes that in an organisation goals are known, tasks are repetitive and fully analysable, resources like human labour are available in uniform quality and so on. Formal administrative theory (Gulick and Urwick, 1937) presupposes that organisational efficiency can be maximised by fixing goals, specialising tasks, grouping them into departments and controlling activities; it assumes further that a masterplan can be laid out according to known goals and production tasks.

These approaches share the hypothesis according to which the level of uncertainty (or lack of information) the organisation and the individuals have to face can ultimately be reduced to zero. The model of the fully rational organisation 'results in everything being functional – making a positive, indeed an optimum, contribution to the overall result, resources are appropriate resources, and their allocation fits a master plan. All action is appropriate action, and its outcomes are predictable' (Thompson, 1967: 6). The management of an organisation focuses on the concepts of planning and control, and the information systems support such a central concern. The conversion of knowledge related to tasks into information and data can be streamlined: a scientific inquiry (that is, a structured analysis and design) can render organisational knowledge fully explicit, rational and transparent. Computer systems can process knowledge converted into data in a more efficient way and ultimately replace humans as more effective information processors for planning and control.

It goes almost without saying that such a view has been the cause of many, large and small, failures of computerisation. One of its implications has been particularly detrimental: the analysts, guided by their scientific method, were thought to be able to penetrate fully any pocket of situated knowledge in the organisation. They just had to be sufficiently skilled at 'stealing' knowledge from the users by adopting 'structured' implementation strategies (Couger, Colter and Knapp, 1982). Unfinished systems, conflicts with the end users, sky-rocketing costs of 'integrated' or 'total' systems and databases have shown the limits of such a perspective.

An appreciation of organisational matters, that is, of how knowledge is actually processed by individuals in organisations, would have pointed out that the dream of the designers guided by this approach, that is, total automation, was bound to backfire: piecemeal automation is often the outcome of totally integrated system designs.

Limited rationality and tacit knowledge

Systems designers, like any decision maker, are information processors with limited capabilities: 'It is impossible for the behaviour of a single individual to reach any high degree of rationality. The number of alternatives he must explore is so great, the information he would need to evaluate them so vast that even an approximation to objective rationality is hard to conceive' (Simon, 1976: 79). This sets limits to the design of any system, especially those that are complex. Not all the knowledge is formalisable, and models can usually include only a bounded set of variables. Their optimisation may have nothing to do with the optimisation of the process modelled. It follows that designs are incomplete, systems are open (Hewitt and De Jong, 1984), and a knowledge gap between the system and the surrounding user organisation must be filled somehow.

Another way of presenting this view is to recall the tacit nature of individual and organisational knowledge (Polany, 1966; Sternberg and Wagner, 1986). Organisations are seen as co-ordination and control mechanisms that cope with the fact that knowledge is by and large not transparent and accessible. In its turn, information technology needs to come to terms with the tacit nature of knowledge in order to find a realistic role in supporting human work.

Limited, or bounded, rationality refers to information-processing limitations in computing optima from known preference or utility information, unreliable probability information about complex environmental contingencies and the absence of a well-defined set of alternatives, especially in a turbulent world that may produce situations that never existed before (Ciborra, Migliarese and Romano, 1984; Heiner, 1983; Knight, 1921). While in the special case of no uncertainty,

the behavior of perfectly informed, fully optimizing agents responding with complete flexibility to every perturbation in their environment would not introduce easily recognizable patterns, but rather would be extremely difficult to predict . . ., uncertainty requires behavior to be governed by mechanisms that restrict the flexibility to choose potential actions, or which produce a selective alertness to information that might prompt particular actions to be chosen. (Heiner, 1983: 561)

These mechanisms are 'rules' that can simplify behaviour (Schotter, 1981; Ullman-Margalitt, 1978). The outcome of this necessary simplification is routinised behaviour and organisational routines that can be more easily observed and predicted.

Routines store co-ordinating information and knowledge underlying effective performance (Nelson and Winter, 1982). Routines, and people who perform them, tend to be arranged hierarchically, according to the principles, inherited from the previous model, of specialisation and functional decomposition of a complex task. Organisations live and remember by repeating such routines, and every time an organisation has to select an alternative, it will select it from a narrow menu composed of idiosyncratic routines. As a consequence, the individual firm is not characterised by highly flexible adaptation. Planning of tasks and control of goal attainment are still central activities in this model of hierarchical organisation, but they cannot be carried out once and for all as a result of *ex ante* design, as the classical administrative theory prescribed. Rather, they have to rely on a variety of approaches, for example control by norms or by feedback (March and Simon, 1958), and they tend to be always incomplete and require continual adjustments.

Adaptation of individual and organisational behaviour occurs through searching and *learning by doing*: knowledge of an idiosyncratic kind is acquired by osmosis, by close familiarity with machines and existing procedures, by appreciating the subtleties of behaviour of other team members, etc. Of a similar kind is *learning by using* (Rosenberg, 1982): systems, procedures and routines being incomplete, or open, are re-invented by the users, that is, they become a testing ground for a variety of minor improvements that ultimately influence the real performance of systems.

Such a view of the deployment of organisational knowledge is not specific to *hierarchies or informal teams*: it is also typical of *markets*, regarded as adaptive co-ordinating mechanisms. To wit, knowledge in society never exists in an integrated form,

but solely as the dispersed bits of incomplete and frequently contradictory knowledge which all the separate individuals possess. The economic problem of society is thus not merely a problem of how to allocate 'given' resources – if given is taken to mean given to a single mind which deliberately solves the problem set by these 'data'. It is rather a problem of how to secure the best use of resources known to any of the members of society, for ends whose relative importance only these individuals know. (Hayek, 1945: 520)

In such a perspective, the market, seen as an organisation, is an effective co-ordinating mechanism because it copes with the fragmentation of knowledge. The *price* is a means to communicate information between a multitude of agents, each possessing idiosyncratic knowledge of particular circumstances of time and place, stemming from unique biographies and contexts of action.

The whole tradition of Decision Support Systems (DSS), for both individuals and groups, is based on the view of limited rationality. (De Sanctis and Gallupe, 1987; Sprague, 1980). Also, phenomenological studies of office procedures (Suchman and Wynn, 1984) and systems use (Gasser, 1986) have stressed the incomplete nature of systems and the adaptive processes carried out by end users around every system. The *raison d'être* for prototyping as opposed to one-shot, straightforward structured methods of systems development can also be traced back to this model of rationality.

Finally user-participation strategies and the socio-technical approach (Briefs, Ciborra and Schneider, 1984; Mumford, 1983) are based on the notion of limited rationality of the analysts and the recognition of the superior knowledge the users have regarding the organisational routines as they are carried out in practice (see ch. 8).

The perspective of limited rationality helps us to abandon the conception of the organisation as a clockwork mechanism that can be fully planned and controlled: it shows that the organisation is a problem-facing and problem-solving device operating in an uncertain environment, where information and knowledge are not fully accessible. However, the notion of limited rationality needs to be specified further in order to build models of organisation and information processing closer to the everyday experience. To wit, there are two hypotheses about the way limits to rationality may condition the behaviour of economic agents.

First, limits to rationality can be made more severe by the intentional manipulation of information, and data, performed by certain agents against others. How can we model organisations and their information systems in a context where conflict of interests cannot be ruled out *a priori* (Cyert and March, 1963)? Second, there are cognitive processes studied by psychologists and intervention theorists for which intentionally rational behaviour turns out to be biased, without the agents being aware of such a bias. Thus, agents make mistakes and fail to adapt, even if they have the relevant information, for their decisions may be flawed in a way they cannot check. When are these phenomena important and how can we design organisations and systems that take into account these knowledge- and information-distortion processes?

Strategic rationality and opportunistic information

If full co-operation is not present among members of an organisation, then it cannot be ruled out that tacit knowledge is used strategically by some of the members, that is, to create and maintain monopoly power, or 'first-mover' advantage in their mutual dealings. In other words, as soon as organisations are seen as mixed-interest co-ordination games (Schelling, 1980), the opportunistic user of knowledge, information and data must be taken into account. Information and data can be manipulated, communicated in a distorted way, or concealed. Knowledge can be used to effect asymmetries in power relationships. Organisations and information systems are now regarded as coping also with the problem of *opportunistic information processing* (Feldman and March, 1981). Correspondingly, models of support systems, and analysis and design methods need an adequate refinement.

The transaction-cost approach (Williamson, 1975) can be of help in this respect, for it provides us with an understanding of economic institutions that takes into account simultaneous bounded rationality *and* opportunism of the decision makers. In the transaction-costs framework the fundamental organisational processes of co-ordination and control are understood in a *bargaining context*. Transactions can be regarded as the basic organisational relationship in which conflict of interests may take place. In an exchange, or transaction, information is used, and produced, for the following purposes: it is a means of searching for a potential partner; it signals willingness to exchange; it contains the terms of the contract; it is the medium of control, enforcement and modification of the contract; and it maintains communication during bargaining (Barth, 1981). During each phase of a transaction, contractors may behave opportunistically, that is, 'seeking self interest with guile' (Williamson, 1975), as long as there is a conflict between them. This means they are prone to gain from knowledge they possess during and after the exchange, or from information they obtain while exchanging goods or services: opportunistic information processing consists of a selective disclosure or deliberate distortion of the factual data to which each party has unique access during transacting.

Organisations are seen as networks of transaction, regulated over a period of relative stability by a set of contracts. The essential difference between organisations, such as markets, hierarchies and teams, lies in the nature of their constituent contracts. Thus, there are spot contracts on the market; the employment relation, and the authority relationship, in the hierarchy; and long-term, unwritten and trust-based contracts that hold together groups or clans (Ouchi, 1980).

Such a view of organisations, and the way knowledge, information and data are processed by their members, has far-reaching implications for the role of systems and their design, as will be shown in the remainder of this book. First, the information system of any socio-economic organisation can be defined as the network of information flows and stocks needed to create, set up, control and maintain the organisation's constituent contracts. The information systems that could support different types of contractual processes of co-ordination and control have distinctive properties: the information system for spot contracting on a market is highly standardised, formalised, a-procedural and responsive: it supports electronic markets (see ch. 5); systems for decision making in a hierarchy are procedural, while those supporting 'unwritten contracts' based on trust are highly informal and idiosyncratic. Second, by suggesting that information technology should be viewed as a *mediating technology* in any socio-economic exchange, the transaction-cost approach is well suited to providing insightful design prescriptions for negotiation support systems (De Sanctis and Gallupe, 1987). Such systems must be conceived as a means to decrease costs of transacting and co-ordinating (see ch. 3).

Note, finally, that the transaction-cost approach is germane to those efforts aimed at building new software based on communication modelling through illocutionary logic (Cohen and Perrault, 1979; Lee, 1980; Searle, 1969); more generally, it justifies from the vantage point of organisation economics the whole communication perspective on the design of co-operative work (see ch. 4) (Winograd, 1986). If, according to such a perspective, the essence of management consists of the communication of speech acts, that is promises, commitments, requests, instead of 'data' or 'decision making' (Flores and Ludlow, 1981; Winograd and Flores, 1986), then systems should be built to support co-operative work understood as communication work (see systems such as Chaos (De Cindio *et al.*, 1986); or the Co-ordinator (Winograd and Flores, 1986)). To be sure, these perspectives and systems emphasise the *co-operative* view of organisations: this is only a special case for the transaction-cost approach, which is more comprehensive in understanding conflicts of interest and opportunistic information processing, by seeing any business organisation as a mixture of co-operation and conflict, of community and contractual arrangements. The interest of the transaction-cost approach lies precisely here: it can reframe the whole MIS/DSS field from the traditional terms of planning and control to those of *community and contract* (Crozier, 1983).

Adaptive rationality and limited learning

The smooth functioning of economic institutions through the execution of orderly routines presupposes the processing of data and information as represented in the models and perspectives provided so far. However, if the process of *organisational change* is considered, it can be concluded that yet another model of organisation is needed. The organisational process of interest here is not the execution of routines but their transformation, that may be required by the turbulent environment. Specifically, it seems that the ways of representing and exploiting knowledge and information in the first three perspectives do not address adequately those limits to learning that favour organisational inertia and hamper organisational transformation.

Several streams of research on cognitive processes have to be brought together to explore the issue of why individual and organisational learning may be limited. First, consider the hypothesis about a dual structure of knowledge (Piaget, 1974): any process of gathering and understanding information is based on a previously developed background knowledge structure (Ramaprasad, 1987). Such cognitive structure has been studied in psychology (Nisbett and Ross, 1980; Norman, 1983), organisation theory (Weick, 1979), artificial intelligence (Minsky, 1975; Schank and Abelson, 1977) and sociology (Schultz and Luckmann, 1973).

It is an invaluable aid to understanding events by framing them in a background of taken-for-granted explanations: it works as a set of ready-to-hand scripts or frames for interpreting and acting in a situation, and for supervising the skilled execution of routines. Research in psychology (Kahneman and Tversky, 1973; Nisbett and Ross, 1980; Tverski and Kahneman, 1974) and intervention theory (Argyris and Schön, 1978) shows, however, that such frames are *misleading* in that they contain poor representations of reality, precluding attention to the details of the actual situation at hand. They are oversimplified schemata, ruthlessly held and easily retrieved, that tend to ingrain mind and action, so that behaviour appears to be 'programmed' sometimes in an unwished-for manner. They are responsible for the cognitive processes that may limit learning, such as resistance to new information, cognitive dissonance (Festinger, 1957), alternative modes of reasoning (Nisbett and Ross, 1980), and ill-structured processes of inference (Argyris, 1985). They maintain the identity of the person, but may diminish his or her capacity for action and creative choice, thus leading to phenomena of weakness of will (Elster, 1979).

In order to understand how the dual cognitive structure, which separates background knowledge from that needed to solve problems at hand, influences individual and organisational transformation, we can refer first to those studies that highlight the existence of different learning loops related to action and change (Argyris, 1982; Argyris, Putnam and Smith, 1985). Single-loop learning is responsible for incremental adjustment to new circumstances that leaves frames, or theories people use in situations to guide their behaviours, untouched; double-loop learning affects instead the governing values that influence behaviour and incremental learning.

To 'double-loop learn' means to affect the level of the 'theory-in-use' and be able to change it, overcoming those defensive routines that keep behaviour within the boundaries of a limited adaptation. The large majority of current information systems, including those discussed in this book, are designed according to criteria that emphasise the processing of information for effective single-loop, that is, incremental, learning; however, the competent adoption of such criteria may lead to design systems that do not help the organisation to implement radical change, nor deal adequately with the process of information creation as opposed to information management (Nonaka, 1991; Senge, 1990).

Another comprehensive way to understand the implications of the dual knowledge structure comes from recent social theory (Unger, 1987). According to such a theory, organisational members, when skilfully executing routines but also when implementing innovations or imaging alternatives to their present work situation, are under the influence of a deep-seated structure, or *formative context*, which accounts for their skill, the inertia of their learning and the unawareness of their actual practices. A formative context comprises both an organisational and a cognitive dimension: it thus differs from the notion of a purely cognitive frame. Specifically, the difference lies in its genesis: the formative context is the outcome of a mode of division of labour in an organisation or, more generally, in the various institutions that populate a given society. Its product is a texture of routines and tasks that possess an aura of naturalness for those who execute the daily routines in that context. A formative context is a *social script embedded in a work organisation*: it influences work practices, but also ways of reflecting on that organisation and its possible alternatives.

A formative context can be defined as the set of institutional arrangements, cognitive frames and imageries that actors bring and routinely enact in a situation. A formative context has far-reaching influences, for it constitutes the background condition for action, enforcing cognitive and practical constraints, giving direction and meaning, and setting the range of opportunities for undertaking action. Such influence is subtle, for organisational members are usually not aware of the formative contexts that inform their practical and argumentative routines: they tend to take them for granted, except in the case of major breakdowns (Bateson, 1972; Schutz, 1964). For example, you can look at the hierarchy as a formative context. It is a supposedly optimal way to divide labour as prescribed by classical administrative theory; it is a contractual arrangement that constrains the behaviour of members, as suggested by the transaction costs approach; but it is also a style, perceived as natural, of looking at the world and of solving problems at hand.

Thus, whenever a complex task has to be faced, the principle of hierarchical, functional decomposition is applied in a taken-for-granted fashion and the conceptual or practical outcomes it leads to are *de facto* legitimised. The very fact of working in hierarchies reinforces such cognitive strategy for problem solving. This means that the hierarchy not only determines the way tasks are assigned, executed and supervised, but also suggests and legitimises the solutions members may come up with to face a new problem. It shapes the culture of the organisation and the individual and group cognitive frames. The formative context becomes the social imprint that generates any amelioration or modification of the work routines, gives the background to reflect on the extant organisation and thus biases any attempt at innovation and imagination of alternatives. In short, it represents the crucial factor for organisational learning and flexibility.

If a formative context is considered as a rigid, all-inclusive package, there would be no way to change it, at least from within; but this conclusion contrasts with the obvious reality of organisations that do change dramatically, of cognitive frames and beliefs that shift significantly. Recall, in this respect, the genesis of a formative context, that is, the sedimentation of practices and reflections about them: a formative context shares the resilience of both institutions and frames, and thus it is a useful justification for the existence of organisational inertia. However, sedimentation is never perfect, or fully consistent, since the interaction between the daily work routines and the underlying formative context to which they are linked is a complex one. Consider, for example, the introduction of a technological innovation, such as a new computer-based system (Ciborra and Lanzara, 1989): it is true that the use of this technology is carried out under the umbrella of a pre-existing formative context, no matter whether the innovation is supposed to reinforce the *status quo* or to change radically a work setting.

But errors in design and implementation are inevitably made: systems, or more generally, technologies, are always incomplete in relation to a specific work setting. Recall that the limited rationality view suggests that systems are open, and in order to function they require the *ad hoc* invention of new routines by designers and users to improve the fit with the surrounding organisation. Such a myriad of small and large unplanned routines generates new knowledge about the system, once again under the bias of the existing formative context. However, being unplanned and unexpected, they may create at the boundary between the system and the organisation a set of innovative practices, and routines (see the cases discussed in chapter 4). Such new routines are fluctuations, disturbances of the old formative context, which reveals itself to be open, incomplete. Some of the new routines may be included in the pre-existing context, some will remain at its boundaries, some may even point at and lead to the emergence of a new context. In the latter case fluctuations may turn into the new prevailing model of thought and work: change of formative context often takes place in this way.

The notion of formative context has several implications for the conception of the information systems, and the role they could play to support more effective learning organisations (Brown, 1991; Nonaka, 1988). Leaving aside the specific implications for systems development, which have been discussed elsewhere by Ciborra and Lanzara (1989), let us consider here the role and nature of systems. On a closer look, systems appear to share some of the properties of formative contexts. As previously illustrated, they are open, need revisions and are formed by both designed routines and those invented by the users of the system (Rice and Rogers, 1980). Systems have a pervasive and subtle influence: they can carry with them into the work organisation new languages and new ways of conceiving work, in addition to new routines. When they are introduced in a work setting, and if they are not pushed aside totally, that is, rejected, they become a permanent feature of that work setting: any restructuring or change of the organisation will take into account explicitly or implicitly the existence of the computer-based system and its exigencies.

If information systems can be regarded as formative contexts, it follows that designing a system would not only concern the implementation of new routines, procedures, databases and information flows. It would not only include the design of a new work organisation, but it would also represent the opportunity for the emergence of a *new* formative context. Information systems appear to be *social scripts*, for they not only automate data flows, decision-making algorithms or databases, but they also could govern the invention of alternative forms of work, new ways of problem solving, the revision of the existing institutional arrangements.

The notion of formative context and the hypothesis according to which information systems can be carriers of a formative context provide a new framework for conceiving and designing systems. Recall that a formative context is responsible for moulding practical knowledge of people at work, perfecting the learning skills and biasing the imageries of those who engage in design and change. Thus, it embeds the knowledge base that constitutes the hidden, background component of skilled performance and orderly functioning of institutional arrangements. An information system seen as a formative context may then touch the following levels:

the boundary between the tacitly held background knowledge and the foreground 'situational' knowledge, that is, the taken-for-granted reasoning and the specific focus of attention;

the new practical knowledge that is invented and applied to 'close' the open system with respect to the needs of the work setting;

the new concepts, language, goals, constraints and problem-solving skills needed to think about and produce alternative forms of work organisation.

Let us consider, for example, a payroll system: its design includes general knowledge of accounting, knowledge of how accounting is actually performed in organisations and knowledge of how to go about the design of a computerised system for accounting applications. After the implementation, new knowledge is added by the local user in applying the system to his or her job. Such knowledge stems from the ineradicable re-invention process that occurs every time a new system is introduced in an organisation. Once the system is in use, it becomes a permanent part of the 'furniture', in terms of artifacts constraining the routines and cognitive frames of the members of the organisation, that cannot be easily disposed of, since it is a kind of 'invisible' or *caché* furniture (Gagliardi, 1990).

Information systems should, then, be designed at two distinct levels: one of the formed routines and one of the formative contexts. When throughout this book we will suggest the design of systems to support team and market arrangements, the design task should be conceived at these two levels. The first is concerned with the restructuring of routines, transactions and the boundaries that define the modes of production, co-ordination and division of labour between the members of the organisation. The second deals with the frames, beliefs and consolidated ways of thinking of those who work in the old, or the new, computer-supported organisation. Though the book presents models and methods that focus mainly on the first level of design, that is, of the architecture of routines and transactions, it should be kept in mind that full-scale change takes place only by intervening at both levels. And the interplay between the two levels is in itself a design variable. For example, one may redraw the boundary between a hierarchy and a market, by changing the employment contracts that govern the transactions between people inside and outside the organisation, as a first, structural step to changing ingrained habits, preferences, belief systems and roles of the members of the hierarchy. This kind of interplay, whereby systems and organisational arrangements are not just treated as technological and economic artifacts but also as formative contexts, is explored and exploited in the case recounted in chapter 11, dealing with the deconstruction of an airline bureaucracy through the joint deployment of networks, team arrangements and a market-like bidding system for the allocation of jobs.

Conclusions

The four models of rationality can highlight the effects of networking technologies discussed in the Introduction. Unlimited and limited rationality allow us to analyse the efficiency and content effects, by pointing out how information technology can improve operations, decision making and information flows. Limited rationality points to the individual learning processes, whereby access to more information helps the decision maker to overcome some of the limitations to its rationality and to the socialisation effects that take place in a hierarchy, seen as the main mechanism for economising on bounded rationality. The model of strategic rationality can be employed, on the other hand, to analyse the socialisation effects in a variety of mixed-interest organisational settings, such as markets, hierarchies and teams. Finally, the adaptive rationality framework is well suited to understand the ramifications of the learning and transformation effects, by employing the notion of formative context.

Another general conclusion is that information technology cannot render economic organisations, such as markets, hierarchies or teams, completely transparent. The models of rationality reviewed in this chapter show some of the reasons why. First, agents have limited rationality in computing their means–ends chains to achieve selected goals. Second, they use idiosyncratic knowledge to create advantages in any kind of mixed-interest game, that is, when organisational co-operation is intermingled with competition. Opportunistic information processing and communication stemming from lack of mutual trust can make information flows in an organisation even more complex and opaque than those yielded by pure task uncertainty. Finally, when laying out plans, designing the means–ends chain of actions aimed at achieving the goals, or finding ruses to cheat the adversaries, agents' choices and interventions are influenced by background organisational and cognitive contexts of which they are often unaware.

Today, the information-systems models in wide currency are designed according to methodologies that embed the model of unlimited rationality, or that of bounded rationality. Strategic and adaptive rationality models still lie largely outside the theory of management information systems. It is the purpose of this volume to explore the analysis and design ramifications of the strategic rationality perspective, as expressed in the transaction-cost view, and more generally by the economics of organisations. By highlighting the intricacies of adaptive rationality, this chapter has focused on some of the limitations of the economic perspective. These are relevant especially in change processes and should be taken into account when designing systems that have a global and long-term impact, such as the so-called strategic information systems (see ch. 9).

2   Teams

Introduction

In addressing a conference on 'Technology and the Future of Work' held at Stanford University in March 1990, Donald E. Petersen, former chairman of the board and chief executive officer of the Ford Motor Company, maintained strongly that the organisations destined to ride the wave of new technologies over the next decade will be those equipped with the 'T-word'. 'T' for technology? Nothing could be further from the truth. In this case 'T' stands for teamwork, as the paramount organisational approach that can support the implementation of new technology. Teamwork can be defined at six levels at least:

between those who put the new technology in place and those who use it;

among work groups at production level, across skills, functions, departments and classifications;

between doers and managers, even at the expense of changing current industrial relations and divides;

within the management group, downplaying or eliminating 'artificial' functional hierarchies so that managers can work together with the confidence of equals, obliterating the dominance of a function over others;

among firms: in global industries firms need access to markets and technologies, to learn about new ways of organising and to support large investment in R&D projects, and they can only do so by integrating competition and rivalry with co-operation and collaboration;

across institutions, for example between business, academia and government, to tackle problems such as workforce education or R&D that may concern the entire productive sector or the economy as a whole.

It is almost ironic, and certainly very telling, that it was the president of the Ford Motor Company who brought forward and implemented such sweeping changes in work organisation that also included the application of the new technology. After all, it was at Ford where it all began, in terms of hierarchical, non-team-based job design and the application of technology (the assembly line) to simplify and fragment work.

Since the appearance of the assembly line and the diffusion of the principles of a Scientific Management by F. W. Taylor there have been attempts to introduce Human Relations on the shop floor. Attempts have been made to enlarge, rotate and enrich jobs. With the most recent discovery of superior Japanese models, these have also been applied. However, it was the socio-technical school at the Tavistock Institute in the United Kingdom that made the first systematic discovery, analysis and design of work teams after the Second World War. Indeed, the school produced the most detailed analysis of the forces that create work teams and keep them together, and new criteria for the design of internal structures, roles, communications channels and task interdependencies. The teachings of the socio-technical school provide the base for our own analysis of teams as viable alternatives to hierarchies.

More specifically, what we are setting out to do in this chapter is to reach beyond the present awareness of the importance of teamwork. Indeed, teamwork has been present all along, under the very eyes of every production manager or office supervisor, but has always been neglected or, worse, suppressed for the sake of efficiency and the principles of Fordism and Taylorism. Our purpose is to forgo as much as possible the current, emphatic preaching on teamwork and concentrate instead on the identification of structural foundations for teams to obtain in a business organisation. The ultimate goal of this exercise is to achieve the teams' viability, self-regulation and growth.

Such foundations can be discerned in the following:

the nature of the tasks to be performed, their interdependence and co-operation requirements;

the characteristics of the technology that supports the execution and control of tasks;

the informal relationships that develop among people working in the same work setting;

the economics of togetherness, that is, in the added value generated by working together and in the economic forces that bind teams or tear them apart;

the cognitive aspects, that is, how members of the team think, define the reality and solve problems collectively.

Our study of teams will highlight the communication and information-processing characteristics that are specific to teams, as opposed to other forms of work organisation. This method should enable us to *design* in the following chapters communication and information systems that support teams effectively – systems that we have come to call groupware or collaborative media, or more generally, mediating technologies. This approach will necessarily be of an interdisciplinary nature. However, at this stage we will omit a full analysis of the role of the technology (to be discussed separately in the next chapter).

Finally, note that terminology has shifted over the years: what the socio-technical school called 'work group' is today mostly referred to as teamwork. One could endeavour to draw a finer distinction between different concepts, such as group and team, the former encompassing the aspects of interdependence, shared purpose, membership and conscious-ness, the latter focusing on the notions of concerted action and common aim (Adair, 1986). In the following pages we prefer to use both terms loosely, since we draw on different literature and especially different disciplines, in which these terms are sometimes used interchangeably and at other times assume a narrow, technical definition (such as teams in economic theory).

The coal-mining studies

The history of the discovery of the importance of teams as a form of efficient work organisation is once again a tale of concern over productivity and new technology. The (black) stage is set in the coal mines of South Yorkshire at the end of the 1940s. At that time a group of psychiatrists from the Tavistock Institute of Human Relations in London was asked by representatives of the newly nationalised coal industry to look into the causes of lagging productivity and high labour unrest that plagued most of the British mines. The directorate of the National Coal Board was puzzled because it had been thought that the major causes of problems in the coal-mining industry had been removed by the nationalisation and recent advances in the technology of coal extraction. Nationalisation was sup-posed to bridge the labour–management divide, while new technology, that is, mechanisation, was to increase levels of productivity in the new industrial-relations context. But neither of the expected outcomes seemed to have materialised.

The Tavistock people, headed by Eric Trist, were trained in the study of groups and their performance, for example in analysing the behaviour of groups of pilots in the cockpit during long flights on war missions. Their background in therapy was based on Bion's (see 1961) theory of group behaviour and Lewin's (1947) social psychology. This background proved very useful in helping them to see and evaluate the dysfunctions of the current method of mechanising the mine operations, the so-called long-wall method of coal extraction, and to appreciate the importance of teamwork in the traditional, pre-mechanisation forms of coal mining.

In positive terms, a former miner and research fellow at the Tavistock, Jim Bamforth, helped the experts to discover and see that working in a group could also take place in an effective way in the mechanised mines: the old tradition of working in a small team was viable, on a larger scale, with the aid of the more advanced technology. For the first time, assembly-line technology was uncoupled from the rigid, sequential fragmentation of tasks: principles of work design that were at odds with Taylor's prescriptions and with the Fordist model of production organisation were shown to be more efficient and more humane.

The discoveries made by the Tavistock researchers were remarkable for their focus on the deep interaction between the technology of the workplace, the tasks and the work organisation. This focus provides a perspective on teams, still valued today, for the redesign of business organisations through new information technologies.

In fact, concern for informal relations on the shop floor and the role of cliques was strong, at least in the welfare departments of large companies on the other side of the Atlantic (recall the Hawthorne experiments by the Human Relations School – see Mayo, 1933). But such informal groups were perceived as an organisation created by the workers in parallel to that based on production, interfering with or supporting the latter according to circumstances. It was within the scope of the prescriptions of the Human Relations School that such quasi-independent organisations could be manipulated to productive ends. On the other hand, such prescriptions would say nothing about the way tasks and jobs were grouped, divided and allocated to people, and in particular, about the way technology was to be deployed in the workplace. Such choices were left to management entirely.

It was the first coal miners study by Trist and Bamforth (1951) that tilted the balance in the division of roles between task execution and task direction as prescribed by Taylor's Scientific Work Organization and left unchallenged by the Human Relations School. As the main methodological premise to the investigation of the causes of lagging productivity and low morale in the British mines, the authors stated that, in order to look for clues to the origin of the deficiencies of new mechanised work methods and the disillusions due to the lack of magic that was expected from nationalisation (in a miner's words: 'My coals don't wear any new look since Investment Day. They give me a look as black as before'), 'the social and psychological can be understood only in terms of the detailed engineering facts and of the way the technological system as a whole behaves in the environment of the underground situation' (Trist and Bamforth, 1951: 11).

With such a premise, the notion of the work organisation, as a *sociotechnical system* was born – the notion that would allow management to look at work practices from a more comprehensive, 'system' perspective (Emery and Trist, 1960).

The socio-technical perspective suggested focusing on the complex and varied relationships between the technological subsystem and the social subsystem, comparing various social and technological arrangements found in the mines and evaluating them according to at least two criteria: efficiency and workers' satisfaction.

High productivity and morale would be the outcome of a good 'system matching', and not of the optimisation of the single subsystem, be it the technology or the human relations between the workers and management. The design of tasks, their grouping into jobs and the definition of appropriate occupational roles supported by effective communications would provide the 'architectural' elements to implement this matching in the permanent structure of the new work organisation.

The results of the early comparison made by the Tavistock researchers between the pre-mechanised work organisation and the new methods promoted by the nationalised industry management showed that mechanisation disrupted the old equilibrium of the traditional work methods without being able to install a new one. The pre-mechanised system was based on a small group of six mates, the marrow group, that would work in couples for each of the three shifts, negotiating the price of extracted coal with the mine management and sharing the income equally. Each miner had multiple skills and could pick up at any point the job as it had been left by the team-mates of the previous shift.

Certainly, strong co-operation above and below the ground was required to ensure smooth operations. In addition, the whole mining community kept each miner in check, so that in re-assembling teams for a new job the reputation of each miner as a worker and as a team-mate was well established and well known. This would not prevent rivalry between teams in competing for the best seams; but again, the community had rules and rituals to keep such rivalry under control. Also, seniority was informally a ranking criterion: the senior miner was better acquainted with mates, supervisors and seams, so that he had the advantage over others when it came to choosing mates, mining methods and bargaining for seams.

The new technology had disrupted this equilibrium. To begin with, the mechanised line that now ran on the coal face was accompanied by an assembly line in an arranged order, or in other words, a long wall: forty to fifty people were now members of a 'cycle group' at the work face, and that required in turn an elementary hierarchy of supervisors (shot-firers and shift deputies). Second, it introduced a detailed specialisation of jobs: workers in each shift performed a specific set of tasks during the various phases of coal extraction. Thus, fixed jobs and work roles were ascertained for borers, cutters, gummers, belt-breakers, rippers and fillers. Each job had different responsibilities and a different pay scale. In practice, the strengthening of this bureaucratic system led to severe grievances, stress and turnover and low productivity.

Briefly, what happened was that at the end of each shift only a part of the jobs planned could actually be performed because of unplanned events, or discrepancies, occurring at the face (such as smoke, dust and brittle roof). The following shift was composed of workers expected to perform other tasks, with different pay scales. They could be redeployed only after renegotiating their contract: this had to be done on the spot, underground, by the supervisors, literally in the dark. If pay was perceived as inadequate, workers would refuse to carry on with their work or haggle for more money. In addition, rivalry and scapegoating *between* the shifts manifested themselves, rendering the work organisation both unstable and unproductive, in spite of the new technology. Thus, by comparison the Tavistock researchers concluded that in the new system the interdependence of the tasks in the coal-extraction cycle was not matched by an integrated social group, as was the case in the pre-mechanised system.

They also identified the cause of such a state of affairs in the implicit reference models employed by management in introducing mechanisation with the work arrangements of the mechanised factories. That is to say, the management did not realise that while in a factory a relatively high degree of control could be exercised behind the scenes of any type of production process, and the assembly line in particular, by ensuring regularities in the supply of raw materials, workforce and subcomponents, the underground situation of a coal mine was much less stable. On the contrary, it was highly vulnerable to unpredictable events. Since the whole production process in any seam was much more prone to disorganisation due to the uncertainty and complexity of underground conditions, any 'bureaucratic' allocation of jobs could easily be disrupted. Coping with emergencies and coping with the coping became part of workers' and supervisors' everyday activities. These activities would lead to stress, conflict and low productivity because they continually clashed with the technological arrangements and the way they were planned and subdivided around them. Dust, falling roofs, hard faces and other, even harder, conditions due to insufficient availabilty of modern technological tools were also part of life in the pre-mechanised mines, causing fatigue and stress.

But these conditions were of a different nature. The traditional, or marrow, group had only to cope with the vagaries of nature. Indeed, the social organisation of the team constituted the moral and practical support for dealing with the uncertainties of the job: senior miners would give advice to younger, stronger members in the group, and each member was ready to take up any task left or forthcoming. There was no room for 'free riding'. Whereas in the mechanised settings, the additional source of uncertainty stemmed from suspicion about lack of co-operation from the previous shift. Also, supervisors who were there to implement modifications in task allocation and corresponding pay, not being able to control (in the dark) the true causes of disruption, whether 'environmental' or 'human', introduced further elements of reciprocal suspicion between management and workers. The net result was that the social organisation turned into an obstacle to effective performance and mutual support.

This accurate analysis would not have led anywhere in particular had it not been accompanied by another discovery. The discovery of new work organisations emerging locally, out of *ad hoc* wage agreements between management and unions, was made by Bamforth, in the very area where he used to work as a miner. To the attentive observer such new arrangements showed explicitly that with the same technology platform a different, and more productive organisation was viable. And most interestingly, it was the *team* arrangement that seemed to have recaptured the spirit and some of the structural characteristics of the pre-mechanised work groups, only on a far greater scale and with an advanced technology. In reporting his discovery back at the Tavistock, Bamforth called these teams the composite long-wall work method.

The new form of work organisation features forty-one men who allocate themselves to tasks and shifts. Although tasks and shifts replicate those of the conventional mechanised system, management and supervisors do not monitor, enforce and reward single task executions. The composite group takes over some managerial tasks, as it had in the case of the pre-mechanised, marrow group, such as selection of members and the informal monitoring of work performance.

Cycle completion, not task execution, becomes a common goal that allows for shared learning and mutual support, rather than rivalry, between mates. In the wage system there is no distinction between specialised and ancillary tasks that have to be paid additionally. There is just a basic wage and a bonus linked to the total productivity of the group throughout the whole cycle, not by shift. Thus competition between each shift that plagued the conventional long-wall is effectively eliminated: each subteam has no interest in leaving the face in a bad condition for the next team. On the contrary, it anticipates the effects of its work on later shifts, trying to forestall the main causes of additional work. As a result, unlike the task group in the conventional system that was consistently lagging behind, the composite teams were often ahead of schedule (Trist *et al.*, 1963).

The researchers point out that in the composite group the re-organisation of tasks and the 'marrow' traditions combine to enhance a common identity of the workers and establish the perception of an equal contribution to the whole production goal. These forces become the strong glue that holds the social system together in coping with the complex and uncertain environment. The source of social uncertainty that plagues the conventional long-wall system is reduced or eliminated, while the more advanced technological infrastructure is kept in place and fully exploited, thus showing significant productivity increases if compared with the marrow group.

Finally, the management structure can also be trimmed down as a result: three overmen become redundant and the deputy can again assume the role of a technical and safety leader.

The team as an open system

The discovery that new mechanised technology could support what the Tavistock researchers called 'organisational choice', and, more specifically, that a work group could perform as well as, or actually better than, a group in the traditional (that is, Fordist) organisation, induced them to look at work groups as a general organisational form, as a work system which comprised a set of activities that made up a functioning whole rather than single jobs into which it was decomposable (Trist, 1981). Such a work system can be studied in more detail, especially in order to trace those universal design principles that could be applied in any industrial setting to create teams adapted to specific production systems.

A few general principles were identified by importing categories from the systems theory. First, the work group, and organisations in general, are seen as 'open system' transacting with the environment. Environments differ for their degree of turbulence, that is, complexity, uncertainty and change. Work groups, being open systems, must adapt their own internal structure and functions so as to cope with environments of varying complexity.

What do these structures and functions look like? The socio-technical school finds a solution to this question in the cybernetic view of organisations. What distinguishes a system from an aggregate of activities and preserves its boundary and integrity is the existence of *regulation* (Rice, 1958). With a view to sustaining their integrity as a group, teams need to carry out regulating activities that maintain them in a stable state with the evolving environment. In order to depict, and design, such fundamental activities, the best analogy is to be found in a control system and the functions it performs (see figure 2.1): decisions and actions are taken so that the production process under control preserves its stable state, that is, its output falls within the range of acceptable behaviour, set by the standards or goals of the whole work system.

The main functions that can be thus identified are as follows:
a knowledge or memory function that contains the work programmes and routines; by selecting the most appropriate routine the work group

is able to implement decisions that keep the process evolving according to the set goals;

a feedback function that monitors output and the state of the system, and communicates it back to the decision-making unit;

a forecasting function able to anticipate and detect disturbances coming from the environment;

a communication function whereby standards, decisions, actions and feedbacks are communicated to each subcomponent.

The role of the technology in such a work system can be of great relevance. Emery (1972: 85) describes it as follows: 'The technological component, in converting inputs into outputs, plays a major role in determining the self-regulating properties of enterprise. It functions as one of the major boundary conditions of the social system mediating between the ends of an enterprise and the external environment.'

Socio-technical analysis and design focus on how to provide the social system with know-how, regulation and communication support, so that it can control the technological component of the work system.

The principle on which this system functions is explained in the cybernetic model of figure 2.1. In order to control the process, the work group will intervene each time there is a deviation or variance of output from the pre-assigned standard. A backward procedure can be employed to empower the team with an appropriate level of regulating capacity:

First, the basic transformation or conversion processes that characterise the work system and the stages when the production technology intervenes are identified; these are called *unit operations*, that is, the changes of states, or transformation of the material or product, that take place.

Second, the disturbances, or main *variances*, that characterise each transformation process are depicted: these variances usually affect the quantity or quality of production, generating costs and stress in the work system as a whole.

How and at what cost, and with which resources the team perceives, controls and regulates such variances is then described in a *variance control table*.

Such a table allows for evaluating to what extent the present work organisation of the team makes way for performing variance control and regulation effectively, or whether it is the case of redesigning tasks, jobs, skills, communication and authority structures for such actions to be executed more efficiently. The socio-technical analysis can also shed light on what type of *information system* (in terms of data flows, files and decision-support systems) may be required by the *work organisation* to function more effectively (Bostrom and Heinen, 1977; Mumford, 1979).

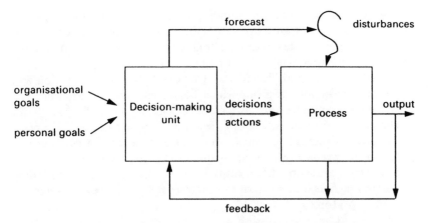

Figure 2.1 A decision-making process represented as a control system

Semi-autonomous work groups

In socio-technical theory the functioning and permanence of teams as a productive organisational form is based on the concept of self-regulation, that is, on its internal capacity to maintain the stable state as a whole system: the more the key variances can be controlled by the group, the better the results and the higher the member satisfaction. For example, in the coal-mines study the composite work organisation was described as one in which the group was semi-autonomous, that is, that took over a large amount of responsibility for the total cycle of operations. No member had a fixed work role; instead, the men deployed themselves according to the requirements of the on-going task (Herbst, 1962).

The viability of a team arrangement as found, and subsequently introduced, by the socio-technical school, depends on its *autonomy*. The team must 'own' to a considerable extent the overall task, the criteria for subdivision and allocation of subtasks, the physical boundaries of the work setting, the measurements available for control and feedback on performance.

Autonomy of a team is best measured in terms of the decisions that can be taken at the collective level. There are decisions that are intrinsic to the production process. A group that is able to make decisions in this area is said to be self-regulating (Sussman, 1976); that is, it has control over the attainment of certain performance standards (typical examples are co-ordination of tasks, allocation of tasks and resources, boundary maintenance and controlling inputs and outputs to the group).

Second, there are decisions of independence whereby the team can

disconnect itself from the surrounding organisations and their requirements, and buffer its own actions from their claims (typical issues that can
be addressed by the team are the following: where and when will the
product be produced, and in what sequence?).

Thirdly, the team can decide about its own internal organisation and
governance (how will the group leader be chosen, and with what powers;
who will represent the group with management and unions?).

The distribution of regulatory decisions depends on the nature of
environmental and technological conditions that the team faces (Sussman,
1976). More specifically, one can distinguish the following:

boundary-transaction uncertainty, that is, the uncertainty regarding
   issues such as the arrival of raw materials, demand, new technologies
   and workforce;

transformation or conversion uncertainty related to the complexity of
   the transformation process (materials, methods, technology) that
   characterise the primary task of the work unit.

Also, the distribution of regulatory tasks depends on the technically
required co-operation, that is, the pattern of co-operation acts required to
attain a technical or production goal, in particular when the sharing of
materials, work pieces or systems is implied (Meissner, 1969).

Co-operation can be grouped into *reciprocal*, *sequential* and *pooled* types
(Thompson, 1967). In the first type, dependence between the members of
the team is mediated by a common tool, work piece or system, which may
have varying degrees of complexity and uncertainty (for example, a rescue
team, a surgical team): the actions taken by a group member may modify
the conditions under which any or all the other members take action. In the
second, such dependence is sequential in time, space or both. Finally, in the
pooled interdependence each member can perform his or her task in an
independent and discrete way.

The combination of the three variables, boundary and conversion
uncertainty, and type of technical cooperation, for example assuming that
each variable can have a binary value (high or low; yes or no), gives rise to
eight cases (Sussman, 1976). The most important are the following:

The assembly line: Tasks are standardised, the environment is certain,
   but some forms of dependence and co-operation are required. It is the
   assembly-line arrangement that makes the three main components of
   group autonomy separable and allocable both within or outside the
   boundaries of the group, thus leaving open the alternative between a
   self-regulated team and an externally controlled team. In the latter
   case the actual autonomy of the group may be so low that the team
   arrangement will have no reason, or intrinsic strength to survive as
   such.

The automated plant: In this case members must frequently share the knowledge about what, where or when to convert inputs into outputs. Though the latter process is standardised, co-ordination about boundary conditions and circumstances cannot be separated from the regulated activities without incurring losses: the cost of transmitting information from an activity or resource to a separate coordinator may be high, relative to the cost of time delays. Thus decisions about boundary maintenance may be spread among group members. This case represents the situation in an automated plant where the conversion activities have been automated, while operators have to face unexpected events coming from outside the automated system.

The surgical team: In a surgical team the uncertainty about the conversion process is high. Mutual adjustment (real-time scheduling) between members is the preferred way of co-ordination. The regulatory activities tend to be delegated to the group. Even if such functions are allocated externally, for example to a supervisor, this will not limit the effective, and necessary, autonomy of the team.

Standards: Given the relative independence of each member who can carry out his or her task fairly independently of others, co-ordination is carried out through standardised routines. Standards provide reference measures for quality and quantity of performance and output, depending on whether the uncertainty hits the boundaries or conversion activities. Allocation of responsibility outside the team can be accomplished if the members decide to share an external resource dedicated to monitoring uncertainties at the boundaries of the team.

If extended as a general design principle, the possibility of allocating regulating functions to the team would help the emergence of work organisations based on constituent work groups (an organisation as a 'team of teams') with jointly shared skills and networked boundary supervisors (see for an application of this concept the case discussed in chapter 11). This would create robust organisational units having intra-group, inter-group and aggregate relations with a whole operational task and within the technology. This kind of organisation would provide considerable room for free movement of the individual, and would also be naturally open to interorganisational networks.

Teams as information processors

The basic assumption of variance control and allocation of regulating decisions within a team is that over the large array of situations, the range of variances controllable by a group is greater than that controllable by individuals separately linked to an external supervisor (Trist, 1981).

Such an assumption can be specified through a more general typology of organisations based on the degree of task uncertainty as formulated by Galbraith (1977). This classification of organisational forms is of interest for two reasons. First, it is explicitly based on the information processing aspects of organisations. Second, it distinctly compares forms of group and non-group arrangements, thus showing in general what the conditions are for the employment of team-like structures.

According to Galbraith, a team or group arrangement is just one of the possible organisational mechanisms necessary to co-ordinate interdependent roles. More specifically, as the amount of task uncertainty increases the organisations adopt co-ordinating mechanisms which allow them to handle more information effectively (see the model of bounded rationality in chapter 1): teams represent one of such mechanisms that should be set up when facing high levels of uncertainty.

For routine tasks, the basic mechanism is given by rules or programmes that contain all that is requested by the situation (events and responses) (March and Simon, 1958). As the organisation faces uncertainty, the hierarchy is employed to deal with exceptions arising from the execution of the rules. However, the hierarchy itself is limited in its capability to handle exceptions: co-ordination by objectives is then the next alternative, for higher levels of uncertainty. Here co-ordination takes place by specifying outcomes or targets instead of behaviours or rules to be followed. Setting goals and planning for their achievement reduces the information processing by delegating autonomy to the lower levels.

For even higher levels of uncertainty the hierarchy must integrate further mechanisms based on two fundamental strategies:

Reduce the need for information processing by using slack resources or creating self-contained tasks.

Increase the capacity to process information by investing in vertical information systems or setting up lateral relations.

Let us consider each substrategy in more detail. Team arrangements will appear in at least two of them, restating the role of teams as autonomous groups (self-containment substrategy) and as non-hierarchical arrangements (lateral relations).

Using slack resources means setting more accommodating goals, allowing production or delivery delays, by increasing inventory levels, budgets and lead times. The use of slack resources results in reducing the amount of interdependence between organisational subunits (increasingly adopting pooled interdependence, as mentioned above) and between the organisation and environment.

The creation of self-contained units corresponds to the divisionalisation strategy. Each unit is dedicated to facing the requirements of a specific product, technology or market. Information processing will thus be more focused on a particular class of problems. The cost of this strategy is the loss of economies of scale and the duplication of many functions and departments. Thus,

the first two strategies reduce the amount of information by lowering performance standards and creating small autonomous groups to provide the output. Information is reduced because an exception is less likely to occur and few factors need to be considered when an exception does occur. The next two strategies accept the performance standards and division of labour as given and adapt the organisation so as to process the new information which is used during task performance. (Galbraith, 1977: 55)

Hierarchical information systems provide those extra communication channels needed to deal with the larger amount of exception, without lowering tasks performance. They allow for the improvement on the number and speed of feedback signals that can be handled centrally, thus facilitating the replanning both at a higher frequency and lower cost. To be sure, information systems may involve formalisation, and the success of this strategy depends on the extent to which information can be effectively formalised.

Finally, lateral relations can reduce the overload of the hierarchy by allowing communication and decision making across the lines of authority. The level of decision making is moved down the hierarchy without divisionalising it. By this process the existing informal contacts are reinforced, widened in scope and institutionalised. Liaison roles may be created to deal with horizontal communication in order to decrease departmentalisation. When it becomes necessary to integrate more departments, tasks forces may be set up by gathering people from different divisions on a temporary basis to accomplish a specific task. Should the need arise for a permanent moulding of the collective decision process that usually materialises in a hierarchy, teams are then established explicitly. How to achieve consensus and how to designate a leader are the crucial design issues for ensuring the good functioning of teams. If horizontal relations become as important as those of a vertical nature, a dual authority structure needs to be put in place. This gives rise to a matrix organisation: the good functioning of the matrix depends on the balance between the vertical and horizontal reporting lines.

Confirming the socio-technical school and Galbraith's conclusions, Aoki (1988) has carried out a comparison between Japanese and American firms, and shows how the Japanese firm has an information structure based on lateral relations that would explain its superiority over the conventional model of the American firm based on the functional hierarchy. Specifically, the internal information structure of the Japanese firm is more decentralized, as it relies on horizontal communication among functional units and autonomous problem solving at individual work units, made possible through the development of workers' integrative skills as opposed to segmented and specialized skills. Such decentralized structure is shown to be effective in adapting the work process flexibly and swiftly to a continually changing market and technological environment. (1988: 4)

Reconsidering the coal-mines studies: the economic dimension

From the socio-technical perspective the economic dimension of a work system always follows the matching of its social and technical components. 'It is of course the socio-psychological and technological which are the substantive dimensions. The economic dimension measures the effectiveness with which human and technological resources are used to carry out the primary task' (Trist *et al.*, 1963: 6).

However on closer examination, it turns out that wage structures, efficiency gains and pay incentives were concomitant not only with the innovations brought to light in the coal mines, but also with those implemented by the Tavistock experts in Indian textile mills, and with the failures of many semi-autonomous work groups established in European and US companies in the 1960s. On the basis of this, in reviewing the socio-technical theory and practice, Kelly (1982) concludes that (a) often under the label of the best match between the social and technical components, the goal is to maximise machine and labour utilisation; and (b) the significance of pay incentives has been systematically downplayed in the socio-technical literature.

Indeed, looking at the coal-mines studies in a different light, that of the pay incentives, is a good introduction to the main aspects of team economics. Let us consider first the wage schemes of the three work systems found in the coal mines over the years by the Tavistock specialists.

In the single-place (pre-mechanised) tradition, the marrow group is a self-regulating unit in contractual status. Each team of six miners makes its own contract with the colliery management. Groups of higher ability contract for a higher pay and payment is based on output, that is, extracted coal. The wage system is so organised because both the narrowness of the work face and the darkness restrict the range of effective supervision. Consequently, leadership and supervision are interwoven in the group.

The operations of the mines are sustained by a rudimentary management system: the deputy, who maintains safety regulations and services the technical needs of the group at the face, and the overman, who checks the output of groups and buys it. A negotiated price is paid for a given amount of coal, with allowances for special circumstances. The price for a ton of coal is fixed by bargaining between the management and the union. Within this quasi-market there exist two possible competition strategies between the groups: competing on inputs and workplaces. It has been mentioned that seniority, hence experience, could systematically privilege groups that were always able to obtain better seams. In order to re-introduce fairness in competition, a ritual procedure, called cavilling, was implemented by the community. Every quarter all work places were pooled and drawn by lot so as to give each group an equal chance of working in favourable or less favourable conditions. In this way, the information asymmetries between the teams were curbed and the folk law of cavilling presented the means to restrain unfair rivalry among miners. Also, cavilling allowed for periodical disbandment of teams and for self-reallocation of miners. This presented a threat to 'free riders', that is, lazy miners who with a new round may have found themselves isolated or were forced to work with inferior groups.

Competition in the supply of inputs was very strong and was described in the earlier study by Trist and Bamforth (1951) as follows: 'Trammers were encouraged to resort to sharp practices to obtain adequate supplies of tubs. As supplies were often short, the amount of coal a working pair could send up depended not a little on the prowess of the trammer . . . In the common saying, it was he who could lie, cheat, or bully the most who made the best trammer' (1951: 8–9). To be sure, intergroup competition never reached the level of conflict that might have compromised the loyalties on which the small team depends. The cavilling custom, the traditional labour–management divide, the knitted relationship of mutual support in the seam community produced a highly organised and stable population.

Thus, the traditional work system can be described as a multiple layered organisation as follows:

At the core there is a team, subject to group pay based on outcome.

The teams operate in a market where the price is decided by the management and union.

The managerial hierarchy is very thin.

The larger community provides the background support for the work groups in the mine.

In the mechanised, long-wall system, the one-man/one-task principle applies. The pay scheme follows suit. Individual miners are paid only for the amount of a specialised task they perform. Any additional tasks have to be rewarded separately. Having no direct financial interest in the outcome of the whole cycle, workers disregard the conditions of the face that do not pertain to their task, nor do they care for the equipment.

However, these conditions must be kept in order to achieve a timely cycle completion.

Cuttermen concentrating on yards cut, which is their basis of payment, do not bother if they crop some of the coal and leave it for the filler to dig out. Fillers concentrating on tons filled, are not greatly worried for the consequences for the pullers . . . All the groups proceed as though the cycle operation were limited to their own task. (Trist *et al.*, 1963: 120)

As a consequence, the co-ordination had to be supplied by the management, which introduced several levels of hierarchy into the mine. Supervisors had to be present at the face to meter the miner's performance. Through collective bargaining prices were fixed for each task, within a certain range of conditions: this is what is known as a contingent-claim labour contract (see ch. 6). Unfortunately, actual contingencies are difficult to evaluate on the face because of darkness and continuously shifting conditions.

Moreover, there are separate agreements for subtasks and ancillary activities. For many of these, prices are agreed on *ex ante*, and negotiation focuses on determining the state of the world which has obtained at the moment of the execution of the task. But for other prices contracting on the spot is required. As a result the deputy has to spend a considerable time underground with a notebook and pencil to determine and negotiate due pay. Thus the pit is transformed from a well-lubricated bureaucracy where everybody is pre-assigned a task and a corresponding wage into a marketplace where everyone haggles.

Competition between workers now affects even the shifts: each shift group aims to maximise its own earnings, not caring about what happens to the following shift. The few team elements left become informal and dysfunctional: that is, such competition does not endanger 'worker solidarity', and collusion over 'made work' provides an escape valve (Trist *et al.*, 1963). No task group finishes its work on time, so that the next group has to be paid an additional amount to complete the work left from the previous shift. Given the limits to supervision at the face, it is impossible to pinpoint the responsibility for delays incurred by each shift and terminate intershift scapegoating.

It is noteworthy that the emergence of the composite work group was due to a wage-system reform, called the 'Manley innovation', based on the name of the seam where it was first introduced. Due to bad roof conditions, the operations of the seam were supported by a short-wall system where groups of six to eight men worked on a face in each shift. The operations sequence was akin to the 'single-place' system, but the group was larger in size. When the roof was finally brought under control, management wanted to switch operations to a conventional long-wall. However, this move was strongly resisted by the miners. After negotiations that lasted a year, an agreement was reached that preserved not only the advantages of the composite work group, but also solved the economic problems of the mechanised work cycle at the longer faces.

Much of the new organisation is determined by the wage system. As mentioned in the earlier section, there is a basic wage in the composite work group set above the legal minimum so as to avoid contingent payments. The rest is bonus on output, to be gained in full if the cycle is completed without additional resources.

The new system achieves the following objectives:
It eliminates those items paid for separately.

It restores goal congruence within and between groups; competition between the shifts is eliminated and every miner is committed to avoiding any cause of additional work.

It gives back supervisors their traditional role of technical support and safety monitoring.

On the one hand, the teams are self-regulating, for immediate cycle control is internal; on the other, they are induced to seek the deputy's technical leadership, which furthers their mission and increases productivity and earnings. The composite organisation resembles that of the single-place form but on a different technological basis: control mechanisms embedded into the wage system allow for an overall reduction of cheating, mutual scapegoating and opportunism.

Does this mean that it is the social, the technical or the economic component that determines the superior performance of the composite group? In trying to address this question, let us now focus on the technology and the economics, leaving the social component aside, at least in our cursory discussion.

Technology seems to affect significantly the scale of operations, the potential level of productivity (extracted coal) and thus the size of the shift group, but it does not determine unequivocally the division of labour. Rather, the division of labour is heavily determined by the uncertainty and complexity of the task at the coal face. The superior performance of the composite group derives from the fact that a different wage arrangement, a different labour contract, restrains conflicts and opportunism not only between the miners themselves, but also between them and the management.

Indeed, let us now imagine a different situation where there would be no cheaters, opportunists and free riders among the miners. The miners would then trust each other in the darkness at the coal face. Even so, the cycle completion could possibly be still far from perfect due to uncertainties and the difficult co-ordination underground. However, an increased specialisation of the task group would compensate for the inefficiencies in co-ordination. On the other hand, the costs resulting from the administrative monitoring apparatus would be eliminated (one could trust a miner and pay for the ancillary work), there would be no mutual scapegoating or psychological stress stemming from conflictual relations. Probably, the two forms would not differ so much in overall performance.

We conclude that in evaluating team organisation and design, economic forces have to be taken into account explicitly. Teams designed without taking into consideration the possible ramifications of self-interest-seeking behaviour of individual members are doomed to be utopian and condemned to encapsulation within the existing hierarchies – the destiny of most socio-technical experiments (Herbst, 1976).

The lesson we have learned from the economic re-examination of the coal mines studies can be summarised as follows:

The employment contract embeds a model of the work organisation that is at least as important as, if not more important than, the constraints posed by the technology or the broader social system.

Conflict over resources and earnings is ubiquitous both between workers and management and among workers themselves; under certain circumstances social control mechanisms (such as institutions and rituals) tend to keep in check such a level of conflict, but competition and rivalry are never completely eliminated unless an employment contract is put in place that is perceived as equitable by the relevant parties.

Agents do not stop short of manipulating information, hoarding know-how, keeping and reinforcing information asymmetries as powerful bargaining means, unless social and economic incentives are set in place to discourage such behaviour (see the model of strategic rationality in chapter 1).

We conclude that it is in the economics of teams that we must look for another 'pillar' to design viable teams.

The team effect

While students of organisations tend to focus on team arrangements aimed at coping with task and environmental uncertainties, economists intent on explaining the genesis and viability of firms and markets justify team arrangements on a combination of task, environment and human-behaviour uncertainty. Their perspective, then, can be of help in designing effective teams because it avoids the deficiencies that were pinpointed in the socio-technical school.

For Alchian and Demsetz (1972) team production is justified when members of the team are able to yield an output larger than the sum of each individual contribution (for example, a group of workers jointly lifting heavy cargo into trucks). The economic problem of joint or team production is that marginal inputs and outputs of team members cannot be directly observable, metered and rewarded.

The two authors hypothesise further that a specific system of metering and rewarding is crucial in stimulating a particular productivity response of the team as a whole and of each individual member: 'If the economic organization meters poorly, with rewards and productivity only loosely correlated, then productivity will be smaller; but if the economic organization meters well productivity will be greater' (Alchian and Demsetz, 1972: 779). This transpires for the reasons elicited in the coal-mines case: lack of trust, complex tasks and barriers to effective monitoring may cause (the suspicion of) shirking, cheating, scapegoating and haggling about actual performance and pay.

Thus, in a team we are faced with at least three situations:

perfect co-operation, while task and environment are complex and uncertain: members trust each other and no metering is necessary as members rely on each other's word; complexities inherent in tasks or unplanned events will not be the cause for team disruption or lower productivity;

diversity of interests, joined with programmable and easily separable tasks and predictable environment: shirking stemming from goal incongruence can be detected at no cost and rewards can be selectively apportioned according to performance; this will maintain a perception of equity and eliminate any incentive to shirking;

fragmentary co-operation due to partial goal congruence associated with joint and complex tasks and uncertain environment; in these conditions detection of shirking is not without cost, but if it is ineffective it will affect output negatively, as demonstrated in the coal-mines case.

The first type of organisation has been studied in economics by Marshack and Radner (1972) in the field of teams theory. In their models a team is made up of a number of decision makers with common interests (utility functions) and beliefs, but performing different parts of a complex task, thus controlling different variables and basing their decisions on different types of information. 'The theory of teams is concerned with (1) the allocation of decision variables (tasks) and information among the members of the team, and (2) the characterization of efficient decision rules, given the allocation of tasks and information' (Radner, 1989: 295). The problem is how best to co-ordinate interdependent individual agents sharing only partial information, and what can be the value of additional information to be provided so as to render them more productive. However, there is no need for incentives to persuade members to implement honestly the optimal decision function and use the information structure candidly.

A typical team problem would be that of travel agents authorised to sell flight reservations in the time before flight-reservation systems came into being: the travel agents and the airline had only partial information about what reservations had been booked by other agents. What would constitute the best information structure for agents to sell seats so as to minimise overbooking and avoid the situation of having too few reservations? And what difference would it make to profits if the information structure were to be modified, for example by centralising it (Radner, 1989)?

In the second case, the best (and most efficient) method for detecting performance is given by total decentralisation through market competition: shirking members could easily be found out because the effort required for executing each standardised subtask can be known *a priori* and easily metered. New members could be hired to replace those of a lazy disposition. Market competition among potential members would determine actual team membership and individual rewards since there would be a market price for standardised tasks attached to their performance. Also, the threat of being replaced through the market process would represent an effective deterrent to shirking for the incumbent members of the team. Inter-team competition would contribute to selecting those teams that through a trial-and-error search are most competent at metering and choosing productive members, so that there would be no real need for managers, organisers or employers.

Teams to be found, and created, in business organisations tend to fall into the third category: they are set up as task forces, work groups or project teams to solve complex tasks or operate in complex environments where it is difficult to detect shirking, because of joint-production or team-effects phenomena, and find adequate replacements that will not engage in shirking themselves. That is to say, such teams operate in market or hierarchical contexts where self-interest and trade-offs between leisure (laziness) and higher income cannot be ruled out from the decision-making process of each member regarding his or her own participation and contribution to the common effort.

In this situation, Alchian and Demsetz (1972) suggest that one method of reducing shirking is for someone to specialize as a monitor to check the input performance of team members, especially if output cannot be easily separated and attributed to individual members. And in order to keep the monitor in check, he or she must be entitled to the residual of the team, so that he or she will have an incentive not to shirk and supervise work effectively. Moreover, to discipline team members and reduce shirking the monitor must be given the power to revise and terminate members' contracts.

Thus, while in the second case the nature of the task suggested a totally decentralised management of independent contracts (the team as a market), in the present case the shirking-information problem of joint production points to a centralised governance of the contracts that keep the team together. In a nutshell, it points to a hierarchy based on a central authority, an appropriate apparatus of supervision and a set of employment contracts. Still, Alchian and Demsetz (1972: 783), emphasise that 'The relationship of each team member to the owner [the central monitor] of the firm . . . is simply a "quid pro quo" contract'.

In contrast to Galbraith, who saw teams as one possible organisational form for addressing the overload in co-ordination structures posed by high levels of task uncertainty, Alchian and Demsetz see decentralised teams (markets) and fully co-operative teams as lying on a continuum of different sets of contracting relationships among individuals. In this sense the behaviour of a hierarchical firm, or of a team, is akin to the behaviour of the market, that is, the outcome of a complex equilibrium of interests, incentives arranged through specific sets of contracts (Jensen and Meckling, 1976).

Indeed, viewing all organisations as sets, or nexuses, of explicit or implicit contracts among owners of factors of production represents a fundamental advance in the theory of the firm due to the institutional economists. In particular, a whole new theory, agency theory, has developed from the original intuition that the firm may be viewed as a team in which a principal employs agents to perform some service on his or her behalf, and there is a discrepancy between the objectives of the principal and those of the agents, which gives rise to so-called agency costs (Gurbaxani and Whang, 1991).

Economic analysis enables us to arrive at a more general model of teams compared to the cybernetic models that inspired the socio-technical theory. If we take the relationship between two individuals (a micro-team) and a task or production process as the elementary organisational unit, the following design approaches can be distinguished (see figure 2.2):

Assuming goal congruence between the members, there is no need for a specialised 'people-control mechanism'. The members will co-operate either through mutual adjustment or in a pooled or sequential way according to the requirements of the technology (of production and communication), the complexity of the task and the uncertainty of the environment. The form which best meets these variables may vary: rules and procedures will guarantee loose co-ordination when uncertainty is low, tasks are standardised and can be subdivided and technology is separable and known. Hierarchy will obtain when levels of uncertainty are higher, while more elevated horizontal co-ordination forms, including semi-autonomous teams, will be preferred when uncertainties and random events make the number of exceptions beyond the reach of hierarchical co-ordination (Galbraith, 1977). A supervisor will be nominated among the three members, and he or she will handle especially the boundary between the group and the external environment, while the group will be self-regulating for internal tasks. Productivity is related to workers' satisfaction in task execution, and this depends on issues such as avoiding fragmented jobs, or having opportunities to learn (Emery, 1972).

If goal incongruence exists, cheating, shirking and other forms of opportunistic behaviour cannot be ruled out. The organisation of the team must thus respond to a double set of requirements: to control the uncertainties of the production process and to establish a monitoring mechanism capable of keeping opportunism in check. The difficulty of measuring individual performance is the central concept that links the two control problems, technical (facing a complex task and environment) and social (checking divergent behaviour). Productivity depends on the effective solution to both problems: perceived fairness in treatment is as important as having a meaningful job.

Different solutions are, then, possible. Goal incongruence may be high between the members of the team, and this leads to two outcomes: a market arrangement, that is, an arm's length relationship regulated by competitive contracts, if the tasks can be unambiguously separated, contracted out and priced, or no organisation at all if the joint task is too complex. A clan form can obtain if goal congruence is very high, and such a closely knit organisation may indeed prove to be the best solution for facing new and complex tasks. The middle case is represented by the hierarchy: the members 'pay' a manager to monitor their performance and distribute rewards (see ch, 6).

Thinking teams

So far we have dealt with teams of various structures as 'self-regulating' social components of work systems (the socio-technical approach) or as sets of contracts between rational agents who may behave strategically. The two perspectives are different, but they show interesting similarities. Both share a concern with the 'structural' aspects that build up a team: tasks, control and co-ordination mechanisms, and incentives.

However, each transaction, each feedback loop that can be identified in describing the functioning of a team from the outside is also attached to a very concrete, touch-and-feel, social relation between human agents. Even institutional economists interested in the architectures of transactions between opportunist 'models of man' admit that productivity and efficiency of team arrangements are strongly influenced by the 'atmosphere' in the group (Williamson, 1975), that is, all the subtleties of the quality of human relationships that emerge in a team (Ouchi, 1981).

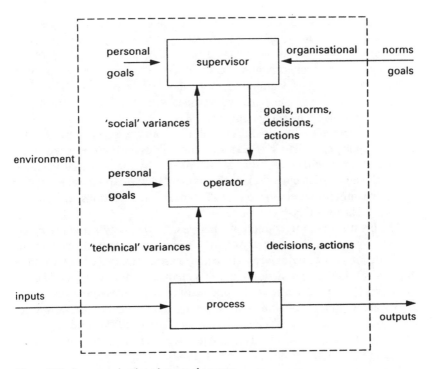

Figure 2.2 An organisational control system

Indeed, for a member of a closely knit group, for example a clan, the group serves functions that go beyond the pure economics of self-interest. Let us consider the following:

The group gives background legitimacy, a 'family feeling', an identity that overlaps with the individual identity of the single member: it provokes the transition from 'I' to 'we', from 'me' to 'us'.

By providing legitimacy, through traditions, a common language and a few shared routines, the group does some of the thinking for the member, both routine thinking and even life and death decisions (Douglas, 1986).

The group is the laboratory where such background social capital that helps the members in making decisions is developed, tried out and perfected. This is made possible by sharing the same work setting and machines, and by facing, that is, discovering, interpreting and solving, the same events collectively. These processes can be so biased that they may bring about dysfunctional consequences, such as 'group think', whereby members are not able to think and choose independently from the collective mind of the group (Janis, 1972; Lewin, 1936).

The team, then, is not only a control system regulating variances or a governance structure regulating contracts, but also a system of interpretation and construction of reality. It is something 'designed' at levels that go beyond those of an economic institution: it is a 'commonsense construct' (Bittner, 1965) that is legitimised every day before the eyes of socially recognised competent members and that supports their everyday activities of classifying and recognising (Douglas, 1986).

The phenomena of co-operation, solidarity and trust, so important for the economic performance of teams, are not maintained by repeated utility computations of members (that may explain why the potential members originally met and decided to join efforts), but by the common identity and 'collective mind' that emerge out of the repeated transactions, experienced as social relationships.

The institutions, for example, teams, sustain themselves and are recognisable by agents because they gain legitimacy continuously and are grounded in some analogy to nature and reason, otherwise they would be highly unstable and put in doubt at every change in circumstances. They set the terms for exploring the world, and legitimize the rules of the game, such as private property, that remain in the background of any organisation seen as a nexus of contracts (Jensen and Meckling, 1973), and especially 'sanctify' the principles of fairness and justice on which economic and social mutual dealings are grounded (Sowell, 1980).

Language, and more precisely conversations and non-verbal communications, provide the raw material for the building of such social relationships. Through conversations a common understanding of everyday reality in the workplace is incrementally built, tested and collectively experienced (Suchman and Wynn, 1984; Winograd and Flores, 1986). This gradually comes to represent the background for any planning and choice that each member sets out to make, that is, it becomes the justification (the *because-of* motives) of any instrumental choice (in *order to* achieve a goal) (Schutz and Luckmann, 1973).

But which of the two minds prevails? The individual or the group? Economics and social anthropology give different answers to this question. The economics of teams indicates that the surplus that results from the team effect (see above) is a public good, that is, a good that escapes the price mechanism, for it is difficult to apportion it according to the individual contribution. In other words, if a member of the team is a free rider, he or she can simulate effort by pretending to lift the cargo as the others, and thus share the result of the collective effort without paying the costs.

The free-riding problem, according to Olson (1965), plagues and thwarts any collective action producing public goods, unless the group is small enough for an individual, the boss or the entrepreneur, to exercise coercion or devise and enforce a set of incentives and a monitoring apparatus to weed out free riders and install a rewarding mechanism that can replace the market price, that is, the hierarchical structure as suggested by Alchian and Demsetz (1972). For economists, then, the survival of a team is determined by scale, or, more precisely, by its internal information system, for scale sets the limits to the ability for metering: the more effective and widespread the information system, the more effective the metering and larger the scale of group operations not infected by the free-riding problem.

The social anthropologists suggest another tack: groups are able to generate their own view of the world, developing a system of knowledge that supports the pattern of interaction, and thus can overcome any limitation by scale and metering.

Mutual convenience in repeated transactions does not generate by itself enough certainty about another person's strategies; it does not justify the necessary trust. The emergence of a team as an institution involves a cognitive process as well as that of an economic, political or technical nature. Members have to have ready-to-hand reasons for accepting the legitimacy of the institution in order to deal with it smoothly.

Even within the most decentralised and atomistic organisation, the market needs some form of legitimacy: 'there is the normative commitment to the markets system itself, the needful fiduciary element sustaining prices and credit . . . [And] in a complex hierarchy, a combination of coercion, multiple cross-ties, conventions, and self-interest explain a lot, but not everything about the commitment of individuals to the larger group' (Douglas, 1986: 42).

The cognitive processes involved in the entrenchment of a team as a resilient institution are concerned with strategies for classification, making analogies between group and natural processes, definition of boundaries, sameness of members and ultimately identity. Douglas (1986: 63) puts it in a very concise way: 'Constituting their version of nature, individuals are monitoring the constitution of their society, in short, they are constructing a machine for thinking and decision-making on their own behalf'.

The team as an institution or, better, as a formative context (see ch. 1) becomes a sort of automatic pilot; it saves energy from institutional coding and inertia (Schotter, 1981). But it does not only save time for members when they tackle routine decisions; it is there to guide members in radical, or life-and-death, decisions, precisely where the rational agent cannot settle the issue unless making reference to some broader context that provides criteria and orientation for the choice to be made.

Conclusions

This chapter has shown that there are multiple levels at which a team can be designed. We may operate with a structured, intentional approach to design at one or more levels: it is important, however, not to forget the ramifications on the other levels, when intervening at one level. Each level can interfere in, but also support and amplify, the design choices carried out at another level. The five levels of impact of networking technologies mentioned in the Introduction can provide a useful way to synthesise the different fields of designing a team.

The socio-technical approach is pre-occupied with the efficiency of the work organisation; it prescribes mechanisms to control variances; identifies links between members of an organisation in order to co-ordinate problem solving around uncertainties (socialisation); and addresses some issues related to learning (learning by doing in controlling variances). The economic view of teams deals primarily with the issue of efficiency in co-ordination, with socialisation through networks of contracts and with the issue of transformation, when it prescribes that a given organisational arrangement should be changed into a more efficient one. The institutional/cognitive approach addresses primarily the issues of socialisation, learning and transformation as experienced, thought and acted by members. Here the team is regarded as a formative context, that is, as a set of routines and behaviours, but also of structures and beliefs that support them.

If there is a design lesson to be drawn from our review of the various facets of team structure and functioning it is that the different levels of analysis and design cannot be kept separate. Thus, for example, when intervening to improve the efficiency of an organisation by introducing team arrangements, following, say, the economic or socio-technical perspective, one cannot ignore the far-reaching consequences of setting up teams as formative contexts, that is, the cognitive dimension of the institution that is not taken into account extensively by the other two approaches.

The same applies to the design of an information system that is supposed to improve the efficiency of an organisation through a team arrangement (see ch. 11). Again, one design question that should be addressed is this: does the new information system affect the institutional, formative context dimension of the work organisation? That is to say, using Zuboff's (1988) terminology, are we just automating transactions or are we 'informating' the world of people at work?

3 Mediating technologies

Introduction

The brief observations on the recent developments in information technology made in the Introduction heighten the awareness that it is difficult to
discuss specific technological systems, and their impacts, without the
danger of becoming almost immediately obsolete. The well-known charts
depicting the steady progress in the miniaturisation and price performance
of microchips and memory components (the so-called Moore's law), and in
communication means, thwart every attempt to anchor established or new
organisations to the successive technological systems, or even paradigms. The
analysis of technology in our study must therefore be raised to a higher, more
abstract level, that is, a level detached from the specific performances of
today's or tomorrow's systems and applications. Though generic in nature, the
study will not ignore the organisational and economic aspects exploited in this
book. On the contrary, it must be supportive of them.

   In most textbooks the prevailing organisational perspective on information technology indicates that computer-based information systems are
cast into and support hierarchies, or bureaucracies, as in the management
information systems models, or market links to hierarchies, as envisaged in
the strategic information systems literature (see ch. 9). One major breakdown of such a view is the consideration of 'co-ordination technologies'
that support groups, markets or hierarchies, whereby the technology, its
design and use, are seen within the broader context of co-ordination
occurring across different economic institutions, and more generally, in an
effort to build an interdisciplinary 'co-ordination science' (Malone and
Crowston, 1990).

   To be sure, this constitutes a major systematic step in moving away from
traditional MIS models and generalising the discoveries of strategic
information systems applications. However, and paradoxically, the concept of co-ordination technology is too linked to organisation theory and

economics, and it misses some of the recent and future developments in technologies that will profoundly affect the nature of co-ordination.

We prefer in this respect another term, that of mediating technologies. While retaining rich organisational implications, this term makes us reflect on the emerging qualities of new technologies, for example those that are media conveying images.

In fact, though the term co-ordination embraces the term 'action', the notion of co-ordination technologies seems to rely on the passive concepts of procedure and organisational routines that must be somehow interconnected. The notion of media, instead, though being rather 'geometrical', through the reference concept of 'middle', is associated in lay and expert language with active roles: for example, the concept of go-between and mediator; the notion of mediating human activity, or computer-mediated work (Zuboff, 1988); up to the technical notions of broadcasting and processing moving images and news.

This chapter aims to define the concept of mediating technologies, as well as to explore its multiple meanings and applications, and to link it to the classifications in the engineering domain, especially the Open Systems Interconnection (OSI) layered model. In general, we will attempt to move away from the vision of the technology as a passive set of tools and methods to one that is able to analyse and design technology as an active medium-in-context. This is grounded in the more general hypothesis according to which technical systems are 'formative contexts', that is, media through which social relations are mediated, reality is envisaged and institutions enacted (Ciborra and Lanzara, 1990).

Types of technologies

We have seen in the previous chapter the importance attributed to the mediating role of technology in the exchanges between a social system and the environment in socio-technical theory. The behaviour of the social system and its internal organisation depend heavily on the uncertainty and complexity of the environment, but as modified by the intervening role of technology, both as a filter in perceiving the 'variances' coming from outside and in being the actuating entity through which the work system reacts to the environment. The socio-technical school, however, has not contributed in further specifying the types of technical system and their influence on organisational action. This task has been taken up by a sociologist of organisation, J. Thompson (1967), who has also deeply influenced the organisational models of J. Galbraith seen in chapter 2.

It is Thompson's comparison of three main technological systems that leads us to introducing and defining the notion of mediating technology.

Technology is seen by this author as the embodiment of tools, systems and methods of instrumental action and rationality, that is, the possibility of achieving desired outcomes through a specified set of actions. Correspondingly, complex organisations are seen as human artifacts set up to operate technologies which are found to be impossible or impractical for individuals to operate.

Different technologies can then be distinguished on the basis of the main pattern or configuration through which the actions aim to achieve a desired outcome. Three patterns stand out in Thompson's analysis: serial, intensive and mediating technology. In order to highlight the latter notion, which is of interest to us, let us briefly compare all three notions in more detail.

Serial interdependence of actions is involved by long-linked technology. The assembly line is the model that must come immediately to mind. Here the means–end sequence that leads from inputs to outputs is well known and decomposable in unit operations linked between them. Repetition of operations allows for further perfecting of tasks, tools and machines and the planning of resources and production, through formal algorithms, such as line balancing. Standardisation of resources allows for measuring each single quantity involved in the process, be it human labour, number of operations or components.

In *intensive* technologies the pattern of actions is defined less clearly. Actions are combined in an *ad hoc* way to achieve the final result, the transformation of an object, but the precise pattern emerges while intervening and interacting with the object itself. Building a plant, or curing an ill person can be illustrative of the intensive technologies. An intensive technology is a project-oriented, or custom, technology.

The pattern that underlies the *mediating* technology is the network. Its purpose is to establish linkages among individuals or organisations that wish to be interdependent. The instrumental actions are not finalised to achieve a subgoal in a pre-defined sequence or a final result, as a therapy. Rather they are aimed at creating opportunities for contact, so that the agents are better positioned to obtain what they want individually or collectively. It is a technology for co-ordination, or more generally, for collective action, but in itself it is not strictly related to the goals of the concerted action: it just provides the support for such an action to take place.

The complexity in mediating technology does not come from organising a coherent sequence of actions or in meshing them effectively to reach an overall goal. Rather it lies in being able to operate extensively in standardised ways, for example with multiple agents distributed in time and space. A few examples can define the concept of standardisation and extension of linkages more clearly.

The commercial bank must find and aggregate deposits from diverse depositors. But however diverse the depositors, the transaction must conform to standard terms and to uniform bookkeeping and accounting procedures. It must also find borrowers. But no matter how varied their needs or desires are, loans must be made according to standardized criteria and on terms uniformly applied to the category appropriate to the particular borrower. Poor risks which receive favoured treatment jeopardize bank solvency. Standardization permits the insurance organization to define categories of risk and hence to sort its customers or potential customers into appropriate aggregate categories. The insured who is not a qualified risk but is so defined upsets the probabilities on which insurance rests. The telephone company became viable only when the telephone became regarded as a necessity, and this did not occur until equipment was standardized to the point where it could be incorporated into one network. (Thompson, 1967: 16–17)

These examples illustrate some of the meanings of mediating technologies that will be exploited in the third part of the book, when we will tackle the task of designing a new business organisation through the use of information technology.

A mediating technology has the function of facilitating exchange. Thus money could be regarded as one of the most widespread mediating technologies (see ch. 6). These are linked to markets, their functioning, their efficiency and, last but not least, their creation. By standardisation, they are able to improve the imperfect functioning of the insurance markets. By aggregating individual demands and by creating a space where individuals can exchange disjointedly, that is, without constraints of time and space as in the case of serial technologies, mediating technologies create a marketplace (Gordon 1989; see ch. 5). Finally, by standardising lower-level routines of establishing contact and communicating by exchanging data, they can mediate informal exchanges taking place within groups.

Technology in context

Thompson's concept of mediating technology is a useful way of characterising information technology that opens a new understanding of its role and impacts in organisations. Diverse systems and applications such as broadband networks, groupware and office automation can be designed and introduced in organisations more effectively thanks to this perspective, as will be shown and discussed in the remaining chapters of the book.

However, one needs to go to a higher level of detail to design different features of network-based technologies and understand fully their implications and effects.

Classifications of the technology oriented towards organisational issues already exist (Francis, 1986): for example, such a classification can be found in the Bright's scale of levels of automation (Bright, 1958), ranging from hand control, mechanical control, variable control and signal response to variable control and action response. The purpose of such a classification was to evaluate the effects of automation on the individual worker and especially the skill requirements. Another classification is due to Woodward (1965): her empirical research focused on the contingent relationship between the production technology and the organisational structure of the enterprise. Production technology was classified along a continuity scale that ranged from job shop, to batch, to machine-paced line flow to continuous flow process. Note that such scales, which have been frequently employed to analyse the impacts of automation on production work and organisation, are carefully crafted in the decision-making perspective, that is, they share the cybernetic view of organisations as developed also by the socio-technical school (see chs. 2 and 6). However, they are less useful for the case of mediating technologies. They can be applied to appreciate the 'automating' effects of computers, less so for their 'informating' effects in organisations (Zuboff, 1988).

This unsatisfactory state of affairs and the interest in exploring more systematically the multiple meanings of the mediating role of technology suggests the search for a new classification, for a new scale of levels able to identify specifically the ramifications of the notion of mediating technology.

To this end it would be useful to have a layered classification of the technology, by analogy with the seven technical layers of the OSI model (Zimmermann, 1980). These start from the hardware and bit and byte level, and reach the application level, in a continuum that is less and less defined to the point where the boundary between the technology and its organisational applications is reached.

We propose to analyse any mediating technology at five different levels, some of which could be further explored by using the OSI model, while others stay on top of the application layer of that model. Our classification shares with the OSI classification the principle according to which each layer (level) supports or 'adds value' to the next higher layer.

The five new levels

The first of our new levels concerns the *scope* of applications. As suggested above, the mediating technology has one clear purpose, as a go-between, but it does not take part *per se* in any conversion process or the attainment of a specific and unique goal of the community served. It is permeable to multiple purposes of individuals, groups and organisations. The extent of such plasticity is, however, constrained by the nature of the messages and applications supported by the technology that we have come to call the scope of the network.

The major characteristics of the scope of the network is what Thompson termed standardisation, one of the prerequisites of the mediating role. Standardisation regards not only the technical sublevels (taken into consideration by the OSI layers), but also what Keen (1991) calls the 'range' of applications, the type of performance in processing data by one or more integrated applications.

In economic terms, the scope level points to the nature and modes of interdependencies that the mediating system actually creates among users, given the range of applications it can support. In particular, it points to the externalities, both negative and positive, that users of certain applications can experience, that is, the incentives or disincentives the user can find in accessing the network.

Examples of negative externalities can be given by the issue of privacy, related to the concentration in one node of a network of data linked to multiple transactions. In positive terms, the very fact that there is a large user community is a bonus to any member of the community or any new member who can, for example, be sure to sell his or her own services to a large number of possible customers. This effect is supported by the 'extension' level (see below), but it is also strongly influenced by the applications running on the network.

The second level, *interface*, specifies the boundary of the user community; that is, it looks at the man–machine interface between the user and the network. This level includes the consideration of human factors in machine and interface design for the user community, and the related ergonomics, and health and safety issues; but it also highlights one of the various meanings of the notion of mediating technology that is strictly related to the media aspect, to the possibility of creating at the different interfaces of the network multimedia applications, where voice, data and images can be transferred and processed. And it can point to specific effects on the work of users, for example, the 'textualisation' effects noted by Zuboff (1988) in her study of electronic-mail usage in a large organisation (see ch. 4).

The third level denotes one of the fundamental characteristics of the mediating technology as identified by Thompson: the physical and virtual *extension* of linkages. On the one hand, it is the physical and geographical extension of the network, and its architecture: it indicates where the data files are, where the processing nodes are, that is, the modes of access. In this way it denotes what Keen calls the 'reach' of the medium, the population of users or customers that can be affected by the medium in a variety of roles:

recipient, information provider, user and so on. It identifies the potential community of users or, better, agents who may interact in some way with the technology across barriers of time and space. At the extension level, any mediating system becomes associated not so much with a transformation or conversion purpose, or with the execution of interlinked routines, but with a community. The behaviour of the members of the community 'colour' the role of the technology and characterise the usage context: for example, in a reservation system, the community may be represented by travel agents or individual customers, that is, a primary and/or secondary market. In an electronic-mail system the group of office workers and professionals who can access the system form its community context. The organisational rules by which the community is governed or self-regulated are of paramount importance for designing the specific applications of the mediating technology and analysing its effects (see ch. 4).

Extension, then, also denotes the type of interdependence among agents that the technology helps create or supports. And, in particular, it delineates the extent to which the technical system is indeed an infrastructure for the community served, and in economic terms, it points to the possible public quality of the mediating system and to the related problems of regulating its usages and allocating its costs (see ch. 5). More generally, it delineates the structure and scope of the governance body for such an infrastructure. Finally, the extension defines the boundary which the socialising (Brandt *et al.*, 1978) and 'informating' (Zuboff, 1988) effects of the technology can reach.

Next is the *function in context*, which deals specifically with the organisational role of the technology. Support and scope specify the possible uses and technical constraints of the network; extension defines the reference user community; interface identifies the interaction modes with the members of the community. Function in context indicates what type of socio-economic interdependence the technology actually favours or supports: a team arrangement, a hierarchical departmentalisation, a market or a mixture thereof. The role of the mediating technology in this case is understood by placing it into its surrounding organisational context. It is at this level that the macroanalysis of the matching between the medium and the social system can be carried out in structural terms (see ch. 6).

The final level is the *reflection* level, where the social and the cognitive contexts of the technology are intertwined. What does the use of, and frequent interaction with, the mediating technology imply for the mind of its users, their behaviour, the executing of their routine tasks or the devising of new ones? Does it change their worldview or the way they solve problems, organise a collective action or think about reforming their community?

The five levels are related to the social and economic impacts of the mediating technology, ranging from the technical to the social and cognitive levels. They do it in a way that differs from that of Bright's scale. The mediating technology connects people, their socio-economic behaviours, the organisational artifacts that they enact and their minds. Not only can a mediating system affect a small or a large community, that is, the number of agents, but it can also provide a highly or less standardised range of services. It can affect the communications pattern and the meanings through which the members of the community define the reality in which they operate and envisage the functioning and development of the community itself. This can be rendered, for example, by mediating the images of the external environment that members of the community perceive, build and share, and by influencing, through the scope layer, the images of the internal functioning, the problem-setting and problem-solving activities that are carried out. In general, the mediating technology can contribute to those 'making-sense' activities through which the community looks at the world and its problems and perceives its own identity and direction. The mediating technology can render the existing network of exchanges more efficient, the network that already defines the community and/or can represent the cognitive maps through which the members communicate with each other and delineate the everyday reality. In the latter perspective the mediating technology may take over a part of the thinking of the community, or at least, explicitly or subtly support and influence it. In the former sense it supports a given institutional form of the community, a hierarchy, a market or a team. In the latter it affects the thought processes and behaviours that lead the community to reflect on any change itself. It thus conditions self-design, self-organisation initiatives of the community, and ultimately its evolution.

The five levels also represent levels of design and self-design. The technical design component is concentrated at the scope level, but affects the following two as well: extension and interface. The institutional design is particularly important at the scope, extension and function-in-context levels. It also plays a role at the last level, to such an extent that institutions supported by the technology do some of our thinking for us in the background (Douglas, 1986). The cognitive level starts at the interface and becomes primary at the last level.

To be sure, each level is characterised by specific tools and methods for analysis and design, touching the technical, the institutional and the cognitive domains. In the rest of the book the institutional domain will constitute the main focus of attention.

Types of impact

The five levels identified allow us to discern different domains at which the mediating technology can make its impact felt on the organisation. They have already been mentioned in the Introduction and now they are in need of a more systematic analysis.

The first type of impact is concerned with the *efficiency* of the exchanges to which the technology is applied. By efficiency we mean the quantity of resources spent to run a socio-economic transaction mediated by the technology. Technical performance apart, levels such as scope (standardisation), extension, interface and function in context can all affect efficiency in determining scale and scope economies. The efficiency effect is determined by the fact that the technology can standardise transactions and multiply, through extension and easy-to-use interfaces, their number. However, the nature of the transactions does not change fundamentally, and more generally, nor does the organisation and its relationships with the environment.

The second impact is that of *content*. The technology enables the organisation that employs it to reach its goals in an improved way, by allowing better co-ordination and finalisation of efforts. The technology through a range of applications (scope) supports the collective problem solving and decision making necessary for the organisation to attain a given goal.

The third impact is concerned with sheer *socialisation*. The extension and function-in-context layers are important in this regard. One of the latent activities of groups (see ch. 2) is also to maintain itself and not disintegrate. This is achieved by a continuous and subtle sequence of mutual adjustments. Maintaining the relationships between a member and the rest of the group is an essential factor at this stage.

The technology is available to support mutual adjustments and mutual co-operation in facing unexpected events that may delay the attainment of the goal. It thus handles communications and feedback loops that are vital for *learning*: this is the fourth type of impact. The scope, function-in-context and reflection levels play an important role here.

The last level is that of *transformation*. The technology may contribute to the change in the way people think at work and think of their work. Through the restructuring of practices, organisational arrangements and cognitive maps, the mediating technology can show how to change the world in which we operate (see an application in ch. 11).

In order to exemplify the meaning of the five levels and the types of impact, let us close this chapter by reconsidering the case of the retirers experiment conducted at the Rand Corporation that was mentioned in the Introduction.

The five levels in the Rand experiment

The support for the electronic group of retired managers denotes the technical infrastructure used in the experiment, such as IBM/XT clones, modems and a server employed by the electronic group.

The five levels above the support infrastructure can be analysed as follows.

1 Scope is determined by the available applications that included word processors, e-mail, databases and statistical analysis programs.

2 The interface is characterised by the 'look' of the various programs running on PCs: for example, the group members did not need to know the DOS commands because the screen menu dealt directly with running the various programs.

3 The extension defines the community of users, with the managers still working in the DWP department, the retired managers and the technical advisers at Rand. In particular, thanks to the extension of linkages, the retirers were not marginalised as was the case in the non-electronic group.

4 Function in context is the level that must be referred to when discussing how the system allowed for supporting a team arrangement (informal groups), a hierarchical arrangement (the initial organisation) and a matrix arrangement (after the re-organisation).

5 The reflection level addresses the phenomena noted by the researchers, whereby applications such as the spreadsheets or the databases suggested to the electronic group different tasks (the survey) and a different work organisation (the matrix).

In figure 3.1 the levels describing the technology and the domains of impact are compared for the electronic and non-electronic group, showing the role of the network and other PC applications as a mediating technology.

LEVELS	Electronic group	Non-electronic group
Reflection	new tasks: survey new organisation: matrix **Impacts**: transformation; content; socialisation; learning	– – – – – -
Function-in context	team, hierarchy , matrix **Impacts**: socialisation	hierarchy
Extension	retired, non-retired managers, technical advisers	retired, non-retired managers
Interface	applications menus main DOS menu **Impacts**: efficiency; content	– – – – – -
Scope	word processor, e-mail spreadsheet, data analysis, databases **Impacts**: efficiency; content; socialisation; learning	– – – – – -
support infrastructure	PC clones, modems server, telephone, mail	telephone, mail

Figure 3.1 Comparison of the two groups and the role of technology in the Rand experiment

4 Team-support systems

Introduction

The design of effective systems for co-operative work in teams must be based on a thorough understanding of the forces that shape co-operation and influence the productivity of the work group (Ciborra and Olson, 1989; Greif, 1988; Johansen, 1988). Co-operative work is not a straightforward social process whose stability can be taken for granted. On the contrary, each case of work-group formation and process is uniquely influenced by its contextual forces. The appropriate type of information technology for the work group and the impact of the technology on work-group performance are also determined in part by that context (Ellis, Gibbs and Rein, 1991).

The objective of this chapter is to investigate how mediating technologies can support the organisational context of co-operative work. In the first part, we describe a few cases of systems used for work-group co-ordination. We employ here the transaction-costs model (to be developed on a full scale in chapter 6) to characterise some economic and organisational contexts for co-operative work. The cases illustrate the impacts of mediating technologies on aspects such as efficiency, content and socialisation of team arrangements introduced in market and hierarchical contexts. In the latter part of this chapter, the application of a groupware system in a non-profit organisation is examined in greater depth in order to show the learning and transformation effects of a team-support system within a hierarchical context.

Teamwork in organisations

Why is teamwork important? From an economic standpoint, we have seen that teamwork is justified because the collective output of a team is greater than the sum of the outputs of each member taken separately (ch. 2).

Teamwork may take place in a variety of settings: a clerical operation of a bank, a research and development laboratory, a university faculty, a workers' co-operative. Each setting is characterised by a social 'force field' (Lewin, 1936). Examples of force fields in the organisational context of a work team are the hierarchical authority system, formal communications channels, the reward system, peer pressures, competitive forces, etc. The life of the team and nature of the group process are conditioned by these forces and the reactions of individual work-group members to them. Thus, even if members are willing to be fully co-operative, external and internal pressures may push them beyond the limits they perceive to be fair and equitable for their participation. Individuals may react differently: some may withdraw or reduce their efforts temporarily, while others may withdraw from the team permanently; some may continue to participate under stress, with the deteriorating quality of their contribution; others may hide their dissatisfaction and simply shirk responsibilities.

The communication structure of the group, the key element of co-ordination of activity, must be able to elicit and signal problems so that the team can respond adequately before teamwork collapses. Specifically, the communication structure can improve the sharing of information, thus increasing the transparency of individual efforts. It can signal the beginning and completion of tasks to all group members. It can support the renegotiation of the terms of explicit or implicit contracts that link team members. It can uncover shirking of responsibilities. It can filter out false information used for cover-ups. It can provide a forum for discussing and exploring the limits of co-operation. It can make the team more open to external incentives and signals; or it can buffer the team from external pressures regarded as potentially disruptive to group performance.

The communication structure described above is not necessarily electronic. The physical proximity of team members and availability of channels determine the medium: face to face, telephone, memo, electronic mail, etc. However, introducing a more advanced system to support work-group co-ordination can have a significant influence in various ways (see ch. 3). First, it can have an impact on the efficiency and contents of the messages exchanged: for instance, it might transform the format of a message, increase its speed of delivery or enrich its comprehensibility. Second, the system can affect the nature of group process and group organisation: the reciprocal contractual arrangements of group members, methods for solving interpersonal conflicts, etc. In the following we concentrate on the effect of information technology on group processes and structures, using transaction-cost theory as a framework for analysis.

Teamwork structures

The transaction-cost model of economic organisations is one of several models of organisations as information processors which can help us understand the organisational context of work groups and the role of information technology in work-group support. Specifically, transaction costs are the costs of setting up, enforcing and maintaining the reciprocal obligations, or contracts, that keep the members of a team together. These contracts can be set by a central co-ordinator or authority, or they can be the result of on-going negotiations directly between group members. Transaction costs represent the 'overhead' of the team and they are linked to the resources (time, skills, etc.) employed to allow a work team to produce more than the sum of its parts.

Information technology can reduce transaction costs through improving information handling and communication (see ch. 6).This may be accomplished by reducing the amount of information required in a transaction (for example, through standard procedures or programmed decisions) or, alternatively, by adding value to the information communicated (for example, through effective utilisation of distribution channels).

There are two main factors in the organisational context that influence work-group process and structure: task uncertainty and goal congruence among group members. Task uncertainty varies in that the more uncertain the task, the greater the amount of information required to be processed by team members for co-ordination purposes. Sources of task uncertainty may be internal to the group (for example, lack of experience with a new manufacturing technology) or external (for example, market turbulence) (see ch. 2).

Goal congruence among members may be thought of as trust. Low levels of trust increase the risk that individual members will shirk their responsibilities or exploit opportunities for individual gain at the expense of the group. As a consequence, more resources are required for monitoring performance in order to ensure group members' confidence in fair treatment. With a high level of goal congruence, a work group can be relatively self-reliant and self-motivated and require little external monitoring; a group of this sort can be considered 'co-operative'. Transaction-cost theory indicates the most efficient (that is, with lowest overhead) organisation of a given team in its organisational context, characterised by competitive forces and the degree of both task uncertainty and goal congruence.

Three stereotypical organisational structures and contexts for teamwork can be identified as follows (see ch. 6):

1 *Market-like*. When task uncertainty and goal congruence are low, the market is the most straightforward arrangement for team organisation: arm's-length spot contracts are sufficient to co-ordinate and control the activities of group members; rewards are allocated according to current prices for service delivered. Competition takes care of shirking and opportunistic behaviour. The role of a market structure as an effective co-ordination and control mechanism in general requires a large number

of participants exchanging standardised services. When this model is applied to individuals supplying products and services, the rules of co-operation are set by market forces, that is, price. Requirements for co-ordination among individuals are low and thus overhead costs are low. The individuals supplying products or services are not a 'team' in the normal sense because they compete on the basis of price rather than work together to accomplish a common objective.

2 *Hierarchy*. These arrangements are best suited when shirking cannot be completely ruled out *a priori*, that is, the level of trust is intermediate, and task uncertainty is neither high enough to require an inordinate amount of exception handling, nor so low that a market mechanism to handle co-ordination is more efficient. Consequently, the overhead costs of maintaining a hierarchy are intermediate.

3 *Clan*. If task uncertainty is high, the most efficient work-group arrangement is one based on high levels of trust; a clan reinforces the sharing of values and goals that facilitate joint problem solving in complex, ambiguous situations. Flexibility in the face of new, uncertain events is facilitated if members are able to rule out at the outset costly haggling and suspicion of cheating from their mutual dealings. The overhead costs of setting up and maintaining a clan are high, but they may be necessary due to high task uncertainty.

Transaction-cost economics provides a contingency view of efficient team arrangements, but it does not exclude the possibility of arrangements that do not match a particular combination of task uncertainty and goal congruence. If an organisation does not match these conditions, the theory predicts that an extra amount of resources (overhead) will be required in order to 'buffer' a team from external competitive forces and keep it viable the way it is. Thus, for example, a hierarchical arrangement may exist where a clan would be more efficient; in this case, the hierarchy will be bogged down by exception reporting and handling activities, and group members (who have high goal congruence) will have to put up with unnecessarily formal and rigid procedures.

Effects of groupware

If an information system purportedly designed to support work-group co-ordination is introduced into a work group, what happens? The transaction-cost model that has been adopted here suggests a contingency view: it depends on whether there is a good fit between the two factors and work-group structure prior to introduction of the new system. A system, if it responds to the needs of the work group, will facilitate exchanges by acting on the fundamental transaction costs themselves.

There are many possible design goals, either explicit or implicit, that might be pursued in the introduction of a system to support a team, all resulting in some sort of reduction in transaction costs:

standardisation of tasks, thus reducing task uncertainty;

standardisation of interfaces between execution of subtasks, thus streamlining co-ordination;

facilitation of reporting, monitoring, etc. of performance, thus reducing shirking;

encouraging communication through creation of new channels or improvement of existing ones, thus reducing hierarchical barriers and allowing these new ideas to flow more easily (Sproull and Kiesler, 1986).

A system may be explicitly introduced to decrease transaction costs and thus facilitate a particular organisation structure: for example, communication channels might be improved to reinforce a clan-like structure; project-management tools might reduce task uncertainty, thus helping the organisation to operate more efficiently as a hierarchy or even move closer to a market-like structure.

Another alternative is that a system for supporting communication may be introduced into a relatively stable structure with no explicitly mandated change in organisation structure; the results of the introduction of the system are dependent on the adequacy of the existing structure and team members' needs for alternative ways to accomplish their tasks. For example, an electronic-mail system may be provided as a bonus by the vendor of an MIS package, and the use of the extra feature (for instance, for lateral communication) may even run counter to the existing hierarchical structure. The use of the system, then, if at all, would be largely informal for at least a period of time.

Thus, the system will have an impact on the organisation, but the changes will go largely unnoticed and informal modes of communication will coexist with more traditional, hierarchical routines. The resulting actual organisation will be a pasted-up set of systems and teamwork practices, with members switching almost naturally from electronic hierarchies to electronic clans, and with the formal organisation remaining apparently intact.

Sample cases

The following brief case studies are meant to illustrate the variety of possible outcomes of introducing systems to support collaborative work. The implications regarding the impacts of information technology on the transaction costs of the main team that has been studied are drawn for each case.

European technology

Several years ago, the R&D department of a European computer manufacturer was assigned the task of developing the proprietary operating system of a new computer line. To increase productivity and improve the organisation of work, two major innovations were introduced. The first was a structured methodology for streamlining software development; that is, a set of guidelines to organise work into stages, define goals and activities for each stage, etc. The second was a 'software factory'; that is, a computer network connecting hundreds of workstations on which software to support programming tasks could be run.

The first innovation, the structured methodology, failed. Its purpose was to standardise interfaces between execution of subtasks. From an organisational perspective, the structured methodology would have reinforced the existing hierarchical division of labour for systems development. Its use required adoption by all development personnel, who did not see it as helping them do their work more effectively.

Once the software factory was introduced, however, it became the basic infrastructure for the daily work of hundreds of programmers. Much of the co-ordination of work took place via the electronic mail and software tools. The messaging system provided an informal channel for direct communication between programmers and allowed the integration of different pieces of code; the network supported large work groups, so that the real tasks, roles and communication lines were no longer governed by the formal structure. The real organisation was the product of informal co-operation and bargaining taking place through the network. Interestingly enough, however, all the agents seemed to ignore the emergent work organisation and to operate as if the formal structure were operational (Ciborra and Lanzara, 1990).

Implications: In this case, the existing hierarchical structure was inadequate to the immediate co-ordination needs of the members of the work group. These were characterised by high uncertainty of the task of developing a complex software product. The group did not adopt a system designed to simplify co-ordination, but they did adopt that part of it that facilitated greater sharing of information. However, the part of the system that was adopted was not explicitly consistent with the existing organisational structure. Thus, the network affected transaction costs with the hierarchy by creating lateral channels of communication. This fact not being acknowledged resulted in slack; that is, a 'pasted-up' and redundant set of co-ordination modes.

A wired alliance

Apple Computers and Benetton are two companies operating worldwide in different markets, with their homes in completely different contexts, the former in Silicon Valley, California, the latter in the province of Venice, Italy. Yet there are striking features in common. They are innovative and young companies; they owe their success to brilliant initial ideas about the product and its distribution and to unorthodox management approaches. The vision and charismatic leadership of the owners have been an important trait of their corporate cultures. In both companies the management structure was established only after their staggering expansion, leading to a flat organisation with wide distribution of authority and information sharing at all levels.

SAFA is a joint venture created by the two companies in the financial service sector. It is a 'wired alliance' in the sense that it sells financial services, such as leasing contracts, loans and insurance contracts, through Applelink, the dedicated network that connects Apple personnel worldwide (and specifically the Apple shops in Italy). In each shop where a customer enters to buy a Macintosh, peripherals, networks or software, the salesperson can sit down with the customer at a terminal, present the financial services available, and fill out all the forms needed. At the other end of the network, Benetton provides the actual services. In this way the financial services division of Benetton through Applelink has access to the market of Macintosh buyers (Ciborra, 1991).

Implications: In this case, a network serves as the infrastructure for the joint venture of the two companies, reducing transaction costs in the chain linking the final customer to the financial services supplier. Thus, we can speak of a network used for the purpose of supporting an electronic market between the two companies and the customer (see next chapter). While it is not an example of work-group support *per se*, it does illustrate the use of networks to reduce transaction costs in a market-like arrangement.

Western laboratory

A well-known US West Coast research laboratory created an 'experiment' to help them understand co-ordination requirements of a work group when face-to-face co-ordination was not possible. They created a 'new' subgroup 400 miles away from the original laboratory. Within any given project, goals, deadlines and subtasks were only very loosely defined and constantly changing, based on new discoveries in the process of research.

A particularly difficult problem was instilling in group members, especially new ones, a sense of what were the most appropriate projects to work on and how to spend their time. Modes of appropriate behaviour needed to be provided and reinforced across a distance. Therefore, the tools the group migrated towards were video-based; they established an interactive audio and video link between the two sites. In essence, they tried to broaden the communications channel between the two sites as much as they could, so that all kinds of information, much of it behavioural cues rather than specific requests or commitments, could be transmitted. There was little demand for more structured co-ordination tools, such as project-management tools, which would standardise or simplify co-ordination requirements, since requirements were constantly changing.

Implications: This organisation has high task uncertainty, because projects and directions are constantly redefined through discovery. It also has relatively high goal congruence, and typically in this type of organisation, attention needs to be constantly paid to maintaining that congruence and maintaining a clan-like structure. Thus the system tools chosen to keep the two sites in congruence may generate slack (they are often underutilised and are expensive), but support the organisation's existing needs in terms of maintaining a communications infrastructure which is rich in behavioural cues.

East Coast high-tech

A leading US East Coast computer manufacturer is well known for its highly matrixed, fluid, organisational structure. The information technology most commonly utilised to support the organisation is electronic mail, which facilitates lateral communication within and between organisational units. There are few systems, such as traditional management-reporting systems, deployed to reinforce hierarchical authority.

The organisation utilises multiple channels for meeting co-ordination requirements, electronic mail, computer conferencing, etc. However, it still relies heavily on face-to-face meetings and persuasion. The co-ordination tools utilised, while rudimentary, have been an accepted method of doing business for a long time. The organsation also exists in an environment which is constantly in flux, and always provides a high degree of task uncertainty. Furthermore, goal congruence is ephemeral; very high level goals are accepted but the ways they should be translated into operational strategies are hotly contested. Thus there is a constant set of negotiations between groups within the firm (for example, between marketing and engineering). The organisation acts in part as a hierarchy with heavy emphasis on lateral channels of communication; electronic mail, computer conferencing, etc., facilitate lateral communication and are highly critical to daily operations.

Implications: This organisation operates as a 'hybrid' structure, with significant overheads (transaction costs) involved in maintaining goal congruence of organisation members. Electronic messaging to support lateral communications within and between groups is essential to its operation. It is, in a sense, a 'networked organisation' whose telecommunications networks reflect its complex, matrixed organisation structure.

An electronic hierarchy

Mrs Fields' Cookies is a well-publicised case of the use of information technology to support a unique organisational structure. This US company has experienced rapid growth, going from one to 500 stores, all wholly owned. The company has essentially a two-layer hierarchy with centralised control; each store co-ordinates extensively with headquarters and there is little or no lateral communication between stores. Management use information technology heavily to maintain centralised control. The systems have two important characteristics: if a machine can do a task it should do a task, and there should be a single centralised database. Thus each store has a personal computer with a limited database of store books; each computer is directly linked with the headquarters computer. Headquarters monitors store production and sales hourly, dictates batch size and orders ingredients centrally. But other features, particularly voice mail and electronic mail, bring the stores into closer contact with the CEO for issues that are not in the database. Thus the network helps to accomplish two things: 'It gives top management a dimension of personal control over dispersed operations that small companies otherwise find impossible to achieve; it projects a founder's vision into parts of a company that have long ago outgrown his/her ability to reach in person' (Richman, 1987: 65).

Implications: This is an example of explicit use of information technology to design a certain organisational structure and a formative context. On the one hand, although task uncertainty is relatively low, a hierarchical structure is preferred by the owners to a market-like arrangement. They utilise information technology explicitly to support a very flat structure with centralised control. On the other hand, they recognise the need for a degree of goal congruence and fully utilise current communications technology to reinforce that.

A commentary on the cases

The cases have shown that there is not a direct, deterministic link between the use of a computer-based system and the arrangement of the team that uses the system. Instead, the actual impacts form the outcome of the interaction between the characteristics of the technology, the pre-existing organisation, the environmental pressures and the choices made by group members and the surrounding organisation. Moreover, even initial plans and designs can be turned upside down if the technology has some side-effects which were not initially anticipated.

At this point we can suggest some normative statements regarding the design of systems to support work groups. First, one should not take a team as a stable set of social practices that just happen to be there. In order to work as a team, members continually solve the structural problems of co-ordination and control, and manage to work out the subtleties of staying together. The complexity of such problem solving depends on the communication structure, the level of trust, the ambiguity of the goals and tasks and the external pressures the team has to face. In an economic context, the analysis of the nature of transactions that link the members of a work group among themselves and with their external environment provides a good start in understanding the specific solution that people give to the problem of 'surviving as a team'.

A system for work-group support should be designed to fit the nature of the transactions of the specific work group. Alternatively, and more creatively, it could be used to transform the work group. Here, one should be aware of the possible limitations of too ambitious designs or the relative efficiency of alternative socio-technical solutions. The approach would warn system designers of the limitations of setting up an electronic market in a clan, or it may indicate that one could replace a hierarchy with an electronic market.

Note, further, that in each of the cases, information technology was used to facilitate co-ordination and information sharing, rather than to simplify tasks or standardised communication as more traditional management information systems are supposed to do. Specifically, technologies designed to support work groups also enable organisation structures that would be inefficient or ineffective without the technology. In one firm, a highly fluid matrix structure is maintained through a telecommunications network and electronic messaging. In another, centralised control is maintained over a very wide span. In a third, an alliance between firms is established and maintained efficiently.

Team support is a reflection of organisation design and vice versa. Teams of the future will look different: they will not be constrained by space and time in their ability to co-ordinate and be productive. Organisations will reflect the same removal of constraints: the 'networked organisation' may be more centralised, or more matrixed, or more characterised by inter-organisational linkages than the traditional hierarchy of today.

Groupware and the evolution of teams

The socialisation effects, and also the learning effects, of groupware, especially asynchronous e-mail, have been the subject of empirical studies, both quantitative and qualitative, regarding large user communities. According to Sproull and Kiesler (1991), e-mail enhances those weak ties that link groups and informal teams dispersed throughout the (hierarchical) organisation. Hierarchical differences in status tend to melt down: users are less shy in communicating, up to the point where uninhibited behaviour, deviance and extreme decision making are practised more on an e-mail-based user community than in face-to-face conversations. Learning and innovation can be the result of groupware use: for one thing, redundancy of channels of communications is important in leading to innovative ideas (Allen, 1977). Synchronous, high-band systems, like the Colab (see the case above of the Western Laboratory, pp. 78–9) have been designed precisely to multiply the opportunities for casual encounter and conversation among scientists, so important as a knowledge-exchange process for generating innovation (Stefik et al., 1987).

But there are more subtle learning effects. Communicating by written text is part of a more general process of abstraction of work (Brandt et al., 1978; Zuboff, 1988). Specifically, the heavy use of e-mail brings in a higher necessity of interpretation of text, an activity that in organisations is primarily collective. Tasks become more abstract, more text-based and at the same time more 'acted with' collectively through the medium (Zuboff, 1988). The shift from face-to-face conversations to written text does not only affect socialisation: the increasing reliance on written or symbolic texts offers raw material for reflection, for more objective discussion and introspection. These processes may trigger learning at two levels: a first level is the incremental accumulation of knowledge, and the second is a radical form of learning, whereby by reflecting in action, existing organisational contexts may be put into question (Argyris, 1982; see ch. 1). E-mail systems, far from impoverishing the interaction between people, may indeed provide the platform for complex organisational learning and change processes. The research by the Rand Corporation mentioned in the Introduction and analysed in chapter 3 is an example in point. Here we present another case to show the unfolding of these important effects, both for organisational and technological design of teams and groupware systems (for a design application see, above all, the systems proposed in chapter 11).

A human-rights organisation, acting on a global scale, in the fight for human rights, against political repression and torture, decided to adopt a PC-based groupware system, the Coordinator from Action Technologies (Winograd and Flores, 1986), to link agents, regional offices and head-quarters throughout the United States.

Soon after the adoption of portables on which the Coordinator and other software was installed, there came an opportunity to use the new techno-logy to cope with an emergency: the fight against the execution of a death penalty in Florida. Actions that were to be taken consisted in organising meetings, having local and national personalities involved, press campaigns, etc. All these activities fell largely within the scope of the organisation, though it was the first time that the organisation itself participated in the United States against the execution of a death penalty. The task was made difficult by the very short time available to influence the judges in Atlanta and at least have the sentence postponed. Four offices were involved: the headquarters in New York and in the capital, Wash-ington DC, and two in the south, in Florida and Atlanta (figure 4.1). The Coordinator, used mainly as an e-mail system (conversation for possibili-ties, see Winograd and Flores, 1986), proved to be a very effective means to keep track of the internal paperwork needed to co-ordinate the press campaigns and, more generally, the various tasks of the small group of people allocated to this mission.

The role of the mediating technology at the higher levels of application (function in context and above) and its effects can only be appreciated by studying the subtle changes in the way the network was used, more precisely by analysing the content of the conversations that took place during the three weeks preceding the moment when the judges decided to suspend the execution. At the beginning of the period, the function in context of the system was simply to confirm and reinforce the existing organisational structure, a functional hierarchy. Communication was mainly vertical: orders came from the top; reports on work accomplished or requests for more information came from the bottom. Lateral communication between branch offices and field agents (especially Florida and Atlanta) was kept to a minimum by the users.

Thus, co-ordination was taking place by sending a message to head-quarters, and from there directives would reach the relevant agent: for example, the two press officers, one in New York and the other in Washington would seldom use the system to communicate with each other; instead, they would communicate through the director of communications. The deputy director for programs would communicate to the director of

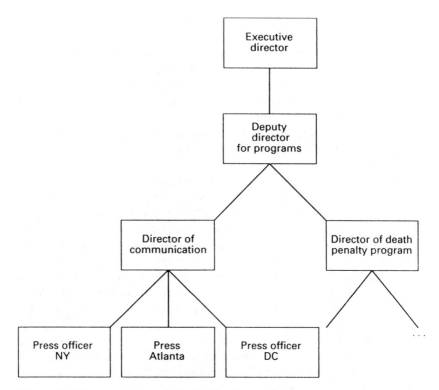

Figure 4.1 The organisational chart of the Human Rights agency

communications and not directly to the press officers, two levels below in
the hierarchy, and so forth. This phase and pattern of usage lasted for at
least the first half of the campaign period, until a major press conference
was held and reports about its successful conclusion were sent up the
hierarchy ladder to the executive director.

In a human-rights organisation one would expect more teamwork and
less hierarchical co-ordination, since members adhere to the same beliefs
and cause. The 'clan' aspects, for sure, must have been present in such an
organisation, but they did not appear from the usage of the system, at least
in the first period, except for one major twist to the bureaucratic pattern of
use just described: while messages were addressed according to the authority ladders and channels, they were at the same time, with few exceptions,
copied to all other users of the network. Thus, thanks to the 'cc' facility,
communication was at the same time formally bureaucratic and totally
transparent. This can be labelled as an 'ironical' use of the technology, that
made its function-in-context role ambivalent.

This is confirmed by another conversation that took place during the subsequent period, concerning a leave for holiday of one of the field employees. She needed a rest, or, as it was expressed, 'time to put away the Christmas tree'. The wish was communicated at the end of a work message as a postscript to a fellow employee, with the request to inform the head of personnel about the holiday. The 'ironic' aspect is that this chat was also copied to the head of personnel. The chat continued over a few days, and the employee kept asking whether the other, evidently located at the headquarters, had heard anything from the boss about her wish. Here, a lateral, and bottom-up conversation is handled at the same time in a totally transparent way. The technology, then, at the function-in-context level not only reinforced the formal and informal structures, but crystallised and made the object of collective reflection the double nature of the organisation as an efficient bureaucracy and a committed community of peers.

During the last week of the campaign, in order to exercise the maximum pressure and gather the highest levels of public mobilisation, the organisation scrambled for condemning statements against the death penalty in general, and on this particular case, from a greater number of opinion leaders. Work became more volatile and frantic. Time pressure and the higher complexity of the task confirmed the prediction of Galbraith's model, introduced in chapter 2: the hierarchical communication mode was replaced by a true team effort and communication structure. Field officers now communicated directly, and higher levels of management were called in only when necessary (though the use of 'cc' was always kept for most of the conversations). The e-mail now fully supported a team arrangement: the technology contributed to the transformation of the actual functioning of the hierarchy.

Finally, the last conversations between the field officers, while they were waiting for the judges to convene and decide about the postponing of the execution, show the reflection role that the system can play, in particular thanks to the 'textualisation' effect of the e-mail system (Zuboff, 1988).

Waiting for the final verdict, the agents chatted over the system about various themes, and in particular they came to formulate their own personal evaluation of the effort accomplished so far, and what it could mean for the future activities of the organisation. Looking beyond the success or failure of the present campaign, the two officers concluded that, no matter what was going to happen, the organisation through this campaign had *de facto* repositioned itself strategically, at least in the United States, by entering a new field: the abolition of the death penalty, instead of taking care of political prisoners worldwide. And the chat went on exploring the strategic implications of such repositioning.

Here the team thinks itself strategically 'through the medium' (see ch. 2).

The system captures these thoughts and makes them available, in principle, as text for all members for further introspection and discussion: it is an instant strategic memo, coming from the bottom of the organisation and made publicly available thanks to the network. The transformation effect does not only concern the way the team members co-ordinate, but also the way they can communicate their thoughts and the way strategy can be formulated. We can conclude, then, that even a narrow-band, asynchronous system for collaborative work can become, if used in an open way and in a 'rich' organisational context, a tool for learning and transformation rather than simply a tool for efficient co-ordination.

5 Market-support systems

Introduction

In this chapter we tackle the market, the other institution that can be supported by information technology and that with teams can be redeployed to the change of hierarchies. Markets play an important role as information-processing devices. As mentioned in chapter 1, according to Hayek (1945) one of the main problems of designing an efficient economic system is 'how to secure the best use of resources known to any of the members of society, for ends whose relative importance only the individuals know' (p. 520). The crucial problem is how to communicate the knowledge on which people base their plans, given that such knowledge never exists in a concentrated form, 'but solely as the dispersed bits of incomplete and frequently contradictory knowledge which all the separate individuals possess' (*ibid.*).

The price system of the market can be regarded as a mechanism for communicating such knowledge in an economic way; that is, the individual participants need to know very little to be able to take the 'right' action. This mechanism is also very quick in registering and communicating changes and discovering emerging opportunities: it acts as a device for diffusing innovation. We look at the market as an institution enacted by the interaction of partially ignorant agents for the need to acquire and communicate knowledge which the individual agent lacks. In order to explore the uses of information technology to create new markets where none existed before (for example, inside a hierarchy; see the case presented in chapter 11), or support and improve existing ones (see ch. 10), one needs to examine a few important aspects of the functioning of markets.

First, markets have to be analysed as information-processing mechanisms. The economics of information can help us in this respect, especially in pointing out where the perfect market and the price system fail because of information imperfections. Such imperfections represent the ground for evaluating the potential impact of information technology on the functioning of the market. Second, a number of applications of computers and telecommunications that today support markets, such as those mentioned in the Introduction, EDI, Electronic Funds Transfer (EFT) and others that go under the labels of Strategic Information Systems (see ch. 9) or Inter-organisational Systems, should be framed as 'electronic markets', for which it is possible to identify a precise evolutionary path. Building electronic markets needs at least three points of attack. First, one should evaluate the scope and nature of an electronic market, in respect of other markets for services, in particular the existing universal services. Second, it is important to analyse the microdimensions of a market transaction that can be made the object of auto-mation: this gives an idea of precisely where and how to apply a mediating technology. Finally, who should set up and design electronic markets? Such markets can be roughly divided into two broad classes: the markets where information services traded can be treated like commodities; and markets for information services where externalities are a relevant factor, like in present and future telecommunication services. While the former type can be dealt with by the *laissez faire* of market forces, there seems to be some scope for government intervention in markets of the latter type, as the theory, and one successful case, the French Minitel (see ch. 9), suggest.

The comparison between different institutions, teams, markets and hierarchies will be pursued in the next chapter within a unifying theoretical framework, while the intricacies of building electronic markets, by them-selves or with teams and hierarchies, are exemplified in the last three chapters of the book.

Markets and information

The market is the social mechanism that integrates the plans of goal-seeking individuals and institutions through the exchange of goods and services. Information is essential to the functioning of markets. Indeed, the price can be looked at as the information system of a market of a given commodity. Using the price, economic agents make up their mind regarding their participation in the network of exchanges they are embedded in: buy or sell; exit or entry.

Price information is crucial to the functioning of the market, to the point that economists call this institution 'the price system'. In fact, the main characteristics of a perfect market are (Hirschleifer, 1980):

  perfect communication, whereby every participant has the same access to information regarding prices and quantities of goods;

  instantaneous equilibrium; thanks to the instantaneous communication of the 'market-clearing' price all pending purchases and sales are executed;

zero transaction costs: exchanges take place without friction of any sort. Extant markets may be more or less distant in their behaviour from such an ideal model, precisely because communication is not fully transparent (there are search costs to find the best price) (Stigler, 1961), equilibrium is not instantaneous (there are haggling processes) and transactions are not costless (Coase, 1937). These information imperfections explain why in the real world markets are lubricated by a series of integrative mechanisms, such as middlemen, brokers, dealers and auctioneers. The imperfections, on the other hand, create a series of opportunities by which information technology can improve the functioning of markets and make them more perfect: by communicating prices faster and to more places (recall the notion of mediating technology put forward in chapter 3); by supporting the work of auctioneers and middlemen in communicating prices and collecting deals, and more generally by decreasing the costs of transacting (see ch. 6).

In order to appreciate better how information technologies can improve the functioning of markets as a knowledge-communicating mechanism, it is useful to identify those asymmetries in information that cause the market to fail as a co-ordination and control mechanism (Arrow, 1974).

First, there can be problems of faulty information channels through which the price is communicated on the market, that is asymmetric information about *prices*. 'To obtain price information, consumers have to search and therefore incur *search costs*, which may reflect the value of time' (Phlips, 1988: 14).

Second, asymmetric information can be generated by the fact that because of limited rationality, unique circumstances and experience of each individual participation in a transaction, the particular individual has knowledge that is different from that of the other parties, and it cannot be excluded that he/she will use it strategically or opportunistically (see ch. 1). Consider, for example, the *quality* of a durable good and the different position the parties (sellers who know the good better than buyers) occupy. Buyers can appreciate the quality of the good only by using it. Warranty schemes can be set up by sellers to provide protection for the consumer in this respect. But further problems can be generated by the warranties: for example, the consumer feels well protected and feels confident in using the good with less care. This is the problem of *moral hazard*, where one party to a transaction may undertake certain actions that affect the other party in the transaction but which this party cannot monitor perfectly (Kreps, 1990); or, suppliers may produce intentionally defective goods in order to sell additional warranty.

Where warranty is not provided at all, as in some markets for used goods, the average quality is lower than that signalled by the price, as, for example, in the used-car market, described by Akerlof as a 'market for lemons' (Akerlof, 1970). Here, the seller knows things pertaining to the good on sale that are relevant, but unknown by the buyer: thanks to this form of asymmetry, called *adverse selection*, cars of less and less quality invade the market, and there is no incentive to sell used cars of better quality. Whenever there is a gap in the communication of information about prices or quality, intermediaries (retailers) can both play a role in diminishing search costs and mediate the transmission of information about quality of goods traded.

Finally, in our brief review, we should mention another type of informational asymmetry: if, say, a monopolist is selling a unique object, for which no market price exists, in order to find out how much potential buyers may value the good, the sale takes place through an *auction*. 'Auctions offer the advantage that the participants reveal their valuations or their costs to some extent through the bidding mechanism' (Phlips, 1988: 16).

Market failures can be generated by faulty information channels, by the fact that knowledge is fragmented and information does not flow and by the information structure of individual economic agents that may cause the phenomenon of 'information impactedness' (Williamson, 1975), or information asymmetry that the parties involved in the transaction are willing to use strategically. The possibility of using the price system is, then, limited by the structure of the information channels and the asymmetry in information, to the point where 'the value of nonmarket decision-making, the desirability of creating organizations of a scope more limited than the market as a whole, is partially determined by the characteristics of the network of information flows' (Arrow, 1974: 37).

Information technology can be used to overcome to some extent such limits of real market organisations. This is the arena of the current building of electronic markets.

Characteristics and evolution of electronic markets

According to Malone, Benjamin and Yates (1987), there are three main effects of information technology on markets:
the electronic communication effect, whereby technology allows more information to be communicated in the same amount of time, at a much lower cost;
the electronic brokerage effect, whereby computers and communication technologies allow many potential buyers and sellers of a given good to be matched in an intelligent way, that is, by increasing for each party to the transaction the number of alternatives, filtering them and selecting the best one;

the electronic integration effect, that is, coupling more tightly (co-
ordinating) value-adding stages of production and distribution across
different organisations.

These effects contribute in various ways to reduce the information asymmetries mentioned above, and thus improve and expand the functioning of
markets. Through the communication effect search costs for prices are
diminished by reducing the cost of accessing relevant price information that
may stay with distant experts or markets.

The electronic brokerage effect improves market signalling (Kreps, 1990)
and the communication of incentives, so that the risks of moral hazard and
adverse selection can be significantly diminished: it is easier to monitor past
performance, check reputation, keep track of customers so as to devise
more tailored policies for the customer service (see below). Databases and
high-bandwidth electronic communication can handle and communicate
complex, multidimensional product descriptions much more readily, and
this curbs the opportunism of sellers and buyers in playing games around
the quality of goods. Thanks to the higher information-processing power,
the complex facets of quality can be reduced to a more manageable, and
observable set of attributes: in a way, the goods become more standardised,
while preserving their complex qualities. Finally, the integration through
just-in-time techniques of different production stages through CAD/CAM
(Computer Aided Design/Computer Aided Manufacturing) technology
can speed up the overall production time, maintaining at the same time
enough flexibility and customer orientation.

To be sure, many of these advantages can be captured by hierarchical
firms, as well as markets (see next chapter). However, some of these are
specific to markets: for example, a number of so-called Strategic Information Systems applications fall in this category (Wiseman, 1988),
especially those labelled Interorganisational Information Systems, of
which EDI is one of the latest applications (Johnston and Vitale, 1988).
These concern linking suppliers and customers, or manufacturers and
retailers, or in general independent organisations that regularly exchange
goods and services. Well-known cases are the network systems through
which American Hospital Supply (AHS) links its client hospitals and
McKesson sells its goods to retailers; or the reservation systems through
which airlines sell their services to networked travel agents (see ch. 9).

Johnston and Vitale (1988) identify the following aspects that show how
such systems may have an impact on markets' structure and functioning.
They

provide benefits of vertical integration (more control, co-ordination at a
  lower cost) without requiring actual ownership of other organisations;
increase sales of company products due to ease and efficiency of ordering;

remove levels of the distribution chain by going direct to customer or user rather than through an intermediary (though middlemen are not eliminated, but shifted, see below);

evaluate quickly the effects of advertising, rebates and other marketing programmes;

extend market reach to customers who could not be economically served by conventional field sales;

ship in more economical lots and receive incoming goods more efficiently by communicating with transportation companies;

deliver products or services electronically, monitoring compliance with policies related to customers;

make products easier to select, order, handle, use and account for;

provide immediate feedback on product availability and price;

improve customer's ability to shop for third-party products that generate fee income or additional sales of primary products;

get the best available prices on purchased commodity materials.

Malone, Benjamin and Yates (1987) call markets where systems like those just mentioned play a relevant role, 'electronic markets'. An electronic market may emerge because of the single or joint action of a variety of actors who are always present in a market in general: buyers, sellers, distributors, financial-services providers and information-technology vendors.

Sellers or producers, for example, are interested in tying customers: information technology, in particular network services related to the sale transaction, has been employed to provide a sort of electronic tie-in. The cases of AHS and McKesson (see ch. 9) can be read in this perspective; in the early reservation systems, travellers were induced to buy tickets from the airline that provided the electronic reservation system.

On the other hand, buyers would like to see their range of alternatives expand in order to be less and less dependent upon one or few suppliers. Buyers can access systems like the electronic yellow pages or many other services available on successful videotex systems, like the French Minitel (see ch. 9) to get information about alternative products or services.

Or, a major firm can have its suppliers linked through a network, so as to be able to choose more quickly and reliably where to allocate a certain job. Sometimes it may be a distributor, like McKesson, who establishes electronic links with the customers. Financial services can take advantage of their role of middlemen in almost any transaction (where they provide money, credit, means of payment to the parties): they can use the information in their hands to set up databases and networks to become electronic brokers of many more transactions, at a lower cost (see ch. 10). Finally, computer vendors may be active partners in setting up electronic networks: the use of Applelink network by Apple Italy for the SAFA joint venture, described in the previous chapter, is a case in point.

In the various cases where an electronic market has had sufficient time to develop fully, specifically in the best-known application of strategic information systems like the airlines reservation systems, Malone, Benjamin and Yates (1987) identify a sequence of stages that generalise the evolution of electronic markets.

The first stage is characterised by the application of information technology to an existing non-electronic market or to the externalisation of internal departments of a hierarchical business organisation, typically as a result of a buy or make decision.

The investment in setting up an electronic link is justified by the possibility of tying in buyers, raising switching costs, building entry barriers and generally modifying market structure to your advantage (Porter and Millar, 1985): for example, thanks to the electronic communication effect, buyers will find it advantageous to use only that supplier, while switching costs will increase correspondingly. The earlier reservation systems did contain some features that created such *biased markets*. In a subsequent stage, however, competition, interventions by the Antitrust authority and buyers' pressure tend to eliminate much of the bias in the system: either other suppliers feel compelled to adopt similar systems, not to be cut out completely from the market, or legal forces will mount because of customers' pressures to eliminate the bias (Clemons, 1991).

On the other hand, *unbiased markets* reduce margins significantly, do not justify any further investment in the technology and indeed may backfire, since they overwhelm the consumer with too many standard alternatives. A further stage, made possible by the new technology, is to move towards a stage of *personalised markets* (Jackson, 1985). Recall that, thanks to the technology, it is possible to profile the customer, track closely his/her buying behaviour and provide a host of electronic services, from special offers to programs, tailored on the exigencies of the specific client (the systems that lie behind the frequent fliers programs are a familiar example). Personalised markets can bring some technology to the buyers, too. Malone, Benjamin and Yates (1987) envisage intelligent aids that can help buyers select products from a range of alternatives; or agents that can act as representatives for the buyers on the electronic market, providing directly to the suppliers information about their customers' preferences, so that better-tailored sales policies can be devised.

This evolutionary model suggests the following implications for setting up strategic information systems that create electronic markets:

Firms should review their make or buy decisions, and thus evaluate whether to externalise some activities, that is, get them through the market (see next chapter for the transaction-costs theory behind this type of institutional choice).

All market participants may envisage the possibility of setting up an electronic market and value the benefits they can reap.

At the same time participants should be aware of the evolution from biased to unbiased, and possibly to personalised markets; they thus should carefully plan their investments, and their timing, so as to be able to reap first-mover advantage, then oligopoly membership, and be ready to re-invest for a personalisation of customer relationships (Clemons, 1991).

In the words of a marketing expert, given the evolution of electronic markets, the successful applications of information technology rest with those that build strong links and high switching costs (biased markets). These systems can cause pain to other vendors, and may be used simply as a pre-emptive move (Jackson, 1985). But competitive applications of information technology are not all equally desirable; some are considerably more defensible against competitors' reaction than others (Beath and Ives, 1986): thus, in order to maintain a biased electronic market to a firm's advantage, a strategic application must be *valuable, inimitable* and *rare* (the ramifications of this point for the development of strategic information systems will be fully explored in chapter 9).

The emerging service idea

On a perfect market, commodities are exchanged by faceless buyers and faceless sellers. The more the market is imperfect or intentionally biased, the more transactions include a flow of customised benefits over a period of time derived from physical goods or human activities, that is, they include the production and consumption of services. Building a biased electronic market, means, then, conceiving and implementing a service idea. Some marketing relationships, however, will stay based on large-volume transactions of standardised commodities and, as we have seen above, biased markets evolve eventually because of competitive or legal pressures into such unbiased markets. Finally, we should not forget the existence of so-called 'universal services', where services are often provided outside a real price system and in an uncustomised way (think of the universal phone service, national medical care and other services delivered by public administration (see ch. 12)).

Building an electronic market means, then, not only positioning oneself along the evolutionary path described by Malone, Benjamin and Yates (1987), but also defining how to carry out the electronic transactions according to one, or a combination of, the three models: relationship-based service, transaction-based contact and universal service. Vepsæleinen and Mækelin (1987) provide an interesting framework for tackling this design exercise by identifying the main dimensions and a typology of the service relationship. In order to build such a typology they list the following generic components of a service:

type of service, or service package: that is, the content of the exchange relationship;

delivery channel: that is, the more or less permanent arrangement that makes the service possible;

the governance of the service transaction, whether long term or short term, personalised or anonymous.

The object of the design endeavour is to find the best fit, when designing an electronic market, between the three dimensions, exploiting the opportunities offered by the technology available and the competitive situation at hand. This requires a more detailed analysis of each dimension and the links between them. Specifically, it is possible to build typologies of markets and services based on the first two dimensions of a service, while using the third as an intervening parameter when exploring the other two.

Service packages and delivery channels are defined in terms of scope and governance. The service package can be defined on the basis of the scope of the service contract, whether broad or narrow (the service to be provided is left largely unspecified vs the service that is strictly pre-defined), and on the governance structure, or customer contact strategy, whether relationship-based, when major investments are made to strengthen the link between the firm and its customers, or transaction-based, when costs vary according to the volume of transactions (Jackson, 1985). The emerging typology shown in figure 5.1 identifies three types of efficient service packages: customised services, that have a broad scope and are supported by an adaptive, close relationship; standard services, that balance transaction costs and production costs; and mass transactions, simple services for which the identity of the customer does not matter.

Delivery channels are defined by the channel system and its governance structure, or channel organisation. Channel system can vary from narrow-band decentralised channels (that usually rely on some 'back office') to generalised network infrastructure. Channel organisation varies from independent agents to internal and field employees, or self-service by direct customer access. Note how the variable costs of delivering a service are highest for an agent and lowest for the direct access; the initial and capital costs have instead a reversed ranking. The typology of efficient delivery channels, shown in figure 5.2, is formed by agency support, corporate mediators and market networks, respectively. Both figures 5.1 and 5.2 indicate the type of costs incurred by non-efficient designs of service

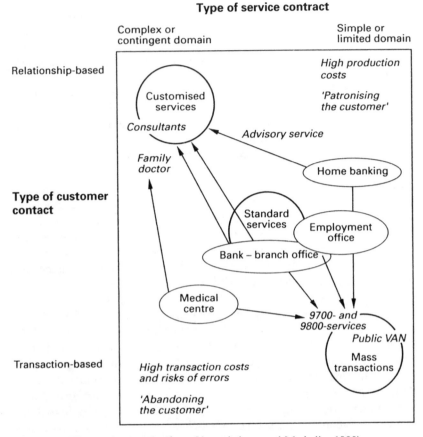

Figure 5.1 The service matrix (from Vepsæläinen and Mækelin, 1990)

packages and delivery channels. For the former the trade-off is between production costs ('patronising the customer' excessively) and transaction costs (high risks of errors, 'abandoning the customer'). For the latter the trade-off is between opportunity costs (by using a substandard network) and out-of-the-pocket costs (by relying on too heavy an organisation).

A typology of service markets emerges if we combine figures 5.1 and 5.2 into a third one, called the service–strategy matrix. Along the diagonal of figure 5.3 are a variety of service markets, ranging from electronic mass markets (bottom right), where human intermediaries are by-passed, to consultants (upper left), where centralised service systems support agents' face-to-face contact. In the middle of the diagonal there are services like medical centres, banks or public services such as the employment office,

Channel systems

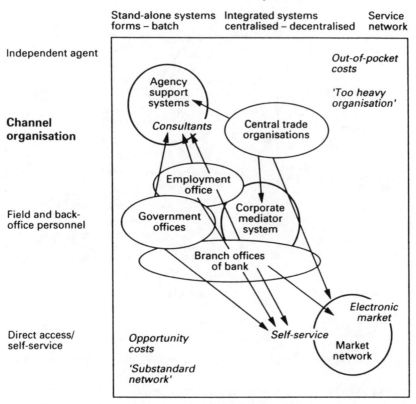

Figure 5.2 The channel matrix (from Vepsælæinen and Mækelin, 1990)

that could be shifted in either direction along the diagonal itself, that is, towards more standardisation (unbiased markets) in the bottom right or more customisation (personalised markets) in the upper left. Once again, the inefficient solutions can be found outside the diagonal: 'overwhelming the customer' (providing complex advice without adequate support) with high fixed costs, or 'exploiting the customer' with low value-added services (a heavy organisation that delivers simple transactions).

This typology leads us to identify the potential role of information technology in transforming the structure of the market. As a mediating technology, computers and telecommunications can have an impact first on the delivery channels. They provide more effective distributed networks, thus, in general, they push towards the right all the markets along the diagonal of figure 5.3: intermediaries can be by-passed, so more electronic

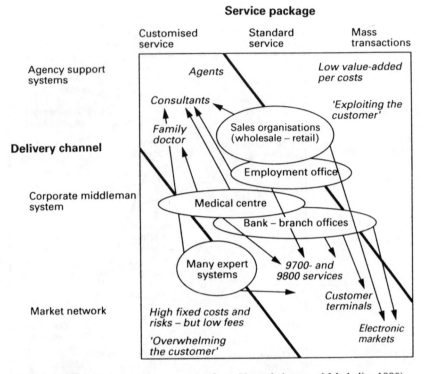

Figure 5.3 The service–strategy matrix (from Vepsælæinen and Mækelin, 1990)

markets can be created. On the other hand, new intermediaries may emerge: those who provide the value-added networks to buyers and sellers. Vepsælæinen and Mækeling (1987) suggest that the channels will evolve first from channels developed around specific products and services to integrated channels, which will deliver a variety of services surrounding a specific good or service; and then towards a new stage characterised by a division of labour along the channels, between organisations that will perform massive back-office activities, and more flexible intermediaries targeted to customers and specific media. Regarding the service package, the trend is to standardise the information content of some services, so as to transform them into commodities for self-service (Gershuny, 1978), or to enrich them with knowledge. Systems for sale support, bidding systems and service hot lines are examples of such applications in marketing.

As mentioned above, however, new service markets are not created in a vacuum, they are the result of strategic change implemented in existing markets. And almost any policy for change in this area must cope with, or even challenge the existence of universal services. Building electronic markets has much to do with transforming universal services. A universal service is based on providing many generic services, with trivial customer relations (no segmentation of customers by needs, costs or profitability) and passive marketing: customers call in or stop by. Often a universal service provider employs a heavy bureaucratic apparatus, with a large back office, high fixed costs and a constant need to expand offerings in response to local pressures (see chapter 12 for the analysis of the expansion drive of the public administration in a pluralist state). The ideal information systems support for a universal service provider is the integrated system, whereby one staff member can handle all customer matters through the same terminal which accesses large databases and centralised procedures. Many Postal Telegraph and Telephone agencies (PTTs), utilities, banks, insurance companies and most public services, but also some large manufacturing companies, can be classified under the label of universal service providers.

These providers are often stuck in the middle of the service–strategy matrix shown in figure 5.4. Information technology can support the differentiation of the universal service towards the electronic market end by offering direct access to standardised services, for example through videotex systems, ATMs in banking, etc., or to more customised service providers like consultants (Vepsäläinen, 1990).

The mediating technology can make services more efficient by establishing direct interorganisational customer services; focusing when needed on professional support for customised services, or establishing electronic markets for fast self-service. Probably, the universal service provider has to implement some internal changes in organisation: decentralisation; establishing alliances with private intermediaries and network service providers; deregulation (see chs. 6 and 12), in the use of information technology (moving from unilateral integration to shared systems that match complex differentiation strategies); targeting different customers on the basis of their needs, opportunities of access and profitability; and finally, abandoning the policy of total ownership of channels to participate in multi-partner value adding channels.

Redesigning the relationship with the customer

The transformation of universal service, either through networked mediators (see next chapter), a fully fledged electronic market or more personalised markets entails a specific effort at microanalysing the transaction with the customer in order to understand where the mediating technology can fit. Data and structured methodologies are lacking in this respect, for at best they are user-oriented and not specifically service- or customer-oriented

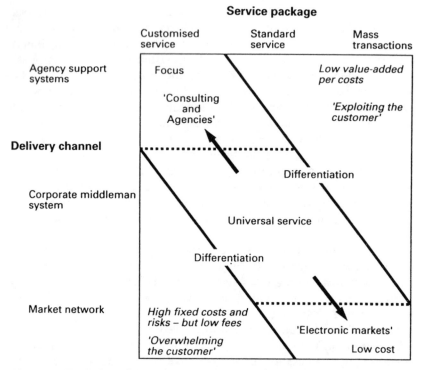

Figure 5.4 Evolution of the universal service idea (from Vepsæläinen and Mækelin, 1990)

(Vepsæläinen, 1990). Also the traditional structured data or decision analysis approaches cannot deliver for such applications, more linked to external exchanges, than internal procedures or databases.

The best methodology, to date, seems to be the one derived from BIAIT (Burnstine, 1980), subsequently adapted by Ives and Mason (1989), and very much compatible with the transaction-cost approach used throughout this volume.

BIAIT focuses on the transaction between a firm and its customer, analyses its main dimensions by asking seven fundamental questions and provides a variety of ways, that is, a subset of all the possible combinations of binary answers given to the seven questions, on how to (re)design such a transaction using information technology as a mediating technology. Thus, the methodology can address simultaneously, at a micro level, the issues of designing a more efficient market, transforming the relationship between the firm and the customer and improving the customer service (for another approach on the latter point, that of the customer life cycle, see Ives and Learmonth, 1984).

The seven questions aimed at analysing how a firm processes a customer order related to any product or service are the following:

Is the product made to order or provided from stock?
Is the product tracked after purchase or not?
Is the product provided now or in the future?
Are customers profiled or stereotyped?
Is the product sold or rented?
Does the producer bill or take cash?
Are terms stipulated or negotiated?

Note how these questions are focused to understand the nature of the relationship between vendors and customers, whether it is a lasting one or a short-term one (see above), or whether it requires an information system to support relationship marketing or transaction marketing (Jackson, 1985).

By posing 'what if' questions about each of the seven business-practice areas addressed by the questions, Ives and Mason (1989) suggest that a firm's management can identify new opportunities and better specify information systems needs. Information technology can play a significant role in leveraging the transformation from one customer service format to another, or simply improve the existing one. In this light let us consider the trade-offs posed by the seven questions.

The first is about made-to-order customer service or standardised service, and reflects the distinction about service packages introduced in the previous section. Information technology, through flexible automation and expert systems can provide solutions that favour a made-to-order customer service, re-introducing a tradition that was in place before the age of mass production and distribution (Best, 1990; Piore and Sabel, 1984). Examples are given by recent projects of Japanese car makers, who will build cars according to customer specifications when ordering the car, or by McGraw-Hill, which assembles textbooks according to the designs of individual instructors. This corresponds also towards the drive towards personalised markets envisaged by Malone, Benjamin and Yates (1987).

Second, information technology can affect the trade-off between tracking or not tracking a product, in favour of the former, more complex alternative. Product tracking offers considerable advantages in terms of information economics, and can reduce the costs customers have to pay for warranties against uncertainty of delivery or performance (sources of moral hazard and adverse selection): for these reasons, they may be willing to pay a premium or simply to let themselves be tied to the vendor that offers such an enhanced service. Companies in the shipping business have implemented systems able to track parcels that provide them with a strategic advantage in getting corporate customers who need to know exactly where a shipped parcel is located (see, for example, the strategic application for the Cosmos system by Federal Express; Wiseman, 1988).

Ives and Mason (1989) indicate that further advances in satellite tracking will give shippers the ability to locate a truck, rail car or ships within moments.

Frequent flyers programs are an example already mentioned of profiling a customer in order to introduce a more tailored, and hence differentiated, service. Again, previously customers were stereotyped as the result of economising on the information-processing capabilities of large vendors (recall Galbraith's model in chapter 2): information technology can bring back the additional resources needed to process the information that can make each client special, and hence offer the opportunity to transform a transaction marketing link into a relationship-based one.

The trade-off between delivery now or in the future depends upon the inventory policies and automation level of the vendor and the desirability for immediate delivery by the customer. As the strategic information systems of American Hospital Supply and McKesson show (see ch. 9), automated inventories are an essential pre-condition for providing quick delivery of goods from distributors to retailers and final customers: telecommunication links are another important technology ingredient to speed up the transaction.

Next is renting versus selling. The former alternative requires more information handling activities, and the use of information technology can contribute to expand its scope. Renting involves keeping track of the product and the customer at significant information costs. For expensive goods worth renting a good information system can keep track of all those data required to reduce to a certain extent the drawbacks of adverse selection and moral hazard. Conversely, for some information goods, for example those contained in large databases, CD-Rom technology can contribute to transform them in commodities to be sold and not just accessed and rented (but not all information goods present on the market of information can be reduced to this case, especially those for which the interdependence between transactors is required; see next section). The bill or cash alternative provides a host of typical applications of information technology. Here, the mediating technology supports banks and mediators in automating transactions between third parties, for example customers who have to pay their utility bills and can do that directly through the banks, or even the utilities access the customers' bank accounts. In general EFT, credit card and EDI applications can address this and the previous trade-offs to a growing extent.

Finally, the market processes of price setting, taking and market clearing are fields where information technology can be applied in revolutionary ways. One example, often quoted, is the 'Big Bang' or automation of the stock-exchange trading rooms (Steiner and Teixeira, 1990). Such systems can deeply affect the roles of the market makers, like brokers and dealers. Chapter 10 contains an example of how the design of new information systems can change the market of government bonds (for other examples of information technology in support of pricing, see Beath and Ives, 1986).

Building an electronic market

The use of the term 'market' in the case of electronic markets hides some of the complexities of the functioning, and especially of the creation of a market for information or knowledge-based goods.

In order to find what the correct policies are to set up such markets for the various participants (see above), it is necessary to appreciate better their special nature.

A market for information differs from an ordinary market for commodities on at least two counts: the type of commodity, that is information, and the rules governing the market. On the surface, information can be considered a factor of production. Actually, the markets for commodities or skills depend on the transmission of information about scarcities and needs in the economy. Both consumers and suppliers will find it worthwhile to invest in the acquisition of market information in order to choose according to quality. This explains the emergence of a thriving private-sector information market (job agencies, advertising, market research, corporate communication, etc.). However, 'despite the willingness to pay for information, private competitive markets are not likely to provide as much of the commodity as consumers require' (Hartley and Tisdell, 1981: 263). Given the scope of such private-sector information markets, one could indulge in plotting quantity of information demanded against price (Emery, 1969); unfortunately, information possesses some idiosyncratic features that make such markets only a part of a more complex picture. For one thing, information can be easily reproduced and sold without destroying it; it is difficult to establish property rights for it; it also shares the qualities of a public good (for example, government statistics), that is, a good the consumption of which by any one economic agent does not reduce the amount available for others (Demski, 1980; Hirschleifer, 1980).

Because of such characteristics, it may well be that less information is collected and disseminated by individuals than is collectively of value. There is scope, then, for government to interfere with the failing information markets by subsidising the collection and provision of information (for example, through publicly funded R&D), or by making the information the legal property of the discoverer through the patent law, so that at least some type of information becomes salable like a commodity (Hartley and Tisdell, 1981).

When we turn to the actual functioning of a market for information goods, we may observe that the rules governing such markets are quite different, also given the special nature of the 'commodity' traded. In the model of the perfect market, each agent makes his/her choice independently of other agents. In particular, the utility of each consumer is unaffected by the consumption decisions of other consumers, if prices are held fixed (Kreps, 1990). However, in the case of information goods, or say telecommunication services, one can observe what economists call externalities, that is, the consumption pattern of a good by one consumer can affect positively or negatively the buying behaviour and the utility of another.

On the information service market, the willingness of a consumer to buy more of an information good, say a videotex service, may depend on how many other consumers are using the network (installed base or critical mass effect; Gordon, 1989). Also the market, specifically the electronic one, requires an infrastructure, a marketplace, which may be another public good to be provided. The crucial design question is: by whom? By the invisible hand? Or by government? Finally, the 'medium' and the 'message' may be interconnected, in a container–content relationship, so that delivering one may require delivery to some extent of the other (there is little reason for selling CDs, if CD players are not available, and vice versa).

Thus, the electronic markets we have in mind are an institution that allows the satisfaction of a collective need (that is, where the satisfaction of the need takes place among agents that have to be interdependent), but the functioning of which does not require that the agents act collectively. The agents can act separately, since they expect in their individual acts the institution itself to provide 'the service of interdependence' with the other potential partners.

Creating an electronic market is equivalent to creating a dance hall, or a veritable marketplace or market square, where people can meet, and make a profit out of it. This is precisely the job of Value-Added Network (VAN) service providers. Gordon (1989) distinguishes three types of possible VAN designs, according to consumer group served, application provided and the role of the VAN operator:

Since the electronic market needs an infrastructure, a first type of VAN consists in supporting an infrastructure to a user community already defined and willing to pay for it; the operator does not intervene in enlarging the community or in the applications.

Since the electronic market needs a critical mass, the operator may, beside providing the infrastructure, contribute to the enlargement of the customer base, by 'creating interdependence'.

Finally, to address the container–content issue, the operator may intervene also in the content of the applications running on the infrastructure, as a condition to promote the use of the service.

In the case of the successful French videotex Télétel (see ch. 9), the French PTT (now France Télécom) was able to intervene at the three design levels; and the intervention at each level, it can be seen at least after the fact, was essential for the take-off of the system:

First, France Télécom built an infrastructure, a public network, based on an X 25 network, called Transpac, to handle the traffic, and provided the terminals, or Minitel, free of charge.

Second, in order to promote the use of the system, thanks to the 'kiosk' idea, it allowed third parties to provide services through the network; with a flexible billing mechanism: the PTT just held the accounting of the transactions between consumers and suppliers of the various thousands of videotex services.

Third, in order to make the system useful from the very beginning, before a critical mass of service suppliers was there at all, the PTT put on line the national directory books of all telephone owners; in fact, this was the only content that the telecom operator was proprietor of, and could put on the network at relatively little cost.

Compared to the French Télétel, videotex services launched in other countries, often according to the logic that free-market forces would have taken care of the growth of the system (see, for example, the US and UK cases; Schneider *et al.* 1990), failed completely. This seems to be in agreement with the idea that for value-added infrastructures that support electronic markets (think of the present and future generations of videophone, ISDN and B-ISDN) there will be a renewed scope for public, government intervention (Egan, 1991).

PART II Design

6 Transaction-cost analysis of information systems

Introduction

In this chapter we set out the general design principles for computer-based information systems according to the transaction-costs approach (Ciborra, 1981). These principles bring together what we have seen so far in terms of the strategic model of rationality (ch. 1), the economic view of teams and organisations (ch. 2), the notion of mediating technology (ch. 3) and the use of information technology to support teams and markets (chs. 4 and 5).

The accepted tradition suggests the analysis of (individual) decision making as the main information-consuming and producing process in organisations. The Management Information System's discipline has embraced this concept (from the principles outlined by Ackoff (1976) to the applications of Keen and Scott Morton (1978)), and has propounded empirical research on the impacts of computerisation in terms of the individual managers' decision-making power and the centralisation versus decentralisation dilemma regarding organisational structures. However, a few problems have been left unresolved. For example, the possibility of generating and using information for strategic misrepresentation purposes in an organisational context of conflict is not assumed as an explicit design constraint when creating a decision support system, despite the fact that in organisations information may be subject to misrepresentation.

We have seen in chapter 2 that regarding information as a resource for the individual and organisation facing the complex task environments is a view that leads to a concept of the organisation as a hierarchy of nested cybernetic control and co-ordination mechanisms designed to cope with the uncertainty stemming from the environment and the technology. This view has a major drawback: control problems regarding the technology and the environment become indistinguishable from those concerning people. To attribute self-interest seeking or opportunistic behaviour to a machine or to the environment sounds strange; on the contrary, such attributes cannot be disregarded when considering human behaviour subject to human control.

In order to include solutions to these problems in a new theory of management information systems, an alternative transactional treatment of the whole matter is necessary. Taking as an elementary unit of analysis the transaction or exchange between at least two individuals, management information systems can be appraised in terms of the reasons that transactions use and produce information. Organisations are not viewed as cybernetic clockworks but as institutional, contractual arrangements to govern sets of transactions. The availability of better information through various data-processing devices may affect the efficiency differentials of alternative contractual arrangements and thus provide a powerful tool of organisational design.

The transactional principles not only give one the opportunity to include interesting results from the economics of information in the MIS field (Gurbaxani and Whang, 1991; Kriebel and Moore, 1980), they may also offer fruitful insights into the role of the new developments in information technology, such as office systems, local and distant networks in determining the nature of the organisations of the future.

The chapter unfolds as follows. The presentation of the argument starts with a critique of the accepted tradition and its implicit, but widespread, assumptions: it is shown that the data- and decision-making views are inadequate and unrealistic because they are based on a concept of economic organisation as a perfectly co-operative system. The need for an alternative framework based on the new institutional economics is then addressed: it is shown that by considering organisations as networks of exchanges and contracts between members, both co-operation and conflict can be taken into account together with the various usages of information that individuals employ while they are in the process of co-operation or conflict. Organisational forms depend upon the costs of exchange, or transaction costs, which in turn are essentially information costs. A characteristic of the behaviour of human agents (opportunism) is important to identify the origin of information and transaction costs. The role of information technology as a mediating technology that lowers costs of transacting is then re-examined, and a closer analysis of organisational and technological arrangements shows how each alternative arrangement can economise on transaction costs.

Finally, two design exercises are carried out as applications of the new framework. A few combinations of technological and organisational forms are evaluated on the basis of their overall efficiency and what happens to efficiency when one combination switches to another is briefly discussed with examples.

A critique of the conventional wisdom

In order to introduce a transactional understanding of computer-based information systems, an essentially preliminary step is to discuss two approaches which are at present very familiar to MIS specialists: the *data approach* and the *decision approach*. According to the data approach, in applying a computer to an organisation it is only necessary to consider (that is, analyse and design) the data flows and files in that organisation. The analyst ascertains management information requirements by examining all reports, files and other information sources currently used by managers. The set of data thus obtained is considered to be the information which management needs to computerise (Davis and Munro, 1977). The data approach ignores the economic and social nature of organisations and may be exposed to the hazards of those economic and social processes which characterise the daily life of organisations and which we, as members of organisations, all know (see below).

The second tradition is more sophisticated from an organisational point of view. It can be traced back to Simon (1977) and was further developed by Galbraith (1977) and Keen and Scott Morton (1978). According to this approach, information technology constitutes support to *decision making*. Managers facing complex tasks and environments use information in order to reduce the uncertainty associated with decision making (Galbraith 1977; Simon, 1977; see also for applications Ackoff, 1967; Huber, 1984; Keen and Scott Morton, 1978; Pava, 1982; Sprague, 1980).

It could be argued that the diffusion of communication and data-processing technology poses some limits to the scope of the decision-making view, which emphasises control and feedback rather than *communication* processes. But, of greater interest here are some puzzling organisational phenomena which challenge that view and invite the suspicion that it is incomplete. Consider the following evidence suggested by scholars in the field of organisations:

Information is gathered and taken into account only after the decision has been already made, that is to say, as *a posteriori* rationalisation (many computer printouts are used as high-tech cosmetics to already made resolutions).

Much of the information gathered in response to requests is not considered in the making of those decisions for which the information is requested (Feldman and March, 1981).

Most of the information generated and processed in organisations is open to misrepresentation, since it is gathered and communicated in a context where the various interests conflict.

When, on the other hand, organisations are informationally transparent, as many data-processing specialists wish, it has been shown that the decision makers in two different departments, say production and sales, could be playing never-ending information games which lead to overall suboptimality (Ackoff, 1967).

Information is not only used as an input for the individual decision maker, but is also used to persuade and induce the receiver to action. It could indeed be argued that this use of communication is the essence of authority and management (Flores and Ludlow, 1981).

Thus information is not simply interpreted data; rather, it is an argument to convince other decision makers. To be effective it must have attributes other than exactness, clarity, etc.: rather than being purely objective, it must be convincing and adequate to the situation at hand.

Flaws in the decision-making view

It should not come as a surprise that the conventional decision-making view cannot explain phenomena such as those just described, since its application as prescribed by current textbooks and methodologies is often biased.

Firstly, the decision-making approach tends to be *individualistic*. Decision-oriented design strategies focus on the information needs and cognitive styles of the individual decision maker facing a complex and uncertain task. Take, for example, Rockart's design method based on the analysis of the Critical Success Factors, which stresses 'the investigation of current information needs of *individual* managers' (Rockart, 1979: 85). While it is worth investigating the role that computers play in individual problem solving, a manager in a particular organisation cannot be seen as a solo chess player whose only opponents are the 'technology', a 'random environment' or 'nature'. In organisations the key issue is *collective, co-ordinative* problem solving (Schelling, 1980; Sproull and Kiesler, 1991; Turoff and Hiltz, 1982). Though this obvious consideration is making its way in the recent Group Decision Support System (GDDS) literature, few practical suggestions are provided regarding its implications in systems analysis and design (De Sanctis and Gallupe, 1985; Sprague, 1980).

Secondly, the decision-making control model ignores the fact that organisations are mixtures of co-operation and conflict between partici-pants; its implicit reference is in fact to man–machine systems (Simon, 1977). When dealing with collective problem solving, the model assumes that all the participants share common goals (that is, they are a team; Marschak and Radner, 1972): information problems related to task execution and co-ordination are considered to be caused by environmental

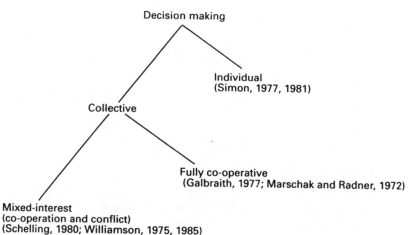

Figure 6.1 Types of decision-making models

or technological uncertainty only. It is, however, more realistic to say that all co-ordinative problem solving and the relevant information processing take place in a *mixed-interest* context (figure 6.1).

A minimal respect for the well-known conflictual processes existing in organisations would indicate that there are other incentives to gather and use information, apart from task uncertainty: information can be misrepresented; promises and commitments can be false; data incomplete; tracks covered, etc.; all in order to induce others to make decisions most benefiting us in the first place. Or another possibility is that information can be selectively disclosed to persuade and bias; what this in fact means is that it can be used as an instrument of power to win or gain a better position in the daily organisational games.

The upshot is that in collective co-ordination and action there is a distinct form of uncertainty besides that characterising the task, the technology or the environment: it is an uncertainty of a behavioural, strategic nature, which has its origins in the conflict of interests between organisation members. The information which the decision maker receives or gathers both within and outside the organisation, may well be 'unreliable' with the result that he/she has to perform a surplus of information processing in order to evaluate its reliability. The fact that it is obtained from human sources means that it cannot be trusted *a priori*. It can therefore be stated that in an organisation at least half of the on-going information processing is dedicated to the solution of tasks and problems by co-operative means, while the other half is concerned with solving problems of co-operation among members who behave opportunistically.

To analyse information requirements and design a system without considering the inevitable opportunistic information processing which takes place in organisations appears to be risky. System implementation can lead to conflict, resistance and other negative attitudes which, far from being irrational, represent the members' response to the attempt to change the way of producing and using information in a mixed-interest organisational setting (Markus, 1983).

Thirdly, and fatal for the perspective espoused in this book, the conventional wisdom is *one-dimensional*: it takes hierarchical organisations for granted, thus ignoring many important facets of the economics of organising. For example, it must be remembered that the boundary and structure of an organisation are not indefinitely fixed: they change every time a manager implements a make or buy decision, or he/she decides to integrate or disintegrate a stage of the production process, an office or a department. Moreover, it is insufficient to consider large pyramidal corporations only, since regional networks of small firms, which are even more diffuse, operate in a manner more like a peer group, or a team, than a formal bureaucracy (Piore and Sabel, 1984). And even within large corporations changes take place at shop-floor level, where work groups are being introduced at the expense of normal hierarchies.

All these developments, which stem from the effort of organisations to respond to the turbulence of the environment, challenge the approach which identifies management and information systems with hierarchies (Arrow, 1974; Simon, 1981; Wiseman, 1988). In fact, many systems, including airline reservation, EFT, remote office work, etc. have little to do with the workings of organisations conceived as pyramids of strategic, managerial and operational control systems. They should be seen as exchange or market-support systems, in that they support market transactions and not the procedures of a hierarchy (see chs. 4 and 5).

Transaction costs and information

This review section sets the definitions for a transactional view of the organisation and its information systems, after having identified the link between transacting and information processing.

Exchange and information

The new institutional economics states that alternative forms of economic organisations, such as markets, hierarchies and teams, are a matter of transaction costs (Williamson, 1975, 1981, 1985). This hypothesis was originally introduced by Coase (1937) to explain the specific nature of the firm in respect to the market. Its implications regarding information processing need further investigation. First, the elementary social process common to all organisational forms is that of exchange among human agents, who are assumed to be prone to behave opportunistically when incomplete goal congruence among them obtains. Fundamental organisational processes such as co-ordination and control, communication and authority are regarded as taking place through a network of exchanges or transactions (Ricketts, 1987).

Transactions differ in complexity. The complexity and cost to carry out a transaction are caused by possible resource losses in defining and implementing the contract which governs the transaction. Resource losses are due to lack of full information among the parties interested in the exchange. Specifically, the information-processing costs related to transacting through negotiation of a contract can be grouped into four main classes, each affecting a segment of the transaction life cycle:

search costs, necessary to set up the minimal social unit for the exchange;

contracting costs, related to the negotiation of the terms of trade and drawing up of the contract which regulates the exchange;

control and regulation costs for the implementation of the contract under conditions of uncertainty, the policing of deviations from the contract terms and the enforcement of sanctions to restore conditions suitable to the terms agreed upon;

maintenance costs of the whole transaction, that is, costs of resources employed to let the exchange develop from one phase to the next.

Only when transactors possess the same information regarding terms of trade and states of the world likely to impinge upon them, and this information is adequate, will transactions go through without difficulty. Asymmetries or lack of information, without the hazard of opportunism, could be overcome by filling the lacunae left behind by incomplete contracts in an adaptive, sequential way. However, if opportunism is admitted as a behavioural property of transactors, then the production and use of information may be the object of misrepresentation for strategic purposes. Or information asymmetry may be exploited by the parties to get an incremental gain in any of the four phases of contracting. Alternative organisational forms are then regarded as a means to curb opportunism of co-operating parties facing a complex task and to let transactions go through efficiently, under different sets of environmental and human contingencies (Williamson, 1975). The most efficient organisation provides, in a given situation, the optimal information-processing structure to carry out exchanges.

The organisation and its information systems

Let us look, then, at the organisation as a stable network of transactions, or better, as a stable network of contractual arrangements to govern a set of transactions among individuals. The contractual arrangements define how individuals join together and co-ordinate their efforts to cope with the complexity of the task environment and the complexity of managing their 'getting together' given the existence of opportunism (exchange uncertainty). Contracts may vary in complexity (Williamson, 1975): 'spot contracts' regulate one-shot market transactions; 'contingent-claims contracts', whereby all relevant future contingencies pertaining to the transaction are described and priced; contracts that because of uncertainty relevant to future environment states require adaptive, sequential decision making to be constantly co-ordinated by parties (for example, the employment relation); contracts that because of their higher duration and complexity cannot be modelled and end up being based exclusively on mutual trust, shared values and internalised norms. These types of contracts, and others, are the molecules which build up from the micro- to the macro-level economic organisations.

The information system of a business organisation can be transactionally defined as the network of information flows that are needed to create, set up, control and maintain the organisation's constituent contracts. The information systems to support different types of contracts show distinct characteristics: for example, the information system surrounding a spot contract will be highly formalised, while that to support 'unwritten contracts' based on trust will be highly informal and idiosyncratic.

Alternative organisational forms

There are a number of organisational alternatives for arranging transactions efficiently. As already seen in the previous chapters, various authors in economics and organisation theory have put forward typologies of organisational forms consistent with the analysis pursued here (see Alchian and Demsetz, 1972; Arrow, 1974; Coase, 1937; Ouchi, 1979, 1980; Williamson, 1975). For simplicity the typology developed by Ouchi – that is, markets, bureaucracies and clans – is recalled below (see ch. 4).

Under different contingencies, markets, bureaucracies and clans correspond to specific contractual arrangements which show distinct characteristics in efficiently organising a stable pattern of exchanges between co-operating individuals.

In the *market* co-operative specialisation is achieved through buying and selling products and services among a large number of agents. The existence and full development of competition (that is, the immediate access to trade alternatives) assure the transactors about the equitability of the trade. There are no barriers to the marketplace and everybody can have access to the relevant information (the price) needed to carry out the exchange. The market thus works as a decentralised control system where the output of each agent is directly metered and rewards are given on the basis of that measurement.

A *bureaucracy* is a hierarchical arrangement of transactions based on the social relationship known as legitimate authority. A hierarchy of decision makers, and not the invisible hand of the market, sets goals and rules prescribing behaviours, meters individual behaviour and apportions rewards according to performance. Legitimate authority is implemented in the contractual form of the employment relation. Such an open contract is more efficient than a spot contract on a market because of its higher adaptability to varying circumstances which may alter the terms of trade and thus trigger transaction costs. Accordingly, bureaucracies prevail when measurement of individual performance is more difficult, transactions are not instantaneous, nor take place among a large number of agents, so as to elicit and eliminate opportunistic behaviours stemming from goal incongruence among them. These problems typically cause market failures such as adverse selection and moral hazard (see ch. 5). Admittance to the organisation is based on selection (formally regulated) followed by formal training.

A *clan* relies on high identification among members, mutual sharing of goals and internalisation of norms, values and traditions. Control exercised at the entrance through careful selection guarantees a high level of homogeneity and trust. Accordingly, clan forms prevail when measurement of individual performance is very difficult, transactions are highly idiosyncratic so that agents tend to be 'locked in' once they initiate a transaction, opportunism is so low that intensive policing of individual output is not efficient, and reliance on trust and sharing of values and norms must be adopted.

It should be emphasised that markets, bureaucracies and clans as described here are 'ideal types' and as such they are seldom discoverable in the real world. More likely, real organisations include a mixture of these control modes. Locally, however, it is possible to distinguish the prevailing one. For example, in a multidivisional company one can identify an overall bureaucratic structure linking through legitimate authority relations the various divisions with the central office. Among the divisions an internal market would regulate the exchange of resources. And both within the departments of the divisions and in the central office, clan forms exist among managers, among workers in production teams, among employees of a specific office, and so on.

Markets and firms are substitutes, and the replacement of one by the other is a common event. Think again of any make or buy decision. A market contract displaces a bureaucratic contract when a travel agency replaces its ticket-delivery person by a messenger service. A hierarchy supplants a market when a firm begins photocopying its own circulars rather than paying for the services of a printer (Hess, 1983).

Given the case with which an economic system, with its essential functions of co-ordination and control, can flow from market to hierarchical organisation and back, it should be clear that there is a need for a framework for defining the special role of computer-based information systems in such a diverse organisational context. If systems do in fact support organisational control and co-ordination mechanisms, what mechanism should they specifically support: the price, the authority relation or a peer relationship? In what circumstances should such organisational mechanisms switch from one to the other, and what criteria are there to tell whether systems are supporting the 'right' – that is, more efficient – mechanism? A tentative answer to these questions is the following (Williamson 1975):

When transactions are fairly well patterned, the services or products to be exchanged are fairly standardised, and all participants possess the relevant information, that is, the price, then the perfect *market* is the most efficient resource-saving way of organising the division of labour, with each person producing a service or product and selling it on a market, where he/she can also buy the necessary inputs: the 'invisible hand' (Smith, 1922) co-ordinates the individual decisions of producing, buying and selling among a large number of independent agents (see chs. 1 and 5).

In some contingencies, however, the use of the price mechanism involves costs, prices must be discussed, transactions encounter difficulties due to the complex search for partners; the contract model specifying the terms of exchange is difficult to develop, and it is costly to control *ex post facto* the execution of the contract. If the product/service exchange is complex and the transaction uncertain due to a conflict of interests, it can be better, or rather more efficient, to use organising agents within the *firm* to mediate economic transactions, rather than to trust entirely the market mechanism. In this case the 'invisible hand' of the market is replaced by the 'visible hand' of management (Chandler, 1978).

Finally, there are situations where co-ordination can take place neither

Product/service

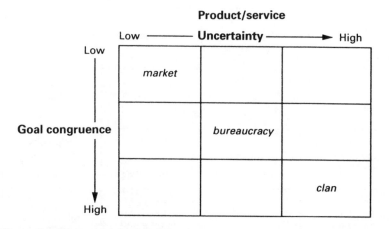

Figure 6.2 Three organisational forms

through a market nor through a hierarchically organised form: products and services are so complex, transactions so ambiguous that the parties involved in the exchanges have to trust each other and give up any attempt at a shortsighted calculation of the reciprocal costs and benefits accruing from the exchange. The 'invisible' and the 'visible' hands are replaced by the 'invisible handshake' (Okun, 1981). The organisational arrangement whereby networks of exchanges are governed in a stable manner by informal relationships of trust, has been called a *team* or *clan* (Ouchi, 1980; see figures 6.2 and 6.3).

Galbraith's (1977) hypothesis (see ch. 2) can be now enriched by using the transaction-costs framework. The more complex co-operation and bargaining are – not only because of the uncertainty of the product/service to be produced and exchanged, but also because of the hazards of opportunism due to goal incongruence among transactors – the more difficult it is to achieve a contract to regulate co-operation and exchange, and the more information has to be processed in order to set up and maintain the organisational relationships between contracting members. This surplus of information can be provided not only by the three main organisational forms just described, or a combination thereof, but also by a variety of computer-based information systems.

To sum up, if the world was certain to evolve according to one pattern only, the co-ordination of activities could easily be streamlined. If people could fully agree, co-operation would be smoothly achieved even in an uncertain and complex world. But when uncertainty, complexity, information asymmetries and lack of trust cannot be ruled out *a priori*, then the multitude of contingencies which affect work in organisations may require

Organisation / Characteristics	market	bureaucracy	clan
level of goal congruence	low	medium	high
type of social relationship	reciprocity	reciprocity authority	reciprocity, authority, shared values and beliefs
type of admittance	none	selection followed by training and monitoring	selection followed by socialisation
informational requirements	price	formal rules	tradition, internalised norms
nature of task and technology	known	partially known	'scientifically' unknown (non-formalisable)
'atmosphere' i.e. quality of the social relationship	'alienated'	partially alienated	'organic'
form of the transaction pattern			

Figure 6.3 Main characteristics of the three organisational forms

the negotiation of complicated contractual plans to arrange co-operation. Depending upon the degrees of ambiguity in the service or product object of exchange and the goal congruence among the parties, the three arrangements – the market, the hierarchical firm and the clan or team – can be employed selectively as the most efficient organisational mechanisms for solving the fundamental problem of organising.

A re-appraisal of information technology

The transactional perspective also justifies the way we looked at information technology in chapter 3, as a *mediating technology*, that is, a technology which, according to Thompson (1967), links several individuals through standardisation and extension of the linkages. The *key feature of a mediating technology is*, in the framework proposed here, *the possibility of lowering the costs of transacting*. Accordingly, data processing can be identified with other devices that lower such costs as mediators and money. Reference to economic analysis illustrates the point. Suppose that two distinct units, A and B, respectively produce and sell a product through an 'intermediate product market'. If for this market the price mechanism can be run without cost (zero transaction cost), the gains (consumer's and producer's surplus) to A and B deriving from the exchange, and the quantity exchanged, will be higher than in a situation where the transaction is not costless, because of the nature of the product and/or the difficulty of writing down a 'perfect' sale contract or enforcing its execution, etc.

The introduction of a mediating technology reduces the costs of exchange and increases gains for both the parties, if the resources it consumes are less than the transaction cost. There are alternatives which could be used in this case:

mediators or arbitrators, trusted by A and B, who would lower costs of information handling, contracting control, and maintenance of exchange;

a 'finer' information system through which the behaviour of the parties and the contract itself could be better monitored, thus standardising the exchange process;

the intermediate market could be abolished in favour of the vertical integration of A and B.

The solution or the combination of alternatives chosen should be the one which economises the most on transacting, if an efficiency criterion of design is assumed. And the most efficient solution, in information-processing terms, is the one which optimally deals with the problems of *adverse selection* in search; *investment in specific assets* in contracting (see ch. 7) *moral hazard* in control and enforcement (see ch. 5) and maintenance of the social and psychological atmosphere of the transaction (Williamson, 1975).

Note that in data processing, specifically in the performance evaluation of different technological systems, the concept of transaction is currently applied, but its meaning is different from the economic one: it is a computer operation triggered by a user message and satisfied by the corresponding computer response. A data transaction is thus an exchange of data carried out partly between the user and the machine, and partly within the computer system itself.

Data transaction costs are determined by the following (Bucci and Streeter, 1979):

complexity of user's requests;

communication costs;

economies of scale in the computing facilities and overhead costs;

congestion characteristics of the system;

interruption costs;

error characteristics and liability;

flexibility;

storage costs, etc.

Factors determining the cost of transacting data within the computer do differ from those affecting economic transactions, but because human transacting involves some information processing, the two can be closely related. In other words, it might be possible to define a *common unit* of *measurement* to assess the costs of handling transactions through a computer, through a computer and an organisational process and through an organisational process alone. Assuming that this hypothesis is workable, a systematic comparison of organisational and technical alternatives is carried out in the next sections, evaluating the different alternatives identified on the basis of their differential transaction-economising performance.

Computer-based information systems

Given the innovative turbulence of data-processing technology, a classification of systems is not an easier task than a typology of organisations. A tentative classification put forward here is based on the subject of (a) the main characteristics of the mediating technology described in chapter 3 (that is, standardisation and type of extension of the linkages); (b) the state of the art of computer-based information systems; and (c) the current main approaches to the usage of data processing.

Standardisation of information processing can affect the outcomes of transacting, namely that information, or data, generated during the life cycle of a transaction by the parties involved, or it may concern the model, the procedure embedded into the contract to be followed by the transactors. In the former case 'historic' data about the transaction are exchanged for subsequent co-ordination among the parties; in the latter an algorithm, a method of a standard procedure prescribes how the transactors ought to behave.

Databases represent the design approach and software products which embody the former type of information standardisation, while more traditional, procedure-oriented application software represents an implementation of the latter type of standardisation. Next, the topology of linkages establishes the connection of hardware and software resources and users, namely the centralisation versus the dispersion of computing facilities. Three cases are of interest in a first approximation: centralised linkages, no linkages and distributed linkages. Five main forms can be identified using these two criteria:

C-form, or centralised systems. Functional programs, dedicated to distinct applications (production control, sales, accounting, etc.) with specialised files, are integrated in a MIS which replicates the hierarchical structure of the firm. Programs and files are supported by large-size computers.

DC-form, decentralised systems, where local files and programs run on separate (small) computers, scattered in distinct organisational units.

The correspondence between hardware and software in the first two configurations is not one to one: a system is decentralised if it runs applications completely separated one from the other, even if they run on the same machine.

DS-form, distributed systems, where local machines support local programs and files, with a network connecting the local processors and files. Data-control instructions and file contents are exchanged through the network. Networks may assume different forms: linear, ring or loop, star, or meshed, determining the degree of centralisation in the execution of functions of the overall system. At the extreme, in a star network, despite the distribution of part of the software resources, the centralisation may be as high as in a C-form (Streeter, 1973).

CDB-form, centralised databases. Data are separated from the single application programs that generate/use it and are consolidated in a large file independent of the applications. A Database Management System manages the sharing of the data among diverse applications, and updating, retrieving and accessing data. A company's large database can be designed to contain an integrated view of the organisation and, in principle, each manager/user can access the content of the database except for security or privacy reasons (Chen, 1977).

DDB-form, distributed databases. Many local databases, each containing a local data set representing an integrated data view of a company's unit (a division, a department), are linked through a network with a central database that contains a generalised management system to access local bases.

If in the last form the network does not exist, a 'decentralised database' would prevail. But this form, according to the database philosophy, is to be regarded as degenerate, because it does not reach the basic aim of the database approach of integrating the data pertaining to a whole organisation. The performance of each of the forms, once tailored to a given application environment, can be evaluated according to efficiency criteria in the use of computer resources. Efficiency for the end user can be measured by output dimensions such as (Ceri and Pelagatti, 1984): average response time; number of transactions processed per unit of time (throughput). The cost of executing a data transaction within a given form can be assessed through simulation, taking into account its main design and operating parameters. Parameters which have to be specified for simulation purposes are size and type of programs to be run, volume, distribution, type of transactions to be processed (user workload), storage characteristics, mean access-path length etc. (for simulations comparing C- and DS-forms see Bucci and Streeter, 1979).

Technical trade-offs between forms can thus be carried out. For example, the database forms economise on data redundancy and direct access to data, while in the C- and DS-forms, each file content is retrieved only through the application program linked to that file. On the other hand, the larger the database, the larger the storage employed and the more complex the database management system: accordingly, the access time increases and the application programs which use that data will run slower.

Two design exercises

The framework developed up to this point can now be used to address two key issues for an efficient joint design of organisational and information systems:

the 'fit' of each technological form with each organisational form according to the economisation in transaction-costs criteria (static analysis);

the effect of the characteristics of each technological form on the differential efficiency of organisational forms and how they may foster/hinder 'change' from one governance mode to another (dynamic analysis).

Figure 6.4 depicts the combinations obtainable from intersecting the organisational and technological taxonomies previously discussed. Note that the bureaucracy has been divided into two subtypes: functional and multidivisional forms (U- and M-form respectively in Williamson's (1975) terms). The two classifications are not independent. After all, each organisational form embodies a characteristic information system and each technological form, as defined above, embodies a logic of usage, an

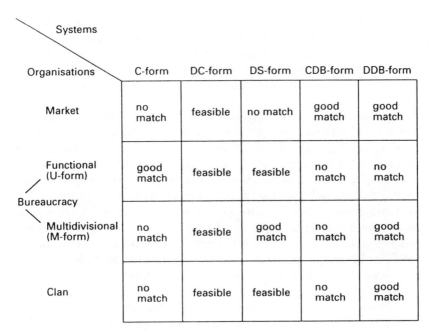

Organisations \ Systems	C-form	DC-form	DS-form	CDB-form	DDB-form
Market	no match	feasible	no match	good match	good match
Functional (U-form)	good match	feasible	feasible	no match	no match
Multidivisional (M-form)	no match	feasible	good match	no match	good match
Clan	no match	feasible	feasible	no match	good match

Figure 6.4 Technico-organisational taxonomy

information processing 'philosophy'. Thus, in the analysis that follows, the task pursued is really an evaluation of the goodness of fit between the information-processing modes of organisational and technological forms.

Static analysis

The market. In a purely competitive market all the relevant information – that is, price, quantity and quality – is fully available and no special 'memory' function is required by the individual agent. Search, contracting and control costs are negligible. Adverse selection, moral hazard and information impactedness (see ch. 5) do not affect the constituent contracts underlying such an organisational form, nor would any further gain in efficiency be obtained with the use of any of the forms.

However, in markets where information is distributed imperfectly and transactors consume resources for search and contracting, databases, CDB- or DDB-forms, which can be accessed by every buyer and seller, improve organisational performance, increase the responsiveness and lower the costs of using the market mechanism (for example, the applications of computers in the stock exchange or airline reservations; see chs. 5, 9 and 10). Technical costs of transacting data within systems help select the most efficient network configuration. On the other hand, instantaneous market-spot contracting does not require any program-oriented (that is, procedural) system, such as the C- or DS-forms. The single agent can, however, improve his/her information-processing capability by using a personal system to scan and compute alternatives (DC-form).

Unitary and multidivisional bureaucracies. A body of rules and routines hierarchically transmitted represents the core information system of the bureaucracy. Rules convey the information on output, pricing, etc., so that decision makers by referring to them can allocate resources in an adaptive, sequential and co-ordinated way. Rules represent the 'organisational memory' which embodies the knowledge necessary to maintain the pattern of transactions. Adaptive, sequential decision making which takes place along the co-ordination and control loops of the hierarchy can be made more efficient by use of vertical, procedural information systems, such as the C- or DS-forms. Technical trade-offs separate the most efficient of the two forms for specific applications (Peebles and Manning, 1979).

The 'fit' between the information system of a functional hierarchy and the CDB-form leads to a paradox, which might frustrate some of the efforts of database specialists. On the one hand, specialists would emphasise that the 'common database' concept offers economy in information channels, closer coupling between activities, tighter co-ordination between decision makers and a common view of the enterprise. In real applications, however, this technical approach does not appear to work. Empirical surveys have shown that in organisations using databases, data are far from being shared in a common scheme. Political problems impeding the centralised standardisation and storage of data are reported by the majority of data administrators interviewed (Davenport, 1979). 'Resistance' to standards, data 'ownershipness' and other such phenomena are usually associated with the psychology of the recalcitrant user and indicate that the implementation of the common database may be at variance with hierarchical organisation (Sibley, 1977). Other signs seem to confirm this conclusion.

Consider first some technical evidence. The growing interest in distributed databases, a technology that has a more complex architecture than the centralised version, can be interpreted as a failure of the latter and a need to accommodate database-management systems to the idiosyncrasies of the extant, departmentalised organisation. Concepts such as 'site autonomy' of a local database in respect to the global one, or as heterogeneous, multi-databases, where different data models coexist, further illustrate the point. Indeed Ceri and Pelagatti (1984) suggest that the organisational and economic motivations are probably the most important reason for developing distributed databases (see also Emery 1977).

That such organisational idiosyncrasies play an important role in determining the system architecture is supported by the experience of leading companies who have pushed database integration quite far: 'Although a homogeneous architecture is attractive at first', writes Beeby (1983: 45), previously at Boeing Commercial Airplane Company's Engineering Division,

it is less attractive over the long run. Factors that argue for a heterogeneous implementation are: diverse applications that impose diverse requirements on data management, need to exchange product data with industry partners and subcontractors who employ different hardware. In the *next* generation systems at Boeing, a homogeneous solution will be pursued whenever practical, but the advantages – and frequently the necessity – of heterogeneous implementation will not be ignored.

And beyond the supposedly technical reasons, experience suggests that important organisational issues are involved.

By using the transaction-costs framework, flaws in database implementation can be understood, and even anticipated. Although the original idea of scholars like Emery (1969), Chen (1977) and others, is technically sound, it contains a hidden organisational dilemma. In order to show it, let us assume that their ideal has become reality, that is, a common database is available to manage the data of a whole enterprise efficiently. Each departmental manager could then, in principle, access the overall system schema to retrieve the relevant data for his/her decision making. Moreover, the output of each decision taken in any organisational unit would likewise be made generally available through the database. But, if all this were possible, *the enterprise would not have any reason to exist according to the transaction-costs view*: its dissolution would be warranted on efficiency grounds (reduction of overhead costs). Namely, the single units or individuals would transact by exchanging services and intermediate products with each other through *market* relationships, with the information provided by the common database becoming the main co-ordination mechanism. The common database would be able to standardise the specialised pockets of knowledge scattered throughout the hierarchic organisation, thus eliminating both existing information barriers and departmental idiosyncrasies.

In this way uncertainty and opportunism play no role, nor is there a need to use a hierarchy instead of a market as a more efficient control and co-ordination mechanism. But precisely because hierarchies are there to cope with the fact that full transparency is difficult to obtain, pockets of knowledge and related information asymmetries are hard to eliminate, etc., the idea of a centralised, common database is doomed to failure, unless, and this might prove exceedingly difficult, its implementation can be so thorough as to eliminate the reasons for the hierarchy to be set up in the first place.

As a second example, consider the award-winning computer-based information system employed by Benetton, the leading Italian company in fashion knitwear. The network of production plants, design bureaux, subcontractors, warehouses, points of sale (hundreds scattered all over the world), which build up Benetton's organisation, is held together by a computer network whose aim is to decrease transaction costs between the various units, and between them and the market. Data links have been established between the central office in Treviso, Italy, and cash registers in the shops: these links enable production and re-order plans to adapt swiftly to market vagaries, by shortening the time lag between customers' needs, as expressed in purchase transactions, and the company's adaptive response. CAD systems decrease the time lag between the design of models and their production. Databases support the quasi-market relationships between the company and its subcontractors and so on. Thus, the system seems to fit the nature of Benetton's organisation, because it maintains and strengthens its flexibility. It streamlines crucial transaction costs instead of superimposing a rigid, pyramidal system configuration.

Teams or clans. The information system of a clan is non-formalised and highly idiosyncratic; information exchange and communication take place through transmission of traditions, internalisation of values and norms. Traditions represent the memory of the organisation, accessible only after a long apprenticeship. 'Tacit knowledge' of the agents cannot be subjected to formalisation, nor can idiosyncratic communications be digitised. These modes of information production, exchange and storage set the limits to most of the present forms of computerisation.

However, new systems are being developed with the aim of at least not impeding and, if possible, enhancing human intuition, informal social exchange and iconic imagination. Such systems are being tested in the school or in the office environment and contrast current approaches aimed at including the work logic and methods of the past in the 'office of the future' hardware and software (Galeghen, Kraut and Egido, 1991). Basically, these systems allow synchronous and asynchronous horizontal communication, that is, they are those systems that support collaborative work discussed in chapter 4.

Dynamic analysis

Further insights into the interaction between computer forms and organisational arrangements of transactions can be gained if two dynamic exercises in figure 6.4 are pursued. Consider first the issue of the organisational change of a U-form into an M-form, in particular reinforcing the U-form. One of the reasons indicated to justify such a change is the economisation on bounded rationality so as to overcome the 'control loss' from the office of the chief executive over the different functions, due to the radial expansion of the firm. As Galbraith has shown, investment in vertical information systems (C- or DS-forms) may represent an alternative to such an organisational change, because up to a certain extent it allows the economisation on bounded rationality (see ch. 2). Thus, the availabilty of systems would shift upwards the size threshold for a switch from the U- to the M-form. Also, the size within which large M-forms can be managed shifts upwards if effective DS-forms are employed.

Second, consider the decentralisation of the U-form thanks to the introduction of teams and information technology. Specifically, costly co-ordination and control are one reason to give a 'peer group', or team, a hierarchical arrangement, but computer-based information systems (compatible with small-group idiosyncrasies) can support the complex communication network of teams, especially large ones.

The dynamic exercise can also be of a creative kind. Transaction-cost considerations allow us to appreciate the role of information technologies as an incentive to explore new forms of organisation, which, though feasible, have been (implicitly or explicitly) rejected; specifically, the exercise deals with the deconstruction of a hierarchy, thanks to the introduction of a market cum information technology.

Consider the organisational re-arrangement, suggested by Strassmann (1985), regarding a large bureaucracy (U-form) oriented to providing complex services to customers. Figure 6.5 shows the functional administrative units (1, 2, 3, etc.) organised on a specialised basis (specialisation is supposed to be necessary because of the unique and complex skills involved in the functional tasks) and integrated by co-ordinating resources (I, II etc.) to deal with customers (A, B). Costs of organising the whole administrative structure depend on the size and complexity of the co-ordinating and controlling mechanisms.

The cost of producing the service is also correlated with these factors because it is assumed that the services requested by the customers must be processed sequentially through pockets of functional expertise scattered in the different administrative units. Given the size of the whole administration, costs due to 'control loss' affect both the efficiency of the internal organisation and the provision of service to the client. In fact, the central office finds it difficult to control the performance of the functions under the effect of a 'team arrangement' among the functions (see ch. 2) and for the customer it is difficult to see the origin of delays or mistakes in the service delivered.

A different architecture for information handling (supported by a suitable information-technology architecture) allows one to achieve greater

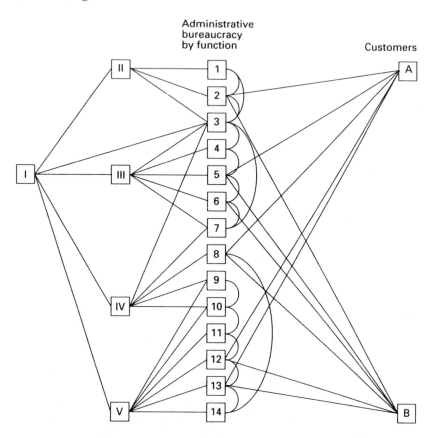

Figure 6.5 Administrative and market transactions between bureaucracy and customers (from Strassmann, 1985)

organisational productivity and higher efficiency in the provision of the service. The alternative indicated by Strassmann is to create 'information middlemen' who can package information products and responses to administrative needs of the customer. Figure 6.6 shows the information middlemen X and Y as interfaces between the customer, whose needs and requests they deal with integrally, and the administrative bureaucracy. This arrangement decreases the information load necessary to co-ordinate centrally the internal workload. Instead, it is the middlemen who selectively access, on the basis of customers' requests, the administrative functions. While policing the performance of the functions is difficult, given the transversality of the work flow and the team effort required, the performance of the middlemen is more easily monitored on the basis of the rate, costs and quality with which the output service is delivered to the customer.

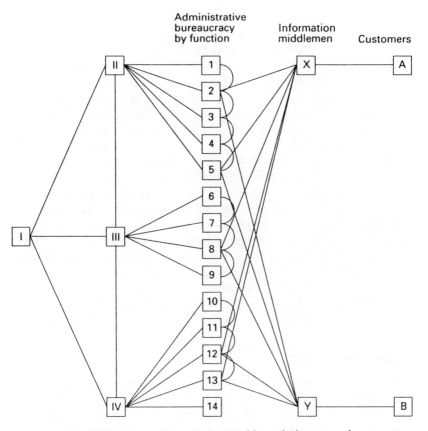

Figure 6.6 Modified pattern of transactions and boundaries among bureaucracy, middlemen and customers (from Strassmann, 1985)

The middlemen act as qualified purchasers of services from the various functions: a market prevails between middlemen and bureaucracy. This market provides an important co-ordinating function: each administrative unit provides the middlemen with a discrete, specific and standardised product, so that monitoring the function's performance is made easier for the central office.

Thus, the newly created market supplies some of the co-ordination which was previously carried out by the central office. Information processing is also reduced for the customer, who faces the single middleman. The cost of creating the internal market is represented by the middlemen. Data processing adds zest and lowers transaction costs in this new market. By using personal computers, the middlemen can easily access, via a communication network, the specialised functions of the very large, even geographically dispersed, bureaucracy. The network becomes a means for the local customer, through the middleman, to aggregate and co-ordinate various tasks to generate the complex service he/she needs.

Also, as soon as the boundary between the bureaucracy and the market has been redrawn in the fashion explained, database forms immediately find a wider domain of application than in the previous hierarchic–functional arrangement. For example, CDB- or DDB-forms, which otherwise would hardly overcome interfunctional barriers, could be a means for the bureaucracy to sell information to the middlemen through the network, which would constitute the technological support of the internal market.

We conclude with Strassmann, noting that quite often an exercise of organisational imagination (here economically grounded on transaction-costs concerns) contrasts with the current approach in administration, where data processing is regarded as an opportunity to increase functional specialisation and centralisation of control, optimising the single-office productivity at the expense of overall efficiency (see also chs. 5 and 12). This kind of exercise lies at the very heart of this book, when we try to identify general design principles to deconstruct and reconstruct bureaucracies through the joint deployment of information technology and alternative organisational forms, such as teams and markets.

Concluding remarks

An understanding of the nature of economic organisations is an essential prerequisite not only in governing the development of computer-based information systems, but also in analysing and designing them in an effective way. The transaction-costs perspective can help design information systems appropriate to the functioning of institutions such as markets, bureaucracies and teams. The foregoing analysis can be summarised as follows:

Exchange transactions represent the fundamental organisational relationship between human agents.

The organisation of exchange transactions depends upon contingencies which are both *environmental* (uncertainty and complexity) and *behavioural* (bounded rationality and opportunism).

Organisations can be regarded as *stable networks of contracts* which govern transactions, enabling co-ordination and control.

Transacting requires *information processing* to identify partners, define a contract, control its enforcement, etc.

Information technology acting as a *mediating technology* can, by lowering transaction costs, improve the information handling needed in transacting.

The application of information technology should not contradict *the nature of the organisational transactions* supported.

Information technology can, in the interests of efficiency, influence the shift from one organisational form to another. The possibility of lowering transaction costs should be considered in any attempt at *joint design*.

Note that this framework does not render obsolete the standard systems analysis methods, be they data- or decision-making oriented. On the contrary, it augments them with a new organisational and economic background, so that when an analyst goes into an organisation with his/her toolbox, he/she has a theory with which to select the relevant organisational phenomena, identify the information requirements and make a sound forecast of the organisational implications of any redesign put forward.

7 Analysing costs and benefits

Introduction

Cost–benefit analysis is aimed at defining the contribution of information systems to the improvement of business efficiency and effectiveness. Cost–benefit analysis should start from an estimate of all the benefits and not immediately of the costs of information technology, though in practice the opposite is usually done. Specifically, the following stages should be followed:

defining the objectives and the range of issues to be tackled;

quantifying the values of the problems, that is, the possible benefits, by separating the information problems from other types of problem;

identifying the mix of solutions, both information-process solutions and business solutions to the problems to be solved;

estimating the costs of each solution by separating information solutions from hardware and organisational solutions;

comparing the benefits generated by the solutions of the problems with the costs, specifying those costs directly related to information technology.

The benefits stem from the achievement of the goals and solving of the problems mentioned as the first point. The costs that have to be estimated are all the costs to be paid in order to achieve those objectives and solve those problems, not just the costs of the hardware. While this procedure is clear in theory, it is not so easy to follow in practice. First of all, not all problems are information problems, and to separate the information-based ones from the others is sometimes an unnatural way of dealing with them because they are so intertwined and they can be valued only as a 'package'. Furthermore, there may be no exact correspondence between an information problem and a computer solution (Strassmann, 1990).

Often computer technology is a solution to problems that are not strictly of an information nature, for example many applications of information technology to gain competitive advantage would fall in this category (see ch. 9). On the other hand, some information problems do not need a computer solution, but an organisational one, as Galbraith's framework described in chapter 2 shows in detail. In this chapter we want to compare two general approaches to the cost–benefit analysis: the first is based on the decision-making model, while the second refers to the transaction-cost approach. Next, we want to show with an analytic model how technology, by influencing the costs of co-ordination and production, can shift the relative boundaries between market-like and hierarchy-like arrangements of transactions. The conclusions reached with the model are also discussed by using empirical, qualitative data.

A typology of the benefits of information technology

While a detailed analysis of the sources of costs for a computer-based information system can be found in any MIS textbook, it is more difficult to analyse the benefits of an information system. It is, then, on the latter issue that this section and the following are focused. A possible way to start is to look at the benefits as related to two broad classes of application of information technologies. These can be labelled, according to Brandt *et al.* (1978), computers as 'work tools' and computers as 'organisational techno-logy', or, which is roughly the same, the two classes could be identified through the two application strategies that Zuboff (1988) defines as 'automating' and 'informating'.

Computers as work tools

The first bread-and-butter applications of computer technology have concerned the administrative areas, such as accounting, payrolls, invoicing, etc. These systems are necessary for the very existence of the firm; some of them actually regulate the key relationships between the firm and its environment. However, the analysis of such systems is in a way marginal: here the problem is to compare different solutions by analysing the costs of the various available technologies, including manual work, mechanisation and automation.

For these jobs computers can be valued as any office machine from the typewriter to the photocopier. They are mainly used to produce documents. They perform activities that before were carried out either through manual office work or through more traditional office machines. The benefits that can be derived from these applications of computer technology are essentially savings on clerical work. Such applications are very frequent in the service sector, banks, insurance, public administration and in the administrative services internal to the firm. In automating, or more generally in the use of information technology as a work tool, what prevails is a concern for efficiency rather than effectiveness, and the economic evaluation boils down to a cost/performance evaluation.

Organisational technologies

We have two organisational perspectives from which to look at the use of computers as an organisation technology. They are, as described in the previous chapter, the decision-making and transaction-cost approach.

Information and decision

Here information technology is used within the scope of management information systems to manage and control business processes, in particular to support or automate fully decision-making processes in the various functional areas of the firm. But what is the economic value of information needed to manage the business processes?

It is difficult to answer this question because information for an organisation does not have an intrinsic economic value, rather it is a resource that contributes to the production or sale of goods and services, and this contributes to the achievement of the goals of the firm. Only in specific circumstances can the value of information be derived from its market value. The value of information is determined from the specific, *ad hoc* use of that information that occurs within the firm. So what matters is more its *use* value rather than its market value. But then, what is the use value of information? The decision-making view can be of help in tackling this complex question.

Recall the individual decision-making model and its organisational counterpart as described in Galbraith's framework (ch. 2). The basic hypothesis is that the higher the uncertainty of the task, the bigger the quantity of information that needs to be processed and exchanged among various decision makers in order to achieve a certain level of performance. Also, to achieve this level of performance, the organisation can be modified so as to improve or adjust its co-ordination capability. Organisations respond to the increase in uncertainty in at least two ways, either by reducing the amount of information to be handled and communicated, or by increasing the capacity of processing and communicating information.

Let us examine the costs of each of these two alternatives. First, reducing the need to process information means essentially decreasing the number of exceptions compared to some pre-planned sequence of events. In other words, it means having standards or instituting slack resources (financial, human or physical) in order to have a certain autonomy in front of the vagaries of demand, supply and other variables outside our control. Thus, deadlines are perceived as less stringent, inventory levels are kept higher, for one builds extra production capacity in order to absorb variations in demand. To be sure, the capacity to dampen and absorb the unplanned event is paid for by the higher cost of the slack resources. In the second case, one needs to create the self-sufficient, semi-autonomous units that can, for example through a multidivisionalisation, leave some autonomy to the units to react to the unplanned events.

To augment the power to process information means either investing in information systems from a technological point of view, that is buying computers to institute vertical information systems, or from an organisational point of view creating roles and functions that facilitate the lateral exchange of information, or the combination of the two interventions. In the first case one invests directly in information technology; in the second in human resources to build mediating roles, task forces, project teams, integrating roles such as area managers, product managers, liaison roles between different departments, matrix organisations. The costs to be borne are those of computer systems and the organisational costs stemming from numerous sources (overheads). Here computer technology allows a different way of organising the productive factors and the business resources by improving co-ordination in the face of uncertainty. The use value of information is related to a better productivity of the resources because resources are employed better. Also information technologies appear as alternative, complementary solutions to more traditional organisational or management mechanisms.

Information and exchange

Let us consider now the transaction-cost approach. According to Galbraith's (1977) model uncertainty of the task determines the information needs. Uncertainty means the variety of events or states a decision maker must face with his/her own limited capabilities of processing information. This is only one of the possible causes of uncertainty, as the transaction-costs approach shows, derived from technology or the environment (see the previous chapter). But there are situations where interpersonal relations represent a new source of uncertainty.

If a decision maker obtains information on the behaviour of both the other decision makers and the environment, this introduces a type of interdependence or externality between the rules according to which the decision maker takes his/her own decisions. This externality compels the decision maker to take into account the uncertainty of all the other players besides that of the environment. And the distinction between the uncertainty and information regarding the environment, on the one hand, and the uncertainty and information regarding other players' behaviour, on the other hand, is a fundamental one.

The second source of uncertainty, or exchange uncertainty, suggests a different approach to the economic evaluation based on the transaction-costs idea. Note, further, that transactions can be a source of uncertainty, but at the same time are a source of new information regarding other people's plans. The information that can influence the dependent decision processors and improve their independence lowers the costs of transacting. This perspective on the relationship between information and organisation allows a different way of looking at the benefits of information technology, specifically as a mediating technology.

A typology based on the decision-making approach

Figure 7.1 shows a possible range of benefits both for information technology as a work tool and as an organisation technology in a range of cases for various functional areas. To be sure, these examples are not exhaustive. We can identify two broad areas of benefits depending on the technology as a work tool and as an organisational technology:

the direct benefits, through the direct replacement of work by technology;

the indirect benefits, due to either an increase in sales or economising the production factors: materials, energy, machines, and personnel. These benefits can be obtained either by changing directly the business areas or through an improvement in management activities like planning and management control.

As a concrete example, consider a summary list of possible benefits generated by a computer-based information system for the purchasing department of an international oil company. The improvements can be grouped into the following categories:

reduction of costs in the purchase of goods;

reduction of costs in the managing of the purchasing task;

reduction in inventory stocks of purchased goods;

improvement in administrative personnel productivity;

improvement of salesmen's productivity;

improvement in programming and control;

increase in sales.

We can classify these benefits according to the two main categories defined so far: computers as a work tool or as an organisational technology. For example, the reduction of purchased materials is a consequence of the use of information technology as an organisation technology. The reduction of costs of the purchasing activity falls into the work-tool category: to save on labour costs. A decrease in the inventory of purchased goods is an application of information technology mainly as an organisational techno-logy. The improvement in the personal productivity derives from the use of information technology as a work tool and savings in labour costs. The

1 Computers as a tool:

Costs saved or avoided thanks to the replacement of work by
machines

	Task	Technology
Organisation	White-collar work • decrease of extra hours • decrease of personnel	• office equipment
Data processing	Data-processing work • reduction of shifts • decrease of workload	• cheaper systems (Cpu, peripherals, telecom expenses, etc.) • less consumption

2 Computers as organisation technology (more profitable mix of factors
of production, markets and organisation):

Finance:
  • Financial expenses saved or avoided (reduction of
    inventories; faster circulation of capital; invoicing;
    credit; etc.)
  • Faster planning cycles

Materials:
  • Improved purchasing policies
  • Optimisation of production scheduling
  • Faster response on critical areas

Plants and machines:
  • Better capacity planning
  • Improved materials handling
  • Better simulation of capacity utilisation

Personnel:
  • Improved production planning and scheduling
  • Better use of workforce

Sales:
  • Better knowledge of demand
  • Faster service (better product delivery and quality)

Figure 7.1 Typology of benefits

higher productivity of the sales personnel is due to managing better the sales force: it is an application of an organisation technology. The improvement of planning and control is obviously an application of organisational technology, while the increase in sales may be due to both effects. It goes without saying that each of these benefits is more or less difficult to estimate and each requires different techniques and resources for investigation.

The benefits in transaction-costs language

According to this perspective information is used and produced during the transaction to help in carrying out and governing the transaction. The benefits of a mediating technology as a tool to facilitate exchanges can be identified by analysing the costs of exchange that can be saved. As shown in the previous chapter, the transaction costs are essentially information costs and they derive from the fact that there are impediments to exchange. These costs can be split further in search costs, contracting costs, control costs and maintenance costs. If we consider the case of the purchasing department, one can note different sources for savings which translate into the following benefits:

Search costs. A possible reduction in costs in the goods purchased is given by the larger number of quotations and prices that can be handled by the system for each item, or by the supporting purchasing staff when they bargain for a reduction in prices according to volumes thanks to an industry database. Also, a purchaser may have more free time to find better deals.

Contracting costs. Among the items that would allow reduction of the purchased material, there is a cost of competition on the economic order quantity for each item purchased. Also, a faster and more reliable communication of prices and contracts may contribute to a faster response to a request for quotations.

Costs of control. A better control over the inventory of stock and a better quality control so as to send back goods that do not conform to quality standards. More generally, a better feedback to the personnel to help them solve problems.

Costs of maintenance. The improvement in documented communication, a better planning procedure and a richer availability of historical data should make purchasing a smoother job.

In sum, to the extent that organisational and management costs are basically transaction costs, to market, compute and communicate prices, to control performances and so on, the application of information technology can decrease such costs in various ways. This can happen directly, for example by reducing the time needed to execute each stage of a transaction, or indirectly by making more advantageous the transaction itself, for example by allowing purchasing employees to get goods of better quality.

An analytic model of economic evaluation

A richer model for evaluating the costs and benefits of information technology according to the transaction-cost approach must include a due concern for comparing different forms of arranging transactions and other production costs. This can be done by adapting the analytic models introduced by Williamson (1985) to appreciate how technology and organisational forms jointly can make more efficient certain ways of co-ordinating the tasks of producing goods.

According to such models the main parameter for the analysis of the shift between market and hierarchical transactions is given by the specificity of human, physical or locational resources. That is to say, if there is no specificity of resources, market contracting will result as the most efficient: in fact, an outside supplier can merge various orders, thus economising in production costs, and costs of purchasing from the market are negligible. If there is a specificity in the resources, it might turn out that the hierarchy is more efficient in that it avoids the costs of haggling or overcoming barriers to exit that transaction, given the lack of alternatives or given the high investments that the partners have made in the specific assets needed to carry out the transaction.

It is, then, possible to compare the costs of having a hierarchy, $CGH(k)$, assuming it produces only one product, with those of the market $CGM(k)$, when the parameter k, 'specificity', varies. In the first instance, let us consider negligible scope and scale economies. Let us assume further that for zero specificity, that is, for the maximum standardisation of transactions, the hierarchy has some bureaucratic costs that are not negligible, that is $CGH(k = 0)$ is greater than $CGM(k = 0)$; also let us suppose that CGM' is greater than CGH' for all k values, that is, there is a lower adaptability of the market to negotiate the terms of the contract and this is true especially when k is large. If we call $\delta G = CGH(k) - CGM(k)$ one can see from the chart in figure 7.2 (the continuous line) that when we have low resource specificity, the market is to be preferred as a form of transaction governance, that is the curve at the left of k', which is the indifference value of resource specificity. When the specificity of resources is high (to the right of k'), the cost of the market tends to increase and δG becomes negative.

If we introduce information technology into the hierarchy, for example as vertical information systems, δG will move towards the horizontal axis and this will lead to an expansion of the role of the hierarchy itself, δG_i. The same effect could be obtained through a purely internal organisational

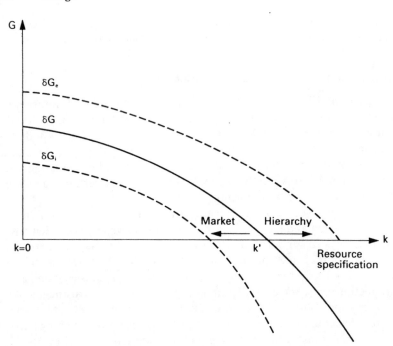

Figure 7.2 Market versus hierarchy trade-off when new technologies are applied

restructuring, for example by moving from a functional hierarchy to a multidivisional form. But note the *relative* impacts of technology on the hierarchy and the market. If the technology is applied to support a market, then δG will move along the vertical axis and become δG_e, given the fact that CGM(k) in the δG difference decreases. And what will happen if the technology is applied simultaneously to the market and to the hierarchy? The curve δG can move in one direction or the other according to the relative impact of the technology on the two variables CGH(k) and CGM(k). However, in general, market transactions by their nature are already standardised and it is easier to automate them. This suggests that the curve δG will move towards the top of the vertical axis, leading to a process of expansion of the markets already discussed in chapters 5 and 6 and to be further explored below.

The model can be made more complex if we factor in the economies of scale and scope, and specifically the production costs, beside the differences in transaction costs. Also in this case the hierarchy will entail higher production costs when we have standardised transactions. The disadvantage in terms of cost will decrease at the increase of resource specificity, going towards zero asymptotically. This is the case of only one good for which there are no scale economies for suppliers who are unable to aggregate the various orders of many buyers (Williamson, 1985).

In this case, when we have scale or scope economies, it can be shown that the market is preferable also with specificity values higher than in the case where scale and scope economies are supposed to be negligible. In this more complex situation one needs to consider the impact of the new technologies also on production costs and standardisation of resources. A similar effect is obtained through the increase of production quantities, considering that diseconomies associated with in-house production will decrease when the quantity of the manufactured goods increases. This leads to a higher vertical integration, that is, the automation of production and information systems will support the expansion of the hierarchy.

A more complex interplay can take place if the technology is applied to both the market and the hierarchy, to production and co-ordination. The final outcome will depend upon specific circumstances (Brosseau, 1991).

The impacts of information technology on organisations: a comprehensive appraisal

An estimate of the costs of running markets, administrative hierarchies and teams in a real economy can be deduced by looking at the percentage of labour income absorbed by the 'organisers' (that is, those who direct, co-ordinate, monitor and record economic activities of production): for the United States it has been calculated at about 40 per cent, roughly equally allocated to those who run markets and those who run administrations (Jonscher, 1980; Porat, 1977).

Information technology, in the various forms of office automation, telecommunications, EDP, etc., will have widespread impacts on the quantitative and qualitative dimensions of the employment (for example, on the subdivision between 'organisers' and 'producers', the creation/distribution of professional skills, etc.), and on the organisations where the work of production and co-ordination is carried out, along the lines of what has been shown with the static and dynamic exercises in the previous chapter.

Specifically, this last section discusses the qualitative change in the population of organisations to be expected as a result of the influence of information technology on the efficiency of different organisational forms (Ciborra, 1983).

Since the classic empirical study by Whisler (1970) of the impact of data processing on the organisational structures of a sample of insurance companies, the development of computer and telecommunication technologies indicates today the need for a broader approach to the evaluation of the organisational impacts of information technology. In what follows some of these developments together with their implications are briefly sketched.

Transborder data flows. The availabilty of transborder data flows (TBDF) deeply affects multinational organisations. Specifically, data flows for control functions of headquarters about affiliates tend to increase the degree of centralisation of the multinationals. Moreover, within the corporate structure new functional firms are created, such as trading companies, re-invoicing companies, etc., which specialise in providing more and more co-ordination services to the group as a whole. The overall structure of the enterprise becomes a complex mix of product divisions, local affiliates and global functional centres (Antonelli, 1981). The growth of TBDF seems to accelerate the process of international specialisation as occurring *within* firms rather than between firms, thus confirming Porat's (1978) hypothesis according to which the information economy is largely bureaucratic in nature.

The cottage industry. Emery (1978) and Trist (1981) see in microelectronics the opportunity for scaling down rather than up, dispersal rather than concentration and self-management rather than external control of organisations. New forms of social and work organisations, such as 'community workshops', and the re-assessment of the household as a socio-technical production system are envisaged. Bureaucracies will give way to self-regulating primary work systems loosely coupled through ephemeral networks. According to Rice (1980), computer conferencing may allow geographic decentralisation with the shift of organisational units to rural areas, especially of routine and information transfer activities. Although the issue is a complex one, involving the appreciation of trade-offs among telecommunication, transportation and energy solutions, preliminary studies do not exclude the advent of a new 'cottage industry'.

A self-service economy. Considering the structure of the whole economy, Gershuny (1978) identifies two main organisational changes which the diffusion of microelectronics may reinforce:

    Goods replace services (the privately purchased and owned washing machine replaces the laundry service), thus creating a different organisation of the economy in which production carried out in the home becomes more important.

    Enlargement of the tertiary sector as a consequence of the increased division of labour in the production of capital goods which substitute services: large bureaucracies needed to provide services will give way to smaller organisations which co-ordinate, plan and control production and distribution of goods.

Emerging markets. Lemoine (1980) indicates that the 'informatisation' of the tertiary sector will

lengthen the production cycle of marketable services;

stimulate the emergence of new jobs such as 'network managers', 'distributors of information', 'suppliers of data banks', etc.;

transform the quasi-markets through which services are provided within the enterprises into real markets where information goods and services are bought and sold; functional departments will turn into small or medium-sized, highly specialised firms.

Thus, informatisation would appear as a driving force which re-inverts the process whereby in the nineteenth century the 'visible hand' of management has taken over the market functions (Chandler, 1978).

This process is not exempted from risks. For one thing, Lemoine points out that the increased division of labour and the allocation of information-service activities to the market may weaken the informal, unofficial exchange and processing of information which take place daily within the firm and which are, for example, of importance for the unions in their bargaining activity.

Will there be, then, more markets or more bureaucracy as a consequence of the diffusion of information technology? The studies carried out so far are split in two directions: those who sustain an expansion of markets and those who see a reinforcement of bureaucracies (Brosseau, 1991; Brynjolfsson *et al.*, 1989). Our data on a sample of Italian companies that have applied since the 1970s technological innovations, ranging from robots to computer-based information systems, show that organisational structures are rather 'turbulent', that is, they undergo changes simultaneously with technological ones (Ciborra and Roveda, 1981).

As suggested by the analytical model above it is difficult to evaluate the net result of the transformations. In Figure 7.3 the impacts of different *technological systems* are shown on the three main *organisational forms* previously examined, plus a fourth one, the hypo-integrated organisation. The latter, to be examined when considering the special case of public administration (ch. 12), represents a set of loosely coupled organisations, for example organisations located on the same territory: firms, families, autonomous work groups, the market and the state. They all interact in various ways (bureaucratically, through competition, through clans, etc.), but no common purpose or way of functioning can be singled out.

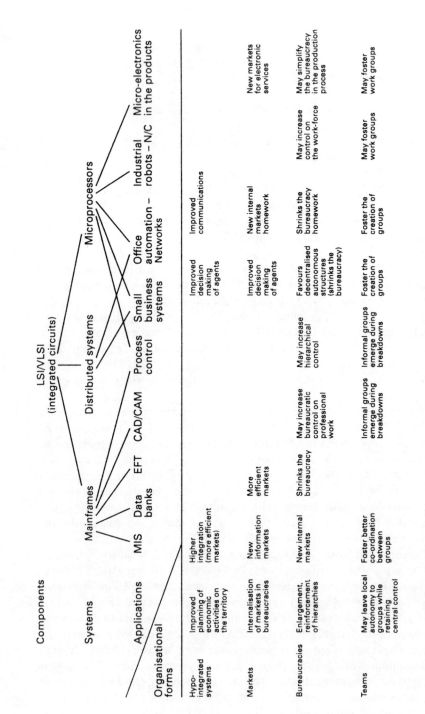

Components / Systems / Applications

Organisational forms	Applications	MIS	Data banks	EFT	CAD/CAM	Process control	Small business systems	Office automation – Networks	Industrial robots – N/C	Micro-electronics in the products
Hypo-integrated systems	Improved planning of economic activities on the territory	Higher integration (more efficient markets)					Improved decision making of agents	Improved communications		
Markets	Internalisation of markets in bureaucracies	New information markets		More efficient markets			Improved decision making of agents	New internal markets homework		New markets for electronic services
Bureaucracies	Enlargement, reinforcement of hierarchies	New internal markets		Shrinks the bureaucracy	May increase bureaucratic control on professional work	May increase hierarchical control	Favours decentralised autonomous structures (shrinks the bureaucracy)	Shrinks the bureaucracy homework	May increase control on the work-force	May simplify the bureaucracy in the production process
Teams	May leave local autonomy to groups while retaining central control	Foster better co-ordination between groups			Informal groups emerge during breakdowns	Informal groups emerge during breakdowns	Foster the creation of groups	Foster the creation of groups	May foster work groups	May foster work groups

(LSI/VLSI (integrated circuits): Mainframes — MIS, Data banks, EFT; Distributed systems — CAD/CAM, Process control, Small business systems; Microprocessors — Office automation – Networks, Industrial robots – N/C, Micro-electronics in the products)

Figure 7.3 Impacts of information technology on the four main organisational forms

The main findings of figure 7.3 can be summarised as follows:

The *hypo-integrated organisations* undergo an integration process. Information technology fills some of the gaps of their 'colander' structure by providing cheap information goods and services to be sold on new, specialised markets. Data banks support and improve markets connecting previously isolated operators on the territory. Planning information systems integrate the workings of the administrative bureaucracy with the socio-economic process taking place on the territory. Also, groups, coalitions of interest and more ephemeral social networks could be supported by distributed communication, through systems like videotex.

Market forms tend to strengthen and expand. Through standardisation of transactions and services exchanged, markets are supported by information technology at the expense of hypo-integrated systems and bureaucracies. New markets are created and old markets are improved, for example through EFT in banking, data banks in the information goods markets and the transformation of universal services to be provided by administrative structures into information products (see ch. 5), the design of computer-based internal markets among bureaucratic functions, etc. (divisionalisation, subcontracting, etc.). The design also introduces market elements into hierarchies, which can be supported by distributed systems, local networks and TBDF.

The *bureaucracy* becomes highly turbulent: on the one hand, communication supports the creation of very large multinational organisations; on the other, these contain more and more internal market arrangements. In innovative environments, such as those where R&D units of the electronic industry operate, the bureaucratic organisation is blended with flexible team or clan features to support matrix patterns. Specifically, it has been found that information technology affects the bureaucracy in the following ways:

Small hierarchies give way to teams which manage transactions through local networks (this is the case of remote office work; see Olson, 1981).

The size threshold between functional and divisional organisations is shifted upwards: computer-based systems can support larger functional bureaucracies.

Multidivisional forms can grow larger, as mentioned above.

In summary, the bureaucracy seems to become more and more a mechanism for distant co-ordination among diversified and scattered units, but it is increasingly mixed with market elements and losses in efficiency rating as a means of local control. Finally,

Teams expand their range of diffusion. In highly automated environments the actual work organisation is the 'work group'. Subcontracting dissolves small hierarchies and departments of large hierarchies into small teams transacting through markets. Computer-messaging systems facilitate the shift from hierarchical organisations to different ones consisting of constantly changing teams when this is required by the failure of bureaucratic co-ordination and control mechanisms.

Conclusion

The empirical data seem to indicate that the relative impacts of information technology on production and co-ordination costs should also be appraised for the qualitative changes they may induce, for example in shifting the organisation that hosts the computer system from a hierarchy to a market or vice versa. If this is the case, then one important class of costs or benefits to be considered includes the change in the governance rules of the hosting organisations.

Appraising the costs and benefits of information technology is more than accounting or auditing tangible and intangible consequences of computer applications. Apart from the easiest cases, each time we carry out an economic analysis of the actual or expected impacts of information technology, we need a point of view and a conceptual framework on which to ground our evaluation. The point of view has been spelled out by adopting the dichotomy: work tool versus organisational technology. The first perspective allows us to look for the 'automating' effects of information technology; the second for the more subtle, but no less relevant, 'informating' effects. The latter perspective, where the sheer accounting of labour or capital cost does not suffice, requires in turn an organisational context to be fully appreciated. We have applied two of them: the decision-making and the transaction-cost approach.

8 Systems development: a contractual view

Introduction

In this chapter we begin to look at the *process* of development of information systems. Systems development is a complex task that requires an appropriate organisation to link various specialists, management, customers and users. Such an organisation tends to be looked at according to the traditional hierarchical, planning-oriented perspective. The methodologies in common currency prescribe a division of labour and a way of carrying out the task that is machine-like and hierarchical. Despite the attempts at proposing more and more 'structured' methodologies, systems development is still in need of significant advancements. The team and market perspective can be useful in approaching the task in a new light. Our aim is to show here the superiority of a contractual approach to the organisation of systems development, on the basis of a hard-nosed economic analysis of the costs of technological innovations (Ciborra, 1987b).

Let us start by recalling the problems that current methodologies often fail to address. Those that are experienced in connection with developing information systems are the following (Bostrom and Heinen, 1977; Nolan and MacFarlan, 1974):

communication and language difficulties between specialists and users;

lack of a commonly accepted framework, particularly in the early phases of systems development, or conflicts between different (individual) frameworks;

lack of effectiveness of the new information system, which does not produce the expected results;

low efficiency of the overall project, and underestimation of costs and development time;

missing, incomplete or unreadable documentation;

very short life of the developed system;

expenditure of large amounts of resources on the maintenance of already developed systems, rather than in the development of new ones.

Survey data show that systems are delivered even at two and a half times the original planned cost and require about one and three-quarters times as long to develop as originally estimated. Often no correlation seems to exist between the introduction of new systems and the effectiveness of organisations. Users are frequently dissatisfied and systems designers feel frustrated.

The problems listed above stem from a variety of sources: some of them relate to the definition of the role of the user, some are due to general organisational factors and others result from failure to manage the process of change.

In such a situation, it is understandable that computer specialists have tried to find methodologies for managing systems development. In fact, in large projects the systems-development work tends to be difficult to control: communications become clouded, schedules are shifted and important goals are overlooked in performing a number of small technical activities.

The primary objective of a structured methodology is to ensure that data-processing resources are used effectively and efficiently in accordance with management's objectives and directives. However, most of the existing hierarchical, planning-oriented approaches and methodologies (including the auditing methods) are not well suited to application in complex organisational environments. By complex environments we mean those situations where social, organisational and technical problems appear to be relevant and interwoven in view of the introduction, use and maintenance of a system.

In this chapter, we focus first on three main topics: the content of standard approaches for systems development and auditing; the analysis of the failures of such approaches in taking into account turbulent environments; the needs and challenges for more sophisticated bargaining-oriented techniques that are emerging from an investigation of actual systems-development processes in companies and public administration in a Northern European country.

From this discussion some guidelines and issues for a new contractual approach are derived, applying the economics of externalities or social costs. Specifically, the design and implementation of information systems are regarded as processes generating social costs. Bargaining for technological change amounts to internalising such social costs through the exchange of property rights in organising work and designing systems. Finally, alternative governance structures, markets versus regulation, are evaluated on the basis of their efficiency in securing the internalisation of social costs.

Structured approaches

A structured methodology includes four main ingredients:

Project organisation: the structure of relationships which connect the participants' roles.

Phases and tasks: various interrelated activities that have to be accomplished in different steps of the process.

Documentation: an output of the life cycle is provided by documents which describe to the participants what has been achieved.

Auditing: management, users and specialists develop routines to review outputs, check expenditures and start possible corrective actions.

A brief description of each item is given in this section, with no special prescriptive aims.

Project organisation. Because systems development may cross the boundaries of several units within the organisation along vertical and horizontal lines, a structure is given to the project to make explicit and control the common framework in which the participants (belonging to the different organisational units) are operating.

Such a structure is usually composed of:

1 an upper-level group, which co-ordinates the overall project organisation;
2 a user-area respresentative structure;
3 the design team;
4 an auditing function.

As an example, the following specifications for a 'managerial' approach to systems development can be given:

1 The upper-level group is generally called the 'MIS steering committee'. The MIS steering commitees serve as a 'board of directors' for the MIS organisation. The steering committees assume a wide range of responsibilities:

   policy-setting activities, such as approving long-range plans, establishing funding levels and budgets, setting priorities for major investments and acting as an arbitrator when lower-level conflicts arise;

   performance-monitoring activities, such as monitoring budgets and establishing performance targets;

   project-review activities, such as major cost/benefit decisions, approving system specifications and monitoring costs and schedules.

The size, structure and roles of steering committees may vary considerably from one situation to another. Each organisation requires its own specific solution to this aspect.

2 In a proactive, participative steering committee there exists a need for a level of involvement and participation from members of functional departments which is additional to the roles and responsibilities of the committee itself. This involvement is of two types:

the routine management of work requests, budgets and priorities for data-processing services;

the monitoring of individual development projects.

3 Systems-development work is 'project'-oriented, that is, it has a definite start or initiation point and a goal which, when reached, terminates the systems-development activity. Managing such work requires that a project-management organisation be applied. Usually, such an organisation structure recognises one individual as primarily responsible for project accomplishment. This individual is responsible for co-ordinating the activities of the various functional elements within the organisation.

4 Each organisational unit should ensure the quality of products resulting from the tasks or activities for which it is responsible. This means that an adequate audit of the efforts should be carried out before any product is transferred to another group.

Phases and tasks of information systems design. Although every application is different, the main functions performed during the development of any system are very similar. The 'system life cycle' concept generally groups these functions into three levels, categorised as phases, tasks and activities.

Phases normally correspond to project stages. Each phase is characterised by a set of limited, clearly definable objectives; a time scale which is short enough to be accurately planned; and measurable outputs which are reviewed before the project progresses. Each phase is subdivided into tasks, and each task into activities.

Any method-based approach to information-systems design consists, then, of a sequence of steps starting from the needs, problems and ideas formulated by the users and the sponsors, to the final specifications for manual routines and computer programs. Hence, by methodology is meant a number of manageable and coherent phases including rules for the description of models and other documentation that are produced during these phases.

Documentation. In general, documentation has the following characteristics;

It is produced during the development activities as a natural output, but it should be constantly updated and formally coherent.

It grows in detail as more is learned about the new system, though one should avoid too large manuals or files.

It is viewed as a verification (*a posteriori*) of activity completion; the systems-development procedure, not documentation, drives the effort. It can be subdivided into two types: process documentation and product documentation.

Process documentation consists of data related to the development and management of the system such as project-authorisation forms, project plans, project structures, schedules and budgets, phase-end reports, cost–benefit analysis, supporting materials and documents. Process documentation can be referenced during the post-audit evaluation and proves useful as a reference guide for future project planning.

Product documentation describes how the new system is created during the systems-development activities, and becomes a 'project file'. Manual documentation tends to become very large and unmanageable, even at a modest level of detail. In the last years, automated documentation techniques have beeen developed as part of CASE tools.

Auditing. The development activities must be checked in the various phases, otherwise their output may not match the initial objectives and expectations. In fact, some aspects of the project organisation have a control content. All the committees or groups (for example, the steering committee and the project team) have among their tasks the responsibility of reviewing and approving the work being done, at fixed checkpoints or at critical stages.

Such committees are also the place where learning about what is being done is (or at least should be) concentrated. Consequently, they are in the right position for contributing to the redefinition of project objectives, scopes, resources etc.

For new projects unavoidable dysfunctions may arise because management involvement in the committees tends to be more important during the early phases, where objectives are fuzzy and risks highest, while learning has not yet taken place. Later, control tasks tend to be delegated to the operative groups. These groups monitor the coherence between the development activities and the standards for quality previously established. Finally, the definition of roles and responsibilities is a component of project organisation which serves as a reference for checking the degree of task accomplishment by individuals.

A critique of current approaches

In this section, the assumptions or the implicit working hypotheses on which current approaches are based are made explicit and discussed, in order to explain why the use of a standard, rigid methodology is ineffective in an organisational environment characterised by a high degree of complexity and uncertainty.

The mechanistic fallacy

One of the key ideas in hierarchical systems-development methodologies is to split the development process into stages or phases, in order to achieve better management control. This segmented approach is particularly important for auditing purposes. At the end of each phase it is possible to compare the actual with the expected results.

The implicit assumption here is that the construction of a system is somewhat analogous to any manufacturing process: techniques developed for shop-floor work and production organisation can then be applied to systems development. However, this tentative analogy is wrong in complex situations, because of at least three reasons.

First, systems designers (and auditors) are characterised, as any human problem solver, by bounded rationality (see ch. 1). They operate in a non-deterministic world where contingencies are known only to a limited extent. Thus, designers cannot rely on a formal methodology which would represent an obstacle to what the situation often requires: *ad hoc* experimentation. Simulation prototypes and field experimentation are needed to replace the straightforward, superficial assumptions about behaviour of users and machines that are often embedded in systems-development methodologies (see next chapter).

Second, as the theory of work organisation shows, the *nature of the task* deeply affects the way in which the work itself ought to be carried out, organised and controlled in accordance with effectiveness and efficiency criteria. Standardised mass production may be organised efficiently according to mechanical principles, but it is highly doubtful that the same approach is valid where the 'product' to be manufactured is complex, uncertain, new and volatile in its specifications (Davis, 1982).

While we agree that organisation, control and auditing efforts must be related to the complexity, novelty and uncertainty of any systems project, it is common experience that simple intensification of the amount of the control and auditing efforts without a qualitative improvement in their sophistication will only lead to more overheads, red tape and slowdowns. More committees, meetings and auditors will make the bureaucracy more cumbersome, without adding much to the effectiveness of the system (Brooks, 1982). It is widely recognised that, even in operations management, when the levels of uncertainty of the process and the product increase, one should rely on work organisations like teams, which are characterised by more flexibility, autonomy and built-in auditing mechanisms (see ch. 2). Such an approach becomes crucial when work is carried out by highly skilled professionals, such as systems specialists.

Third, the *nature of the product* makes a difference. Constructing a system is not simply building a car; it is definitely something more, and not only because the product may be more complex, uncertain, abstract or new. The final outcome of a system project is in fact a real *organisational change*. People's roles, skills, decision-making power, career patterns, work organisation, communication, etc., may be affected by the use of a new system.

A better analogy can, then, be found not in car manufacturing, but in organisational development projects, where the focus of interest is in identifying and facilitating actors, situations and collective learning experiences. The analysts become 'change agents' who help the organisation to change itself, to self-organise. Again a mechanical approach is intrinsically unsuitable to cover self-organising processes to be carried out by the users utilising the new system.

The a-conflictual fallacy

Systems design is not only a complex problem-solving acitvity; it is also a political process (Markus, 1983). Systems designers are not merely problem solvers, they are agents of political change. The functional decomposition of the systems development effort and the assignment of fixed objectives, roles and activities to management, designers and users simply miss the point that system design means organisational change that has to do with power processes taking place in the organisation (Keen, 1981).

If the actual use of any routine, the practical application of rules, or the integration of any data-processing procedure are the outcome of a daily negotiated order within the organisation (Strauss, 1978), then systems development is no exception. It is an organisational process to be understood as a mixed, conflict–co-operation game, where actors having different goals, values, knowledge and interests interact (see chs. 1 and 6).

The end product (the system), the way it is produced and the way it is evaluated are the result of this interaction process, which, it should be emphasised, constitutes at the same time a knowledge-building process, a work process and a bargaining process.

While one can ignore all these features for the construction of a simple and stable application, it seems highly risky to indulge in the mechanistic, functional perspective (that most of the existing methodologies suggest) when complex systems have to be designed within turbulent organisational contexts (Briefs, Ciborra and Schneider, 1984). Unfortunately, and interestingly enough for a new, contractual perspective concerning the development and use of information systems in organisations, new systems (distributed systems, expert systems, office automation systems) tend to be of the complex type. And the increasing awareness of the different actors (within and outside the organisation) about the side-effects of automation contributes to make the picture even more complex and turbulent.

A case study in Norway

In a sense, Norway has been in the late 1970s and 1980s an interesting laboratory where explicitly contractual systems-development projects have taken place. As in other Scandinavian countries, the Norwegian unions, employers and government have tried to take into consideration the effects of technological change on work. Norway was the first country to adopt negotiated labour–management agreements on computer-based systems. Such technology or data agreements establish a variety of rights for workers in the areas of information, training, participation and bargaining concerning the design and use of systems in the workplace (Schneider and Ciborra, 1983).

How do existing methodologies behave in such a contractual environment, where institutionally it is recognised that 'designers' are not the only data-processing specialists, but also the unions' representatives, the company management and the workers?

Results are mixed, depending on the company and union experience in applying the agreements: the new unions' rights do not automatically guarantee increased influence over technological change. However, trends and challenges for existing methodologies can be distinguished.

In companies where both employers and unions have implicitly agreed on an 'after-the-fact' approach, current systems-design methodologies are used with no special problems. In these companies systems are designed, tested and applied by a management-controlled design team (including user representatives selected by management). However, once the system is in use, the post-audit phase is much richer. The agreements give the unions the right to evaluate the system according to criteria not usually taken into account: social needs of the workforce, training and education requirements, impacts on work organisation, skills, etc.

Modification of systems is then the object of *ex-post* bargaining. A union 'auditor' is deputed to this task: this is the 'data shop steward' as defined by the Norwegian agreements. While the company auditors are expected to be technically competent, this is not the case of the union auditor, who has the right to get information regarding the system in a format and language free of any technical jargon and understandable to a non-specialist (so goes the letter of agreement). In some organisations, this fact poses challenges to existing methodologies, which in practice have been abandoned, to rely on more pragmatic, *ad hoc* approaches at the bargaining table. As a result of such an enlarged approach, systems procedures were modified (for example, control routines on individual performance have been switched off).

Even more complex is the situation in those companies which decided to apply the agreement in full. By allowing 'before-the-fact' participation of the data shop steward, the whole systems-development process reveals its contractual nature from the beginning. Not only is a different auditor present, but also a new designer representing different interests and values in the organisation (the data shop steward as an elected designer). Strategies for dealing with the new situation must change: blind reliance on current methodologies leads usually to local and global conflicts which may stop the whole system effort. This is a proof, we submit, of the soundness of the theoretical concerns that were expressed above.

The practice has been to extend the framework provided by existing methodologies to include new features: strategic plans are defined within committees where unions are also present; problems of interest to unions are explored and dealt with by special subcommittees; enlarged evaluation committees are set up to audit the system once implemented, and so on.

One of the most interesting features that have emerged is the need for relying not only on 'plans', but also on 'systems contracts' which specify what the expected characteristics and impacts of the new systems are. Such contracts work as reference documents for the audit phase.

The auditing process here becomes the control phase of the complex contractual arrangement which leads to the use of the new system: its main goal is to check for discrepancies in the allocation of the costs and benefits among management, union members and clients at large that is brought by the new system. In its application, the auditing process must welcome the possibility of opportunistic behaviour and information concealment by parties who are not neutral in the process of organisational change. In investigating responsibilities for wrong design, unexpected consequences or undesired impacts, the auditors have, then, also to take into account the moral hazard caused by the opportunistic behaviour of conflicting actors.

In order to face this and other complexities, committees and control apparatuses are proliferating. However, as expected (see above), this seems to lead more often to heavier bureaucracy rather than to better systems.

Management and unions have become aware of the unsatisfactory state of affairs and have been looking for better methods. One interesting development is the application by the unions of 'checklists' to identify from the beginning what the social and organisational consequences of data-processing systems will be. In one case, an important decision has been taken by the company management: any system project is not allowed to start if a document (contract) listing the economic, social and technical features of the system is not compiled by the data-processing manager and signed off by all the interested parties (unions included). In other words, a business case for a system cannot be approved if it does not include a 'union case' for the same system.

Given the advantages and drawbacks of the Scandinavian experiences with the data agreements, we submit that a further advancement in devising appropriate strategies for managing systems development must be based on a comparative institutional assessment of the governance structures dedicated to technological change within organisations. Once again, reference to economics can contribute to clarify the issue.

The social costs of information technology

Technological change in production and administration carries externalities or, broadly speaking, social costs: that is, an economic agent applying for its productive purposes a new machine or system may affect in an uncompensated way other agents who are in direct or indirect contact with that machine or system (Arrow 1974; Dahlam, 1979). Pollution is a well-known case of an externality provoked by industry. Typical questions related to externalities are: who is liable and should pay for the damage? What is the best solution to reduce the damage (to introduce an air cleaner, a tax, a new zoning scheme)? How and through which organisational arrangement can affected individuals react (Salomon, 1981)?

The point of view assumed here is not that all such problems are easily cleared away by market forces or simply by letting the 'polluting agent' pay for the damage. The question is much more intricate and warrants attention to the bargaining processes necessary for allocating the social costs among the parties involved. The problem of social costs has a reciprocal nature. In devising and choosing between different solutions, one should take into account the 'total effect', that is, what the costs and benefits are which have to be borne by all the parties and what the specific costs of the social arrangement selected are (Coase, 1960).

Information technology is not an exception. Many of the negative consequences originated by the introduction of computer systems can be regarded as externalities. Consider within an organisation which uses a computer the effects of decision-making control and autonomy (Whisler 1970), on qualifications of blue- and white-collar workers (Bravermann, 1974), or on pace of work and health and safety at the terminals. Or, in a wider context, consider the consequences of computerisation on employment and privacy.

Many of the negative effects are borne by people outside the computer-based organisation; in the following we are mainly concerned with the internal environment of the firm. There the main impact of systems is on the key contractual relation of the hierarchy: the employment relation.

The employment relation is governed by a contract according to which the employee agrees to give up the right to govern his/her productive behaviour during the working day and accepts for that period the authority of the employer to specify sequentially the actions he/she must perform and to determine that actions are carried out according to plans in exchange for a set of tangible and intangible rewards. Computer-based information systems, no matter what they are dedicated to, allow the employer to perform more precisely the planning, monitoring and controlling of work, thus altering the implicit or explicit balance (or equity) embedded in the execution of the traditional employment contract.

The internalisation of social costs

General

The preceding section has shown how a factor of production such as information technology may have harmful effects or social costs to be borne by different individuals. These costs may be paid implicitly given a set of property rights (that is, a given social arrangement). For example, a firm which employs slaves does not take into account the full cost of its own activity, because it can rely on the availability of cheap slave labour paid at a subsistence level. If the legal system of slavery is abolished, slaves can bargain with their owners, offering an amount of money to buy their own freedom. Such a sum becomes an 'opportunity cost' for the firm to use slave labour. In this way, a cost emerges explicitly in the use of the labour factor.

The bargaining process which makes a cost explicit, which is allowed by a change in the system of property rights, is called internalisation of social costs. Internalising social costs scattered among various individuals means converting a cost, which is difficult to fix and allocate, into something measurable and allocable at a sufficiently low bargaining cost. Usually, the internalisation of social costs occurs through a change in property rights, either because a legal system is changed or because property rights themselves are the object of trade among the interested parties (Demsetz, 1967).

Given a set of social costs, the problem of internalisation is to find the best institutional arrangement of property rights to allow the allocation of costs such as the total product yield by this arrangement to be highest. It is not guaranteed that the optimal arrangement is going to be reached: the exchange of rights might be very difficult and not get through. The economic analysis distinguishes two cases:

In a world where transaction costs are zero, that is, where negotiating and exchanging rights can be performed at zero cost, thanks to a frictionless market, the end result in the allocation of social costs will be independent of the legal position of the parties. The initial delimitation of rights does not matter: whether it is the 'emitter' or the 'recipient' of the externality who has the liability to carry the cost of the harmful effect, an optimal bargain will be struck by which parties take into account the harmful effect and the value of production is maximised (with a corresponding fall in the value in order to pay the social costs).

In real situations, transaction costs differ significantly from zero. In fact, there are costs to discover the parties with whom to exchange, conduct negotiations, draw up the contract, control its execution, enforce modifications, and maintain the exchange relationship (Coase, 1960). These costs, which are due to imperfect information present in an exchange between opportunistic parties, can prevent certain bargains or trades which would be mutually beneficial if carried out. Two consequences obtain: the optimum pointed out by the frictionless market is not reached in practice because the costs of the negotiation of rights is so high to discourage any internalisation of costs; on the other hand, when there are transaction costs and informational differences between opportunistic traders, then it matters to whom liabilities and rights are assigned (Dahlam, 1979).

In such an environment, the analysis and choice of policies come to the forefront: that is, which is the best re-arrangement of liabilities and rights to achieve a higher valued global output? How much does the new re-arrangement cost? And how much does it cost to operate it compared to the costs to be internalised? (There are various policy alternatives: agreements; agencies or arbitrators to govern contracts; legislation and an enforcement apparatus; the establishment of appropriate markets; etc.) At the worst, if bargaining costs offset the social costs, no internalisation will take place, and the *status quo* is maintained until impediments to trade are eliminated or reduced.

Bargaining costs in the case of information technology

In the case of information technology, transaction costs cannot be ignored. This means that policy issues, property rights, etc. are a relevant factor and, in the case of the firm, that the existing modes of representation such as unions can play an essential role as bargainers of technological change.

First, consider an organisational inertia factor. Organisations, both private and public, will work for reduction in social costs only under limited conditions, that is, they have no incentives to reduce the external costs of their productive processes, nor to search for and identify the depth and extent of external costs borne by individuals within and outside the boundaries of the organisation. Management are not likely to respond favourably to efforts to alter behaviour, rules or structures in system development when such changes imply increases in the costs of systems. If this is true for any technological change, it is even more relevant for the case of system design, where both a new technological core is introduced into the organisation and the rules of running the organisation itself are affected.

The interests of individuals and groups bearing externalities will be taken into account only to the extent that the organisation is exposed to the demands of those individuals and to the degree that some influence can overcome the incentives of organisations to buffer demands for change. Influence can be exercised through environmental factors, such as legislation, and/or through exercising 'voice' or collective action. We can conclude that at least one important actor, management, may be prone to behaving opportunistically and so increase the costs of bargaining for technological change.

A second factor is the nature of social costs in the specific case of information technology. They are reciprocal, difficult to assess and talk about. It is often the case that a new system brings both benefits and costs to management and workers, and it is difficult to separate them. For example, a production-control system can allow better production scheduling and smooth production runs, so reducing the amount of overtime required, at the expense of increased monitoring of individual effort. Costs are often also subtle, 'costly' to identify and communicate information about: for example those related to the organisational impacts of computers on decision making, centralisation, certain forms of deskilling, etc. Especially when an investigation has not been carried out before the system is implemented, it is difficult to identify and account for such impacts.

Information and language asymmetries are another feature arising during system development. For users potentially affected by computers it is not only a matter of ignoring relevant information on systems, but of difficulty in receiving, evaluating, discussing and communicating such information. It can be mind-boggling to extract from a flow chart or a structured tree describing the main system functions what the consequences for skills, job content, social contact, etc. will be. This is due to the fact that while education for users is often inadequate, education for specialists is mainly centred on the machine rather than its social and organisational consequences. The provision included in Scandinavian agreements that all information regarding systems must be in an understandable form to non-specialists can be seen as a crucial step in reducing friction in bargaining due to language barriers (Nygaard and Bergo, 1975).

A fourth element is technological progress itself. Information technology is a highly uncertain subject. New hardware, new software, new design strategies, new organisational solutions are coming up at a very fast rate. This requires continuous learning, adaptation, appropriate bargaining strategies and means.

Finally, various difficulties arise from the need for collective action. Given the diffuse character of social costs, a brief analysis is warranted of the conditions under which collective action of individuals and groups bearing external costs can be expected and the conditions under which the representation of the interests in reducing external costs is likely to be effective. Systems users face various impediments. They need to co-ordinate their voice to change an integrated system, but they are dispersed horizontally and vertically in the hierarchy. Moreover, reduction of social costs is a collective good: the 'free-rider' problem arises as a consequence; there may be incentives for some individual users or groups not to reveal their true attitude towards a system so that others will bear the costs of trying to change it to the benefit of the whole user community (Olson, 1965).

For the broader publics of customers and citizens outside the organisation, information asymmetries, impediments to collective action are even worse. Within the firm, however, problems related to collective action can be solved efficiently by employing the existing union machinery. Unions permit individual or group interests of users to be superseded; they dispose of a structure ready to deal with problems of representativeness and so are the best mechanism to exercise voice to influence the allocation of costs falling on a large group of users. Unions also deal with various aspects of the employment relations, through collective bargaining agreements and all the relevant adaptive mechanisms regarding wage changes, labour adjustments, assignment changes, refinement of working rules, qualification structures, etc. (Williamson, 1985).

Efficient bargaining in systems development

It is now possible to reconsider the issue of how to manage systems development within a broader context, that of internalising social costs. As explained above, internalising social costs requires bargaining among the parties affected: management and employees, the latter organised by unions, and citizens at large (Brooks, 1981).

Of the various possibilities concerning the relationship between management and employees, three situations can be illustrated with references to the European environment (Evans, 1982):

no formal bargaining;

explicit contracts, outcome of bargaining between unions and management;

state regulation.

The alternative forms can be compared on the basis of their efficacy and efficiency as contractual arrangements dedicated to the governance of technological change.

The 'no formal bargaining' alternative corresponds to the case where the existence of social costs due to information technology is not acknowledged; the right to use computers lies exclusively in the hands of management, who dispose of its consequences by fiat: adaptations are required of the employees to follow instructions from the top regarding changes in their work organisation. This was thought to be the most efficient solution for introducing computers before the user-participation theme was ever played. At the extreme, it was claimed that computers had no impact on work organisation, qualifications, employment, etc. But inefficiencies emerged under the forms we all know: user resistance; adaptation problems local and/or global conflicts during and after computerisation; slow-downs in project execution and so on. Frequently such problems were attributed to the users' psychology, outside the domain of rational organisational behaviour that could be controlled by specialists and management.

In the perspective outlined here, these are all inefficiencies related to the process of internalisation of social costs (recall also the slavery example, where cheap labour went along with low productivity). As mentioned above, information technology affects the balance embedded in the employment relation. If equity does not obtain, then employees withhold effort in various ways, mainly exploiting uncertainties around the new technology. For example, they can refuse to tap their knowledge and skill to the formal procedures running on the new system, so hindering its efficacy. The opportunistic use of job knowledge can be an intentional reaction to the perception of inequity in the employment contract, brought by the increased sharpness in monitoring and control.

Resistance can, then, arise at any point of the organisation: individuals, groups or organisational units can block the whole system, or more frequently can lower its efficacy. As a consequence, individual bargains regulated by *ad hoc* contracts must be continually struck by the organisation with different parties in order to continue to develop the system. Bargaining and implementation costs will rise.

The second contractual alternative portrays a variety of solutions (Beath, 1987), only a couple of which are discussed in the following paragraphs. The need for *explicitly bargaining* the consequences of systems is acknowledged and a formal machinery is set up between unions and management, usually in connection with collective bargaining agreements, at company, industry and national levels (see again the Scandinavian experiences as an example; Nygaard and Bergo, 1975). In the present perspective, the object of the contracts is to achieve a re-arrangement of the property rights (management prerogatives) related to systems and data. More specifically, the property rights concern (a) the systems-development process and (b) the use of the system once implemented. How the re-arrangement is to be carried out in practice is a complex task, given the high transaction costs previously discussed.

By examining the Norwegian case two basic approaches have emerged: an *ex post* and an *ex ante* bargaining process. Both have been applied within the same framework of the national data agreement between the Norwegian employers confederation (NAF) and the unions (LO). *Ex post* contracts are market-like, of a contingent claim type: once the new system is operating, unions and management strike a bargain at company level concerning its modes of usage. Items included in the contract are as follows: the scope of the system; operating modes; user training; qualifications; use of personal data filed into the system; work organisation. Such 'system contracts' are easy to draw up and enforce because they can be based on a joint description of the system's characteristics and effects as evaluated by those who directly operate it or use it. Any uncertainty about the social costs can be reduced, if not eliminated, by investigating the features of the system while it functions.

The bargaining machinery needed is rather slim. A (data) shop steward can collect information about the system and about the attitudes and interests of its direct users, and take them to the bargaining table. The users are a rather well defined group both because of the boundaries set by the system and because of union membership.

Objects of exchange are not the rights of designing the system, but of using it, and possibly designing the surrounding work organisation. Such contracts become recurrent as more and more systems are implemented. Parties have the opportunity to develop successively their own bargaining experience and competence in system use, so becoming able to draw up realistic contingent claim contracts.

Some inadequacies are, however, present. First, the scope of the changes is limited, and only a part of the social costs can be internalised. On the one hand, it would be too costly to find alternative designs of the system which would eliminate sources of costs once the system is already designed. On the other, it would be excessively expensive to negotiate the modification of already existing software. (There is an exception to that, which is widely used in *ex post* contracting: the exclusion from operation of routines originally designed into the system. An example is given by routines for the monitoring of individual performance included in production-control systems.) Second, the user community is too narrowly defined. A production-control system can have interdependencies with administrative departments, or inversely, a financial system can have an impact on the way operations are organised. In both cases, *ex post* contracting tends to disregard cross-effects which overcome organisational boundaries or union membership. All this makes narrow and inefficacious the internalisation of costs when integrated, or conversely, when highly decentralised systems are implemented.

Ex ante contracts can be of two types: contingent claim, where both parties try to specify all the features of the new system, its consequences, the reciprocal behaviour when the new system will be adopted and the modification plans; or more open, long-term contracts as far as the system characteristics are concerned, but with specific clauses regarding the modes of participation during system design.

With the former approach, a risky forecasting exercise is needed to anticipate and agree on the future system; in the latter procedural rationality is employed so that the framework for a bilateral (team-like) relation is established during system design: in that process the parties find solutions, negotiate and execute them as specific events and choices unfold. What is traded in the latter approach are the rights to influence decision making in relation to system development, and via this to influence the system itself and its consequences. Given the high degree of uncertainty and specificity of system development, it is obvious that a contract that includes the second approach is to be preferred because it allows more adaptive decision making.

Costs of alternatives should be compared; a longer design process versus haggling around contract execution and control when a system is designed. The complexity of the system could discriminate between the alternatives.

Finally, regulation through legislation: reference is made here to the legislation regarding the organisation of work and system design (the Norwegian Work Environment Act is a good example). First, given the high bargaining costs related to technological change, regulation does have an impact on the application of computers and the organisation of computer-based tasks. Establishing regulation should be made taking into account the economic impact of the resulting legal arrangement: for example, making the employer (the employees) totally liable for externalities might not be the optimal (from a global point of view) solution.

In the case where organisations do not have incentives to reduce social costs borne by individuals inside and outside the organisation, regulation is a means of forcing them to alter their structures, rules and norms so as better to internalise those costs. This role of regulation is important especially in those cases where (a) because of the 'public good' or 'bad' character of the consequences of the technology, that is, the impossibility of excluding anyone from the impacts (such as privacy of the citizen's personal data), and (b) because of the gap in resources and information between organisations and the public, it would be difficult to initiate and maintain a coherent collective action by citizens, employees, etc. aimed at influencing the use of computers.

Regulation can be the means of modifying the status quo, the inertia due to the impossibility for large groups to influence the organisation. But there are difficulties in using regulation for such a purpose. For one thing, regulation is emanated by a political body, the representation of interests within this body can be problematic and the difficulties in organising a collective action may be shifted from the economic arena to the political one. For another, regulation may be too general, and in many cases, generic, because of its comprehensiveness.

In fact, either very specific aspects are regulated because of the existence of minimum standards (for example, working time at VDUs), or 'principles' are simply stated, the detailed application of which has to be carried out by other contractual arrangements. Also, regulation is rigid (see ch. 12). The time needed to prepare, implement and evaluate rules is longer than the pace of technological change. So regulation valid for a large, centralised data-processing centre may be totally irrelevant for a distributed office-automation system. Finally, costs of enforcement have to be faced. The establishment of clear-cut standards and an enforcement apparatus is required (such as special units in the labour inspectorate dedicated to information technology). New bureaucratic agencies have to be created, external to the organisations to be monitored. More resources have to be employed than in the case of an internal control apparatus (like the data shop steward).

Our appraisal has not stated ultimately what arrangement is the most efficient and effective at internalising social costs. It all probably depends on the contingencies related to the development of a specific system. What is certain is the inefficiency of disregarding a detailed comparative analysis, in a specific situation, of the alternatives available. Economic forces at work around the management of systems development should not be ignored. One of the first important consequences of considering them is to establish that bargaining for technological change always takes place under one form or another. Secondly, that, given the high bargaining costs stemming from the parties' conflict of interests and uncertainty of the technology, agreements and regulation have an impact on the allocation of social costs and the global production yield generated by employing a new system. Maintaining the status quo is one of the alternatives, but there is an assumption that this alternative is more costly to implement than others which explicitly recognise bargaining, especially when information technology brings considerable changes and uncompensated side-effects obtain.

Towards a contractual methodology

We can now outline an alternative project-management system suited to face situations where, like those in Norway, traditional approaches are inadequate. In order to do this, we follow the list of problems addressed by conventional methods.

Essential elements for project control. A successful project control is based on the definition of long-term plans and goals, related organisational and project budgets, authorisations and a set of standards (criteria of evaluation).

The previous discussion emphasises that plans and goals are the outcome of negotiations, agreements and compromises among partly conflicting and partly co-operating parties. Their function is thus highly political and their validity subject to the perils of possible conflicts arising during or after the development of the system. Plans and goals express *commitments* and must be based on *trust* to be really effective and operational. Otherwise, they will simply be the source of many bureaucratic games. As noted above, most plans are likely to be *contracts* regarding the system to be designed, its expected characteristics, etc., and/or the process which leads to its construction (in the 'before-the fact' approach). The contracts explicitly express the commitments of the parties on how the system should look and/or how the design process should be organised. Their specification should be clear, unambiguous and jointly shared because they represent the reference document according to which systems will be evaluated.

Standards also turn out to be a very important issue. They must be extended to cover items so far left out (Is there a participation standard? What about the performance of a data shop steward?); but they must not be too constraining in order to limit the risk of endangering a participative process. A reasonable, although qualitative, standard for evaluating a development project is whether 'good' systems were produced by it; whether 'better' people (the participants in the design) have emerged as a result of the system effort; and whether the private and social costs generated by the new system have been allocated to the satisfaction of the parties involved (Mumford, 1979).

Finally, auditing in this context must be mainly internal, or better, built into the project organisation. External auditors do not have access to the relevant knowledge and documentation and they risk being cut off by the opportunistic behaviour of some of the parties. Moreover, if the whole organisational-development effort has to be based on trust to be effective, it cannot rely on strictly bureaucratic, external controls. Auditing here changes its role from being a bureaucratic control procedure to a fundamental step in the organisational bargaining and learning processes taking place during the implementation of the new system.

Project control organisation. The setting up of committees to govern the automation is emphasised even more by the contractual view. With the presence of union representatives, committees become what handbooks seldom suggest to their readers: they are the place where highly political issues, such as defining the goals, plans and impacts of systems, are dealt with. The overall organisation may be complex: strategic, project and operational problems are to be discussed at various levels depending on the scope of the problem.

The chemistry of participation, the Norwegian cases show, is far from being straightforward: should *users* participate in the strategy committees? Should unions be involved in direct design? How are participants selected? Who drafts the agenda of the committees? At what point in time should the committees start to work? (When a system is approved? When its feasibility is explored or as soon as someone has the idea of a new system?) How should communication be organised when opportunistic use of information among the designers, sponsors and would-be designers must be assumed as a likely event? These are just some of the issues that a contractual project organisation cannot ignore.

Project documentation. The one-dimensional perspective held by current methods should evolve into a pluralistic perspective. It is understandable that we will see more and more diverse but coexistent documentations of systems, each expressed according to the values, goals, culture and background, language and expertise of the parties involved. Though heavier, a pluralistic documentation of this kind may lead to the design of better systems in the future. That is to say, not only technical details regarding the programs, the functions performed or the architecture of the systems will be filed, but also the subjective and qualitative impressions of users of systems and of participants in the design effort will be recorded. Such qualitative assessments of the design and its product are important in order to learn from mistakes and design *qualitatively* better systems and development processes (Lanzara and Mathiassen, 1985).

Conclusion

Although a mechanical model of the design process and of its controls appeals very much to the tidy, neat and scientific management-oriented view of the world of many data-processing specialists, it is rare that this model offers a sound representation and guide for the organisational events which take place during an actual systems-development process. It is sufficient that the contractual nature of the design process is made explicit, in order to show the unsatisfactory state of the art as far as systems development and auditing strategies are concerned.

Alternatively, more flexible and realistic approaches must be found: in order to reach this goal we must study the phenomenology of the development process, identify its very nature as distinct from any other 'manufacturing' process and draw from the experience of other disciplines. Economics has first of all provided, through the analysis of social costs, a way to justify the action of the forces that lie behind any contractual process connected with computerisation. Second, it has allowed us to compare various institutional alternatives for managing the systems development process.

9 Tactical information systems

Introduction

Efficient bargaining is not all it takes to create successful and innovative applications of information technology. It is also important to enact and nurture effective innovation and learning processes in the organisation when introducing and using the new technology. In this chapter we examine this other dimension of systems development by considering the important case of how to generate ideas and build strategic information systems. Our aim is once again to show the inadequacy of the structured, planning-oriented approaches and the need to adopt a more complex organisational perspective on these matters. Only by valuing the informal activities of team and individual tinkering can one achieve innovative applications; for complex organisations and for complex systems, tactics are the source of strategic systems.

If we look at the current practice today, after the pioneering years of American Airlines' SABRE, McKesson's Economost and American Hospital Supply's ASAP, building a Strategic Information System (SIS) entails a systematic, planning-oriented approach to generate top management awareness, identify applications that may generate competitive advantage and implement them. The systematic approaches are based on two main ingredients: a set of guidelines indicating how information technology can support the business *vis-à-vis* the competition, and a planning and implementation strategy. The guidelines are grounded on models of competition, while planning and implementation are ruled by the understanding of how an effective business strategy should be formulated and carried out (Bakos and Treacy, 1986; Cash and Konsynski, 1985; Ives and Learmonth, 1984; Porter and Millar, 1985; Wiseman, 1988); All of them make reference to an established set of model cases, from the early adopters, like McKesson (Clemons and Row, 1988), American Hospital Supply (now Baxter; Venkatraman and Short, 1990) and American Airlines (Copeland and McKenney, 1988) to those companies that went bankrupt because they did not adopt SIS, like Frontier Airlines and People Express. There are various frameworks that indicate how to identify SIS applications: the strategic thrusts (Wiseman, 1988); the value chain (Porter and Millar, 1985); the customer-services life cycle (Ives and Learmonth, 1984); the strategic grid (McFarlan, 1984); transaction costs (Ciborra, 1987a; Malone, Benjamin and Yates, 1987); and electronic integration (Henderson and Venkatraman, 1989).

More difficult to tackle, however, is the problem of how an SIS can provide a *sustainable* competitive advantage, so that a pioneering company can extract from a strategic IT application 'rewards substantial enough to justify the costs and risks associated with being the prime mover' (Feeny and Ives, 1990: 29). In fact, even the SIS success stories often show that such systems provide only an ephemeral advantage before being readily copied by competitors (Vitale, 1986). That this is the reality is confirmed by empirical evidence on the patterns of diffusion of SIS.

A study of thirty-six major interorganisational systems in different US industries shows that though the goals set by large corporations differed considerably (decreasing costs, electronic integration, etc.), the driving force pushing for the introduction of such systems was primarily that members of the same industry had similar applications (75 per cent of the cases); other systems were developed in collaboration with companies in the same industry (8 per cent), while for another 8 per cent they were individual initiatives soon to be copied by competitors. In sum, more than 92 per cent of the systems studied follow industry-wide trends. Only three systems are really original, but they will probably be promptly imitated (Brousseau, 1991).

A sort of industry determinism seems to play the overriding role in the diffusion of SIS: *ex ante* market structures and technical and commercial needs strongly influence the firms' agendas and the systems' main features. Then, aiming at sustainable competitive advantage requires generating continuously innovative and competitive applications and successfully protecting the quasi-rents stemming from unique, new systems. For example, Clemons (1986) mentions customer adoption rate as a critical factor that can introduce barriers to entry, at least for those systems that establish customer switching costs. The innovators must be able to apply swiftly the new system to pre-empt the market before others jump on the same application. Feeny and Ives (1990) recommend, further, that a firm, in order to reap a long-term advantage from investments in SIS, should carefully analyse the lead time of competitors in developing a system similar to the one being considered, and look for asymmetries in organisational structure, culture, size, etc., that may slow down the integration of the new SIS within the competitors' organisation.

Even more radically, we submit that effective ways of developing SIS must challenge the planning-oriented approaches to strategy formulation and competition that have been imported into the Management Information Systems field. The critique of such approaches, together with a closer analysis of how some of the 'legendary' systems were originally built, suggests new tactics for designing strategic applications.

Shifts in strategic thinking and models of competition

Consider what we may call the 'mechanistic' perspective on *strategy formulation*, imported by authors like Porter and Millar (1985) from the business-strategy literature into current SIS frameworks. According to such a perspective, management should in a first phase engage in a purely cognitive formulation process: through the appraisal of the environment, its threats and opportunities, and the strengths and weaknesses of the organisation, key success factors and distinctive competencies are identified and translated into a range of competitive strategy alternatives. Once the optimal strategy has been selected, agreed upon and laid out in sufficient detail, the next phase of implementation follows.

This approach is based on a set of premises or assumptions to be found in SIS models, such as the Critical Success Factors (Rockart, 1979), the value chain (Porter and Millar, 1985), the strategic thrusts (Wiseman, 1988) and the sustainability analysis (Feeny and Ives, 1990). Specifically, the approach can be characterised as being the following (Mintzberg, 1990):

Conscious and analytic. Strategies emerge through a structured process of conscious human thought, rigorous analysis and by accessing and modelling factual data. Implementation can follow only when a strategy has been formulated analytically. All strategic thinking is aimed at structuring any intuitive act and skill that is involved in strategy formulation.

Top–down and control-oriented. Strategy is formulated at the peak of the managerial pyramid. Responsibility for strategy rests with the chief executive officer: he/she formulates the strategy and then monitors its application throughout the appropriate layers of hierarchical control systems.

Simple and structured. Models of strategy formation must be explicit and kept simple: data analysis and appraisal of internal and external intervening factors must be synthesised in clear, simple models (for example, the value chain; the strategy–structure relationship; the Boston Consulting Group matrix (McFarlan and McKenney, 1983), etc.).

Separating action and structure. There is a divide between the process of thought that leads to fully blown, explicit strategies and their implementation. Consistent with the classical notions of rationality diagnosis, prescription and action, the design of the organisational structure must follow the formulation of the strategy.

Unfortunately, in everyday practice strategy formulation differs from such prescriptions and assumptions, as the following dilemmas point out.

Making strategy explicit? The rational bias towards conscious thought and full, explicit articulation of strategy assumes, implicitly, that the environment is highly predictable and the unfolding of events is itself sequenced so as to allow an orderly alternation of formulation, deliberation and implementation. Often, however, during implementation surprises occur that put into question carefully developed plans, so that the need for continuous, opportunistic revisions clashes with the inflexibility of the formulation and implementation sequence. Strict adherence to a rigid and explicit strategy-formulation cycle may hinder flexibility, learning and adaptation to a changing environment, threatening the very achievement of that fit between the organisation and the environment which represents the main purpose of the mechanistic approach.

One-way relationship between strategy and structure? In the conventional perspective, the strategist is regarded as an independent observer who can exercise judgement and disconnect himself/herself from the entangled everyday reality of the organisation. Thus, for example, when evaluating strengths and weaknesses of the organisation, or the critical success factors, it is assumed that the strategist can think and make choices outside the influence of frames of reference, cultural biases, paralysing double binds or ingrained, routinised ways of acting, behaving and thinking. Though conspicuous literature shows that such biases are at work in any decision-making process (Tversky and Kahneman, 1981; see ch. 1), they are assumed away by the quasi-scientific orientation of the mechanistic school. Reality, on the other hand, shows that organisational structure, culture, inertia and vicious circles influence the strategy-formulation process, not just its implementation. Assuming that one can conceive a strategy in a vacuum and then mould the organisation accordingly implies disregard for the mutual influences between structure and the cognitive and behavioural processes of strategy formulation (Weick, 1979).

Thinking or learning? Strategy formation tends to be seen by the mechanistic school as an intentional process of design, rather than one of continuous acquisition of knowledge in various forms, that is, learning. We claim, on the other hand, that strategy formulation is bound to involve elements of surprise, sudden, radical shifts in preferences, goals and even the identity of the actors, as well as paralysing vicious circles that may stifle its development and implementation (Argyris, 1982; Bateson, 1972; Masuch, 1985). Hence, strategic decision making must be based on effective adaptation and learning (Fiol and Lyles, 1985), both incremental, trial-and-error, and radical, second-order learning (Argyris and Schoen, 1978), whereby basic ways of seeing the environment and strengths and weaknesses of the internal organisation are continually reshaped (Ciborra and Schneider, 1992; see ch. 1).

Consider next, from an economic point of view, *the models of competition* that are implicit in today's SIS frameworks. Most of them rely on theories of business strategy (Porter, 1980), derived from industrial economics (Bain, 1968). According to such a line of thought, returns to firms are determined by the structure of the industry within which firms operate. In order to achieve a competitive advantage firms should manipulate the structural characteristics of the industry through IT, such as barriers to entry, product differentiation, links with suppliers, etc. (Porter and Millar, 1985).

However, as Barney (1985) has noted in the field of strategy and Wiseman (1988) in the field of SIS, there are alternative conceptions of competition that may be even more relevant to SIS development.

First, recall the theory of *monopolistic competition* put forward by Chamberlin (1933); firms are heterogeneous and they compete on the basis of certain resource and asset differences, such as those in technical know-how, reputation, ability to enact teamwork, organisational culture and skills and other 'invisible assets' (Itami, 1987). It is such differences that make some firms able to implement high-return strategies. Competition is then about cultivating unique strengths and capabilities, and defending such uniqueness against imitation by other firms.

Next, note Schumpeter's (1950) perspective on competition as a process linked to *innovation* in product, market or technology. Innovation is more the outcome of the capitalist process of Creative Destruction than a result of a strategic-planning process. Ability at guessing, learning and sheer luck appear in such a perspective to be the key competitive factors (Barney, 1985).

The Chamberleian and Schumpeterian concepts of competition are consistent with the alternative models of strategy formulation depicted by Mintzberg in his critique of the mechanistic school.

More precisely, we can identify and contrast two different 'packages' in business strategy that can be applied to the SIS field. According to the first, strategy is formulated *ex ante*, based on the analysis of competition, and consists of a series of moves, which can be planned and subsequently implemented, to gain advantage by playing the competitive game defined by the industry structure. According to the second, strategy formulation is difficult to plan before the fact, and competitive advantage stems from the exploitation of unique characteristics of the firm, and the unleashing of the firm's innovating capabilities.

Looking more closely at some well-known SIS applications, it can be seen that there is a wide gap between the prevailing SIS approaches, close to the former package, and industrial practice in strategic applications, definitely closer to the latter. Such a gap invites a new approach to SIS development more germane to the second package.

The classic cases revisited

At a closer look famous SIS cases, such as Baxter's ASAP, McKesson's Economost, American Airline's SABRE and the French videotex, Télétel (better known by the name of the PTT terminals, Minitel; see also ch. 5) indicate the discrepancy between ideal plans for SIS and the realities of implementation, where chance, serendipity, trial and error or even gross negligence play a major role in shaping systems that will, *but only after the fact*, become textbook or article reference material.

Compare the novelty of the first SIS in respect to what conventional MIS models were prescribing. Before American Hospital Supply (AHS) and McKesson introduced their computerised order-entry systems, which turned out to have strategic value, those very applications were regarded by MIS specialists as bread-and-butter, transaction-processing routines: 'strategic' was a label reserved for those yet-to-come systems that would support top management decision making. A plain order-entry system would be too far removed from the top of the corporation and from the glitter of advanced technologies such as expert systems, Executive Information Systems, etc. to qualify for any academic or business-strategy attention.

One may wonder, then, how such systems emerged at all, if theories and textbooks did not pay any attention to them. ASAP, the system launched by AHS Corporation (subsequently acquired by Baxter), started as an operational, localised response to a customer need (Venkatraman and Short, 1990): because of difficulties in serving a hospital effectively, a manager of a local AHS office had the idea of giving pre-punched cards to the hospital's purchasing department so that the ordering clerks could transfer the content of the cards expeditiously through a phone terminal. From this local, *ad hoc* solution the idea gradually emerged of linking all the hospitals in the same way through touch-tone telephones, barcode readers, teletypes and eventually PCs. AHS management realised only at a later stage the positive impacts on profits of such an electronic link with the customers and was able to allocate adequate resources for its further development.

McKesson's Economost, another order-entry system, started in a similar way. Its former IS manager admits that 'behind the legend' there was simply a local initiative by one of the business units: the system was not developed according to a company-wide strategic plan; rather, it was the outcome of an evolutionary, piecemeal process that included the ingenuous, *tactical* use of systems already available. Economost, which later became the herald of the new SIS paradigm, was 'stumbled upon', the outcome of what the French call *bricolage*, that is, tinkering and serendipity. Note that the conventional perspective on hierarchical MIS not only was responsible for the initial neglect of the new strategic applications within McKesson, but also, subsequently, slowed down the company-wide learning process which could have led to a global redesign of McKesson's information systems.

Also SABRE, the pioneering computerised reservation system built by American Airlines, was not originally conceived as a biased distribution channel in order to create entry barriers to competitors and tie in travel agents. In fact, it began as a relatively simple, *ad hoc* inventory-management system addressing a specific need which had nothing to do with ensuring a competitive advantage. On the contrary it was supposed to address internal inefficiency: American Airlines' relative inability, compared to other airlines, to monitor the inventory of available seats and to attribute passenger names to booked seats (Hopper, 1990).

Another telling case, this time at national level, is represented by Minitel, one of the rare, if not the only, successful public videotex systems in the world, which gives France a still unmatched competitive advantage in the *informatisation de la société* (Nora and Minc, 1980; 7 million terminals in French households and an average of eighteen calls a month per owner). Once again, the origins of the Minitel, the timing and the nature of the design choices that favoured its diffusion and distinctive qualities indicate how large-scale innovations follow the twisted paths governed more by happenstance, serendipity and tinkering, than by the orderly formulation of strategic plans.

The initial concept of Minitel was similar to other videotex systems: mainframes allow the creation of large centralised databases that can be accessed by and sold to a large number of customers through dumb terminals (teletypes or television sets). Videotex systems promoted according to this perspective have failed both for early adopters, like the UK PTT, and for latecomers, like the German Bundespost, who could have benefited from a better technology, more careful planning and the experience gained by other PTTs. France Télécom (formerly, Direction Générale des Télécommunications, DGT) moved into videotex relatively late and with a technology which was not on the leading edge. However, there were significant differences in the way the system was promoted to the general public: the vision of the *informatisation de la société* convinced the government to make the Minitel a success story, through the diffusion of millions of free terminals. In fact, its free distribution is seen by observers and competitors as the main success factor of the French videotex.

This is only half of the truth: the free terminals were at the time a necessary condition for success (the launching occurred before the diffusion of the personal computer), but not a sufficient one. In fact, at the beginning the use of Minitel was stagnating, for the same reason other videotex systems never took off, that is, knowledge in society is too fragmented to be included even in the largest database (Hayek, 1945). On the one hand, knowledge that matters for action is linked to the here and now, to the specific circumstances in which the individual makes a decision, to his/her unique biography. On the other, standardised knowledge stored in databases is frequently outdated, too difficult to access and almost always too expensive, if compared with information gathered through other public media, such as the yellow pages, the train timetable, the local newspaper, the television news or the the latest gossip (see ch. 1). While in absolute terms the videotex may sound an interesting idea, its success depends upon the relative capacity to perform better than other, more commonly available channels of information.

To be successful, the Minitel had to be different from other media: it had to be 'active'. As a matter of fact, the system was a public e-mail service in a nutshell, but was never promoted as such by the DGT. Only through an act of hacking, which for its scandalistic overtones happened to attract the interest of the national press, was this potential discovered and enacted nationwide by millions of users. During an experiment in Strasburg, when a local newspaper automated the consultation of the classified advertisements section, a hacker, probably located at the data-processing centre of the newspaper itself, started using the Minitel to respond to the advertisements, establishing a direct, electronic dialogue with their authors. The Minitel began to be used as electronic mail, (*messagerie*) and not just as a dumb terminal to access a database (Marchand, 1987).

Only at that stage did the number of terminals in the homes turn out to represent the critical mass that could start a 'virtuous' circle: for one thing, it created a new market for many independent service companies to sell their services on the network (see ch. 5). Customers immediately used the 'new' medium to the point that the national backbone packet switched network, Transpac, broke down due to overload. France Télécom was flexible and pragmatic enough to adapt the infrastructure technically and commercially to the new pattern of usage which emerged outside the initial vision and plans, 'moving from the logic of storage to the logic of traffic'. The Minitel's more decentralised network and system architecture, if compared to other systems like Prestel or Bildschirmtext, helped such a transition significantly (Schneider *et al.*, 1990).

All the cases seen so far recount the same tale: innovative SIS are not fully designed top–down or introduced in one shot, rather they are tried out through prototyping and tinkering. Strategy formulation and design take place in pre-existing formative contexts that usually prevent designers and sponsors from seeing and exploiting the systems' innovation potential (see ch. 1).

Nobody can specify completely SIS features *ex ante*. Their design and operation consistently show unexpected consequences: events, behaviours and features of systems and the people who use them fall outside the scope of original plans and specifications. The development of SIS seems to have more traits in common with the tactics of end-user computing and prototyping than with most of the current strategic-planning methodologies. Finally, SIS emerge when early adopters are able to recognise some idiosyncratic systems features that were initially ignored or unplanned. We conclude that the development of SIS should be closely associated with innovation in the perception of businesses and the role of information technology in supporting business renewal.

Developing new applications

The preceding discussion on the models of competition has pointed out three general characteristics that an SIS must show to generate a sustained competitive advantage: first, it must be able to create value; second, it must be built by only a small number of firms; third, it must not be perfectly imitable, that is, other firms stand at some disadvantage when implementing it (Barney, 1986).

It is the joint effect of such factors that allows a firm to create a real strategic application. If the application does not generate value, it may not be worth considering altogether. If it is not rare, it may just be a competitive necessity in order to obtain normal, not superior, returns. If it is not imperfectly imitable, it can only deliver a short-term, contestable advantage (Beath and Ives, 1986; Wiseman, 1988).

The question is, then, how to achieve rarity and imperfect imitability in designing an SIS. The analysis of the competitive environment as prescribed by Porter (1980) is lacking in this respect. Collecting information about the environment and analysing according to popular theories of strategy are 'non-proprietary' methods that can be purchased on the market through databases, books or consulting services, so that firms adopting them will come to approximately the same conclusions about how SIS can generate value in a given industry.

On the other hand, factors that could be harnessed to find genuinely strategic IT applications are the following (Barney, 1986):

Chance: firms can stumble upon new information during their data-collection effort; or unexpected events can occur during implementation, where some unique and rare assets and capabilities may come into play that happen to be well matched to the chosen strategy.

Guessing about highly uncertain strategies that no environmental scanning would easily identify; if the guess turns out to be the right one, the firm may gain a first-mover advantage; for the temporary superior performance to be sustained, however, the advantage must be rare and imperfectly imitable.

Analysis of the firm's internal assets and capabilities, to identify unique and rare qualities, and matching them with the competitive opportunities at hand.

In the latter perspective, developing SIS that deliver a sustained competitive advantage is a process of *innovation*, whose management must be based on approaches that have proved to be effective in achieving product and process innovation (Nonaka and Yamanaouchi, 1989; Takeuchi and Nonaka, 1986).

To innovate means creating new information about resources, goals, tasks, markets, products and processes. The skills and competencies available in the corporation represent at the same time the source and the constraint for innovation (Prahalad and Hamel, 1990).

The adequacy of the existing stock of skills and competencies is indeed crucial to tackle a new task. Every time a firm engages in an innovation it faces a knowledge gap between the task and routines it can perform with competence and new tasks which have undefined and uncertain contours, for which new knowledge must be provided, or achievement will be poor.

The creation of new knowledge can take place along two alternative routes. The first is to rely on local information and stick to routine behaviour by extending it gradually when coping with a new task (learning by doing; myopic, incremental decision making; muddling through). To wit, accessing more diverse and distant information, when an adequate level of competence is *not* present, would generate errors, and further divergence from optimal performance (Heiner, 1983).

The second alternative is to attack the competency gap at its roots, by unfreezing the existing core competencies and allowing new ones to emerge and consolidate. This is a process of radical learning that entails restructuring those cognitive and organisational backgrounds that give meaning to practices, routines and skills at hand. It can be a painful and difficult experience for an individual or an organisation, since it requires one to slow down the execution of the routines about which one feels most confident, and to intervene in the background context, practices and beliefs that legitimate those very routines.

The strategic application of IT can be, then, the result of tactics, tinkering, *bricolage*, the bubbling-up of new ideas from the bottom of the organisation, or it can be the outcome of an act of quantum innovation, whereby the existing organisational reality, the environment and IT applications are seen in a new light by the members. In the latter case SIS are intimately associated with business renewal.

Note how the development of an SIS touches in both cases the 'grey zones' of work practices, beliefs, values, routines and cultures that lie at the core of the organisation (Hedberg and Jonsson, 1978). Along the incremental tack of tactics these provide the background conditions, the culture bed for tinkering: new systems applications emerge from the enactment and reinforcement of a local innovation. Along the radical tack, the awareness of the background organisational context, its cultural and institutional arrangements, and the ability to re-invent them pave the way to systems that may support very different contexts and routines.

More generally, the two approaches can be spelled out as in the following subsections.

Bricolage

This approach requires tinkering, that is, the combination and application of known tools and routines at hand to solve new problems. No general scheme or model is available: only local cues from a situation are trusted and exploited in a somewhat myopic and unreflective way, aiming at obtaining solutions by applying heuristics rather than high theory (Brown and Duguid, 1991). Systems like ASAP or the Minitel were developed in this way: even when big plans were present, it was *bricolage* that led to the innovation. The value of tinkering lies in that it keeps the development of an SIS close to the competencies of the organisation and its on-going fluctuations in local practices.

It is based on 'looking within the organisation, to discover those unique attributes that can be created by IT' (Feeny and Ives, 1990: 36). It focuses the attention of developers on fluctuations, odd practices, serendipitous applications of IT that bubble up daily in the user environment and that are often ignored, not valued sufficiently or even repressed. Recall that the hacking in the Minitel experiment in Strasburg, or the first initiatives of the AHS local office could have been ignored, or wiped out, by the enforcement of company-wide technical policies and state laws: those systems were actually built under such threats.

On the other hand, some limitations of this particular approach should not be ignored. *Bricolage* is based on tinkering and learning by doing, which lead to an incremental increase of the actors' and organisation's competencies, and possibly to an original recombination of existing routines (Nelson and Winter, 1982). But it can also lead to a competency trap: the confidence gained by executing skilfully suboptimal routines may generate disincentives to explore radically new venues (Levitt and March, 1988).

Furthermore, generating new systems by a strictly local activity needs adequate resources and support to become an organisation-wide innovation. As mentioned for the McKesson case, the new order-entry system fell short of affecting their other information systems. Also, AHS top management were not quick, at least initially, in realising the global ramifications of an *ad hoc* solution.

Indeed, in the perspective outlined here, the boundary between end-user computing and SIS is very thin. To avoid dismissing a potential strategic application as just end-user computing, top management must be able to 'listen' to the local fluctuations and through effective learning be able to transform them into the 'new order'. Without this awareness, which has been at work in the ASAP and Minitel cases, the local innovations and systems will not infringe the prevailing practices and routines, and never acquire a global momentum.

Finally, the approach must be integrated with the analysis over competitors' lead time and asymmetries, before engaging in any effort at amplification of the local innovation to a strategic solution. It may be, for example, that similar systems are bubbling up in many organisations belonging to the same industry, since they are engaged in the same task and share some common cultural traits. Such a 'sustainability analysis' (Feeny and Ives, 1990) could be carried out more realistically using as a proxy variable the competitors' previous experience in dealing with process and product innovations.

Radical learning

This approach leads to new systems and arrangements not by random walks or tinkering; quite the opposite, it intentionally challenges, and smashes, established routines, in particular those that govern competence acquisition, learning by doing and learning by trial and error.

Designing an innovative SIS involves more than market analysis, systems analysis, requirement specifications and interest accommodation. It should deal primarily with the structures and frames within which such exercises take place, that is, with shaping and restructuring the context of both business policy and systems development. Such a context can be brought to the surface and changed only by intervening in situations and designing-in-action (Ciborra and Lanzara, 1989; Schön, 1979).

Note that the logic of intervention is in many respects different from the logic of analysis, and the heuristics of *bricolage*: its epistemology draws on the theory of action (Argyris and Schoen, 1978; Argyris, Putnam and Smith, 1985). SIS design as practical intervention aims at creating conditions that help managers and users to question and gain insight into contexts, while actually designing or executing routines in situations.

Once the background context is restructured-in-action, members are more free to devise new strategies, and to look at the environment and the organisational capabilities in radically new ways. Different strategic information and systems will be generated, based on the unique, new worldview the designers and users are able to adopt. As an outcome, one can expect organisations and SIS to diverge from standard solutions and to be difficult to imitate, for they imply that competitors abandon not only their old practices and conceptions, but also the contexts in which they routinely solve problems, run systems and build new ones.

This is precisely what has happened in the Minitel case: despite the fact that its success is by now known to everybody, its imitation entails that competitors learn effectively, and abandon, or at least discuss, their entrenched beliefs about the function of videotex, their role as monopolists, their current practices in conceiving and developing systems and so on. Rather than questioning such beliefs and the relevant arrangements that support them, so far they have reacted in a defensive way and prefer to find *ad hoc* reasons to explain away the Minitel success, indicating the free terminals as the key factor of success (but forgetting that today in most industrialised countries there is a sufficient installed base of PCs to make the free distribution of terminals almost superfluous) or suggesting that a crucial role is played by porn e-mail (the latest statistics show that the *messagerie rose* has been only a temporary, though important, use of the system). These 'competent' explanations are the cause of that skilled incompetence (Argyris, 1982) that often undermines any real commitment to innovation.

Conclusions

Our enquiry into the models and methodologies for SIS confirms what a practitioner, Max D. Hopper, director of American Airlines' SABRE reservations systems, stated recently: the era of conventional SIS is over. Worse, it is dangerous to believe that an information system can provide an enduring business advantage. In a word, it is high time to realise that 'The old models no longer apply' (Hopper, 1990: 119).

Miniaturisation, standardisation and connectivity contribute, as far as the technology platform of SIS is concerned, to increasing the levelling effect of imitation. The source of advantage cannot lie only in the possession of a sophisticated system. On the contrary, economic and technological forces push companies to develop such systems jointly, open them to competitors (as the cases of SABRE, Minitel and ASAP show) and sell them or the competencies to build similar ones.

The new challenge, then, is to harness IT to tap the core competencies of the organisation, to create new information and knowledge (Nonaka, 1991): if companies can build similar platforms and access the same data, the competitive advantage related to IT can only stem from the *organisational* capability of converting such data into practical knowledge for action.

Tactical applications are those that are developed close to and serve the grassroots of the organisation, where its core competencies and skills are daily deployed and perfected. This entails a different style of design, more germane to the tactics and intricacies of prototyping, learning and intervention than to the structured analysis of a business strategy and its straightforward translation into SIS requirements. The arts of *bricolage* and effective quantum learning can be applied separately or jointly, contingent upon circumstances, to generate tactical information systems in ways similar to any product or process innovation.

PART III   Applications

10 Creating electronic markets: the case of fixed income bonds

Introduction

It is widely known that information technology is being heavily applied to automate financial markets, specifically the stock market. A good example is the case of the Big Bang at the London Stock Exchange. It is in this field that the market-creating and -modifying effects of the mediating technology can be seen at their best (Steiner and Teixeira, 1990).

In this chapter we examine the fixed income bonds market in the United States as it was evolving at the end of the 1980s, in order to gain a deeper perception of how different technological solutions can modify to a great degree the structure of this market. The American fixed income bond market is the largest and most liquid in the world. The bonds issued by the federal government, and in particular by the Treasury Department, represent around 80 per cent of all of the volume and value of all exchanges; approximately US$25 trillion were exchanged world-wide in 1985.

The global fixed income bonds market can be divided into two different submarkets, with *primary dealers* on one hand and *institutional customers* on the other. Both these classes of participants in the market need a huge amount of information, information that must be accurate and in real time. The information is needed not only for selling and buying of bonds, but also for creating reference prices for the various types of bonds. It is this factor that sets a course for the opportunities offered by information and communication technologies that are of relevance to the market players. However, before considering what the main applications of information technology are in this industry, it would be worthwhile to analyse the structure of the fixed income bonds market in more detail.

The structure of the fixed income market

Primary dealers

The US Federal Bank has authorised forty primary dealers to supply and maintain a liquidity in government bonds and other financial tools. These primary dealers must comply with the requirements set by the federal government as far as their capitalisation and reporting procedures are concerned. Furthermore, there are thirteen dealers who are not directly authorised, but who comply with federal-government regulation on a voluntary basis. These fifty-three firms create the daily bonds market, and specialise in long-term and short-term bonds. They receive profits from the following activities:

distribution for the sale to investors, that is the difference between the price of sale and the price of buying;

position, that is by accumulating bonds until their price increases.

To be sure, these firms own the most updated and accurate information related to prices and rates of the various bonds; and many of these firms have begun to regard such information as a resource *per se* that can generate value by putting it into online information systems through which it can be sold on the market for the institutional investors.

Institutional investors

Customers of fixed income bonds can be defined at three levels: distributors and market movers, active transactors and demand. All the secondary market participants buy and sell bonds through the primary dealers, although it is only the latter who are the largest buyers of bonds and thus major users of information systems on this type of financial service.

The dealers and the first two investor levels are interested in buying and selling bonds quickly to acquire a profit, while the supplier is likely to buy and keep bonds to enjoy interest within a planned period. Investors comprise commercial banks, government agencies, international banks, investment funds, private firms and local authorities. The information needs of this market grow whenever the market becomes larger and more complex. Thus in the last few years various software packages have been developed with the purpose of providing online updated information round the clock. To be sure, information on prices and rates is not enough by itself. There is an additional need for sophisticated applications for portfolio analysis such as expert systems and systems for decision support. The main applications used in this market are as follows:

provision of data on prices and rates;

analysis of services to appreciate a potential profit in any bond exchange;

online communications that include news and comments on the behaviour of markets.

The nature and scope of this online system can be interpreted and analysed by applying the transaction-cost model. Consider, for example, that one of the main characteristics of information market on bonds in the late 1980s is that the investors do not have access, apart from very few exceptions, to the pricing services used by the dealers.

In order to understand the function and the role of information systems, the transactions that occur on such a market have to be analysed in more detail. The majority of the participants acquire a profit by speculating on the increase or decrease of the price of the bonds, and in a strictly related way on the evolution of the interest rates. A small shift in the interest rates can result in reaping big profits or in incurring severe losses, given the fact that the average size of an exchange of bonds is about US$5 millon (1987).

The dealers can get a spread between the buying and selling of bonds. Such spreads are not the same for all the bonds and they vary with time. The spreads are very low on bonds that are frequently exchanged, such as treasury certificates, while they are very high on long-term obligations. In order to maximise profits, participants in the markets must be continuously aware of even the slightest changes in the spread and in interest rates. For this reason all the participants use various kinds of electronic information systems.

The electronic information systems

The market for financial information amounted to $150 million in 1985. In 1990 it grew to $290 million. The high cost of access to such information services is pushing the need to implement more basic services, which can be sold at affordable prices, and this can be done only by enlarging the current customer group. Seven brokers have the monopoly of the online distribution of bond prices. Furthermore, this service is available only to the primary dealers, who use it to announce current prices and to exchange bonds between them on an anonymous basis. For the period considered Telerate is the market leader in the sale of information, with 27,000 terminals in the United States, and 42,000 terminals world-wide. Telerate distributes information through the Dow Jones news service and through a broker of federal bonds, Canter Fitzgerald, who has a contract to announce prices by using Telerate screens until the year 2006. All the participants in the market can subscribe to Telerate and receive the counter quotations. The cost is rather high for an individual customer: $800 per month, even if only a few screens of the service are used. This factor places small customers at a disadvantage.

The primary dealers have developed internal information systems oriented to their own traders and sellers in order to enable them to monitor the margins and spreads of the various bonds. An in-house development of systems lessens the dependence upon expensive systems such as Telerate. In 1987 at least twelve dealers were developing their own in-house system. Examples include the Citibank, Chemical Bank, First Boston and Salomon Brothers. Besides information on pricing, these systems also contain analytical tools and historical databases to support decision making especially in relation to portfolio analysis.

However, the in-house system development is still expensive. In addition, it is not fully clear if it is more convenient in comparison with the purchase of outside services like Telerate, Reuters and Quotron. One of the most successful in-house systems developed by a dealer is Bloomberg of Merrill Lynch. It was originally developed for internal use only, and was subsequently put on the market to sell information to institutional investors. Bloomberg is an online system that offers decisions support: it provides customers with 'suggested' prices, those advised by Merrill Lynch. This system enables customers or institutional investors to perform operations such as

comparing spreads even on historical data;

analysing the yield curves and other financial tools;

other computations on the stock market.

The system has been extremely successful because the secondary market needs data to integrate those of Telerate. The cost of Bloomberg is still high, around $1,500 per month; beside that, the Merrill Lynch quotations are not official and cannot be utilised to exchange. Finally, the company allows access to only a restricted number of dealers.

As a matter of fact, by 1989 there was not a fully fledged online information system that could provide to any institutional investor valid quotations to carry out transactions and means to communicate directly with their primary dealers. To sum up, information technology is applied to support the existing structure of the vertical market (Baligh and Richartz, 1967), that is, to reinforce the hierarchical distinction between primary dealers and all other investors. This leaves room, however, for the creation of a more perfect market. Information technology can be put to work, and through its mediating effect can indeed improve the functioning of such markets. In order to appreciate this kind of effect we have to turn to the new systems that are being designed by a number of firms operating in the financial information markets.

The new systems

Current systems, regarded as the standard in the fixed income industry, have some disadvantages. These disadvantages include lack of good-quality quotations, access that is limited to counter prices, the source of which is a non-specialised broker in the field of fixed income bonds, and absence of quotations from other financial markets beside those held by the Treasury. By examining the transaction costs for an institutional investor, the following can be identified:

Search for a price. This activity is difficult because the investor, once having ascertained, for example, the Telerate indicative price, is obliged to get in touch by phone with other dealers, or use difficult and costly access systems like Bloomberg to compare various offers. Thus the market structure is far from being transparent and an investor has to search for a price by looking into various systems and getting in touch directly with the dealers.

Contracting. Contracting can happen only by taking into account quotations of other bonds and stocks, and through an analysis of the current portfolio.

Control. What matters here is an instant and reliable recording of all the quotations and prices.

Maintenance. Naturally, there is a need for communication services to maintain the communication that would support the actual transacting.

If the market is imperfect, then the institutional investors have to bear the costs. It is not, therefore, surprising that a big institutional investor takes an active stand to render the market of fixed income bonds more transparent. Citicorp buys the leader firm in the distribution of stock exchange data, Quotron, and through it is developing a new information system aimed at deep restructuring of the market for information on fixed income bonds.

In general, the new system should collect all the prices that are present within Citicorp, and then distribute them in real time with specific prices to the investors of the secondary market. Quotron will also distribute data which are coming from various dealers so as to enable customers to compare different prices. This will significantly decrease search and contracting costs. The system should bring numerous advantages to Citicorp and turn into a powerful and competitive weapon. For example, Quotron can penetrate the industry of fixed income bonds, and thus reach new desks and widen the range of financial data that it distributes electronically. As for the case of Merrill Lynch with its own system Bloomberg, the new Quotron system should increase the volume of transactions for Citicorp itself, because many customers of the new information service will be able to place orders through the system directly with the bank.

The access to the data of various dealers seems to constitute the strongest feature of the new system, for it must be taken into account that each dealer, bonds apart, manages a whole array of other stock items. The new system will include an historical database for specific analyses that can be carried out by the customers themselves; it also includes an electronic-mail system that supports communications between dealers and customers during the transaction, and in addition allows for an informal exchange of comments and opinions on market behaviour.

The new Quotron system can also be regarded as a strategic move to place it in pole position in the liberalisation of the information market on the fixed income bonds. This liberalisation is a consequence of the new law of the US General Accounting Office. According to these new rules, brokers and dealers must give information on prices they own to whoever operates on the market of fixed income bonds. This measure paves the way for the abolition of the monopoly on the information market related to this type of bond. The building and diffusion of such a new system also entails a series of alliances, both with software houses and with workstation manufacturers, thus enabling Citicorp to assume the role of the first and largest provider of data and processing power on the market of fixed income bonds.

The impacts on transaction costs

The Quotron system respresents an application of computers and telecommunications as a mediating technology that spurs the standardisation and ramification of linkages. The system will standardise transactions making available online to everyone the dealers' prices; it will also extend linkages, allowing the participation in the market of small investors. In general, it will render the entire market more transparent and efficient.

Moreover, the system will provoke a decrease of the transaction costs for the bonds. The spreads will diminish in this way by providing more information to a larger number of participants: the volume of transactions will increase. The more such a volume increases, the more liquid a bond becomes. Consequently, its spread will diminish, and so will the cost of transacting the bond. Also, the possibility of comparing prices of various dealers directly will increase competition, which will lead to a decrease in prices. These will in turn increase the volume of exchanges and diminish the spread further. As a result, dealers will obtain their profits from higher volumes rather than from higher spreads between buy and sell.

Quotron has an additional advantage in that it already has a large installed base of terminals and workstations dedicated to the stock market. It will be in a position to provide the new service for the fixed income bonds through the existing infrastructure, thus by-passing a specialised system like Telerate or Bloomberg. In this way, it will be able to carve out a new niche in the market with those customers who have been active so far mainly on the stock market, given the unavailability of reliable data on the fixed income market prices. Also, Quotron can be transformed into an electronic broker on the fixed income market. The automatic trading will improve contracting and decrease search costs: for example, customers will no longer have the need to shop around for quotations by phone. Finally, all the transactions will be more reliable, given the fact that quotations will be fed into the system only once.

In the future, one can envisage the arrival of other firms, for example the same brokers, who will develop systems similar to Quotron. Competition between these systems will be based on the service provided, speed, reliability and completeness of quotes, in addition to competition over prices. This competition on the information market will first of all decrease the cost of financial information. The result will be that the mediating technology will give new operators the opportunity to create and improve new markets, that is, the markets for information. This in turn will improve the market for bonds, render it less hierarchical and no longer dominated by proprietary information. Finally, the market will also not be biased by barriers to information of various nature, including electronic, such as those created by the pre-existing information systems of the primary dealers.

11 Groupware, teams and markets in an airline

Introduction

In many industries a strategic issue in work organisation is how to enhance the 'team effect' generated by co-operation between members. Maintenance of team cohesion is paramount to achieve such an advantage. As shown in chapters 2 and 4, cohesion depends upon a variety of factors, such as effective allocation of tasks, effective communications, good knowledge sharing and accumulation of joint experience and fair allocation of rewards so as to maintain a consistent perception of equity among team members.

A technical system like groupware can never be a substitute for the social and organisational integration of team members, but it can fill many of the inevitable logistical, knowledge and communication gaps that always arise, especially in large and/or dispersed teams performing complex tasks.

Such is the case of a large workforce composed of more than 3,000 flight crew in a major European airline (Benson, Ciborra and Proffitt, 1990). Each pilot has a complex set of interactions with various departments of the company and his colleagues both when he is flying and when he is on the ground, at home or during training courses. The co-ordination problem is compounded by the fact that flight crew are a largely absent workforce and its management are flying as well. A whole industrial culture has evolved around the logistics of the pilot's job, that is pilots are considered, and regard themselves, as 'the other side of the airline', an 'odd breed' or plainly as highly competent but isolated chaps who work almost as self-employed individuals. Changes in the airline industry are putting this culture under pressure: more integration is required at a time when the scale of operations is increasing in size and new pilots are being hired.

It is hard to design groupware applications in such a context using data-flow diagrams or other conventional structured methods. There are at least two reasons for this:

The enhancement of team performance may depend more upon increased cohesion among team members (for example, increasing trust, hence motivation; improving flexibility, etc.), than upon the provision of more data.

Groupware deals not only with data, but also with voice, text and images as essential ingredients of human collaboration.

In chapter 6 we have shown that the transaction-cost approach focuses on variables such as trust and task complexity, and extracts the relevant information requirements out of the exchanges among team members. Used as an information-requirements analysis method, the transaction-cost perspective can identify first the main transactions that characterise the flight crew management area, describing their nature, dimensions and evolution over time. Second, it looks at the bottlenecks, breakdowns, gaps and inefficiencies that characterise these transactions. The mismatches identified allow us to envisage what type of groupware support may be needed to streamline transactions, to improve them or even change their organisation.

Specifically, it can help us not only to see the flight crew organisation in a different light (as a 'team of teams'), but also to construct the new, groupware-supported organisation, by recombining team and market arrangements, already existing, though in a latent way, in the present airline bureaucracy, in order to achieve a more effective and humane work organisation.

The requirements analysis records the main dimensions of the contract between the pilot and the airline. A system model captures the regularities in information processing and communication in a form that allows for their subsequent re-use. The model can then be translated into an executable specification (prototype) of a technical infrastructure for collaborative work.

Requirements analysis

In chapter 4 we examined various types of teams and groupware support, using a broad definition of 'teamwork'. In the same spirit, here, we can look at flight crew as a 'team of teams', instead of relying on what the industry culture keeps repeating, that is, the airline administration is a bureaucracy and the pilots are a loose bunch of well-paid professionals. What justifies such an act of organisational imagination?

Despite the highly individualised contractual relationship between pilots and the airline (see below) pilots are indeed a large 'invisible' team: they share the same education, highly refined training, the same routine checks and certifications that occur so frequently during their professional life. They are trained, checked and led by fellow pilots. Within this large unsegregated team one can identify specific, task-oriented teams. The fleet is a relatively smaller team; so is the fluctuating group of training captains.

Figure 11.1 The three dimensions of the transaction between flight crew and the airline

Finally, the flight crew management managers are another team. All these teams intersect and interact.

In order to analyse the nature of the teams, it is useful to proceed from the micro to the macro, thus starting from an investigation of the nature of the contractual relationship between the pilot and the airline.

Figure 11.1 depicts the three main dimensions of the contractual relationship: economic, task-related and socio-organisational.

The *economic dimension* deals with the way rewards for performance are given by the company to the pilots: performance evaluation, incentives and career ladders.

The *task-related dimension* deals with operations, flying and all the communication and co-ordination links involved, including briefing, feedback on operations and training (becoming qualified to do the job, etc.).

Finally, the *socio-organisational dimension* includes aspects such as the culture of independence of the pilots, team spirit, perception of equity, informal links, grapevine communication, etc.

In what follows, the main characteristics of each dimension are highlighted, together with the communication processes and possible groupware solutions that might support it.

The economic dimension

Workload, salary and incentives are decided by the pilots through a bidding process (*the bidline system*). Based on seniority, the bidline rules allow pilots to lodge bids for flights and training periods with the logistics department. The company reserves the right to allocate some of the flights directly and to draft pilots when a flight is still not covered a few days before departure. An 'open time' book, which is not distributed, contains the 'last-minute' offers that pilots can choose to take up.

A first groupware solution envisaged to decrease costs and increase the efficiency of the bidline is an asynchronous system that streamlines the conversation with the logistics department, providing a support structure when breakdowns occur and establishing a link based on structured electronic mail to speed up the exchange of offers and bids. Recall that, as described in chapter 5, this solution is equivalent to the establishment of an electronic market between the airline and the pilots: the incentive for the pilots to come to the market is given by the lower transaction costs and better service that in principle can be provided by the electronic bidline.

The significance of structured e-mail lies in its record of the state of the conversation. This enables both parties to have available at any moment a summary of the conversation so far, and enables the system to prompt each party to keep them informed of deadlines, pending requests, promises due, etc. To be sure, the proposed structured e-mail can be employed as a general communication link between the airline and the pilots, where messages are exchanged that go beyond the bidline, but relate closely to the task and socio-organisational dimensions of the transaction (see below).

Finally, looking at the groupware support here proposed as a mediating technology (see ch. 3), it appears that the electronic bidline touches the levels of scope, extension and function-in-context (it supports a more transparent market relationship between the pilot and the airline). Its impacts are on efficiency and content, but also on socialisation (if it is used as a ubiquitous communciation system).

The task dimension

The increased emphasis on self-help and punctuality that airlines are contemplating as the next challenge for flight crew, requires support in the form of information and expertise as good as the existing ones for technical and safety matters. Indeed, such a support system needs to be more flexible, in order to be responsive and adapt to the contingencies of ground operations.

Groupware could enhance task-related communication at the following two levels: asynchronous and synchronous.

Asynchronous

The electronic link established for the bidline could provide both a faster and a more reliable feedback related to operations. Structured conversations would allow more effective acknowledgement of voyage reports and other flight feedback.

Bulletin boards would permit the exchange among pilots and between pilots and management of information on specific topics such as cabin-crew procedures, maintenance, interaction with terminal personnel, etc.

Synchronous

At times there is a need to consult the same file and discuss issues related to it. This task involves typically training/technical managers, crew managers or a chief pilot. Normally, all these people are located in different facilities.

A synchronous system would allow conferring and co-authoring on such occasions. Remote managers could use Integrated Services Digital Network (ISDN) to take part in these simultaneous sessions. Managers currently on a flight trip could participate via the phone line through which they would have access to fax and voice.

Here, the asynchronous and synchronous mediating technologies would intervene at the scope, extension and interface levels, and would have impacts on efficiency of the transactions, enriching their content, enlarging socialisation among the crew, and enhancing learning.

Socio-organisational communication

This is the most complex area of communication and yet the most crucial in its long-term implications for the motivation of the crew, healthy industrial relations, performance and ultimately safety.

Communication between the pilots and the airline has been undergoing a significant change as a consequence of modifications in the employment relation, company organisation and the airline industry. The following three vignettes represent this transformation.

In the past, pilots had to deal very closely with the airline bureaucracy: the hierarchy of command was pervasive, but in a way flexible and benevolent. Red tape, low productivity and high overheads were the outcome of this type of organisation. On the other hand, in the corridors of bureaucracy, 'everyone knew everyone else'. This was the consequence of an organisation operating in a placid environment, where technology, workforce attitudes and market conditions were changing incrementally, without major discontinuities.

Today, airlines look quite different. Their bureaucratic structure has been trimmed down. Market mechanisms such as the bidline system have penetrated to the very heart of their relationship with the pilots. All this has brought lower overheads, higher productivity and less red tape. Inevitably, the relationship with the pilots has moved towards an arm's length one. The increase in crew size and the flattening of the command hierarchy have necessarily given rise to more anonymity, slower case handling and delays in receiving and providing feedback.

In the future, the flight crew community will need to be more *integrated*. Over time, despite the greater reliance on equipment, the proportion of accidents attributed to pilot error has not significantly decreased. This has led to a reconsideration of the roles and relationships that should apply to the crew – with greater emphasis on interpersonal skills and team working (Hackmann, 1986).

Although this has been recognised for some time, the process of change is generally felt to be too slow. Jobs are highly individualised, rigid and rule-based and this is reinforced by extant organisation and training. In most other environments in which this style of work is found – such as the military – the organisational focus is on keeping the team together. In commercial environments this is not possible for economic reasons, and therefore the airlines may find themselves in the position in which staff are isolated and potentially alienated.

A strategy of reinstating a fully fledged hierarchy of command has too many drawbacks to make it feasible. Such an organisation would not be flexible enough to respond to environmental changes; restoring the old rostering system would cause discontent and a decrease in productivity; higher overheads would make the airline less competitive.

A more realistic alternative envisaged here consists of a trimmed, flexible and competitive organisation built as a 'team of teams' supported by electronic communication. In this form of organisation the internal market (the bidline) would be made more efficient through asynchronous system support (structured e-mail). We have called this system Flyline.

The same system would be available to strengthen the ties among pilots, between pilots and their fleet management and between fleets. From it could grow a sophisticated multimedia system, AMY, which could support the flight crew management team and improve its connections with the rest of the airline. In short, thanks to groupware, the traditional team spirit and organisation of crew would be reinforced. On the other hand, efficiency would be enhanced through a faster and more transparent market process (the electronic bidline).

Groupware as a mediating technology would be applied, then, not only to improve the functioning of existing organisational arrangements, but also to design new ones (function in context), thus having a transformation effect. Specifically, a pre-existing market and latent team arrangements would be better supported, and 'given a new life', at the expense of the bureaucracy. If this transformation is successful, then most probably there would be scope for further reductions in overheads and trimming down of the bureaucracy itself, without losing effectiveness and integration.

Modelling, prototyping and evaluation

The roles and communication flows which form the central bidline conversation can be described by mapping the negotiation between the airline and the pilots onto a 'conversation for action' (Winograd and Flores, 1986). This represents the domain as several 'state-change conversations', each concerned with allocating a pilot to a cockpit seat on a particular trip.

More specifically, four categories of workflow can be identified: a message, a contract cycle, a mediation loop and a negotiation loop (Medina-Mora, et al. 1992). These, similar to the decomposition of the 'conversation for action', can be used to design the mediating application at the scope and interface levels.

The 'atomic' workflow can be modelled as a synchronised *message* between two roles (that is, people or programs). A *contract cycle* consists of a pair of two such messages, where the initiating role suspends processing, until a subsequent message indicating the completion of its task is received from its counterpart.

Two further communication structures can be identified that comprise multiple contract cycles. A *mediation loop* has initial contract cycles with a third party (for example, to obtain authorisation) followed by the substantive cycle. A *negotiation loop* has preliminary 'staging' cycles with the counterpart to agree parameters for its task.

Having decomposed the transaction in this way, a system model can be built. The domain consists of two workflows; firstly an *announcing message* from the schedule-distribution office to the crew followed by a *scheduling contract cycle* between the crew and a resolving program.

The model can provide the basis for both the design of a computational projection of the new system (Ansa, 1989) and the economic evaluation of the existing and proposed systems. We focus here on the latter. The transaction-cost approach directs our attention to the resources consumed in the execution of each transaction. Two categories of cost are associated with a message, and a further two with the contract cycle (see ch. 7).

Search and maintenance costs are inherent in any message transaction; *search costs* concern the identification of a counterpart offering the appropriate service, and *maintenance costs* relate to the resources required to establish and perform the communication.

Additional overheads are involved in the creation of a contractual cycle;

contracting costs are incurred by the need to specify and record the contract terms, while *control and regulatory costs* arise from the supervision of the performance of the contract.

The cost data can be collected into a spreadsheet – the transaction-cost spreadsheet. Actually, two spreadsheets can be filled in: the first lists the costs of the transaction for the airline; the second contains the cost items paid for by the pilot. The spreadsheet is a table whose rows describe the invocations of the bidline process and whose columns represent the four phases of the conversation between the company and the pilots concerning the schedule for the period. A search phase consisting of a set of concurrent announcing messages is followed by a phase for negotiation and regulation. Maintenance activities form the fourth phase of activity which sustains the process.

The cells in the spreadsheets represent the cost to the company or the pilot of carrying out the specific phase: costs of executing the activities when the phase goes through with no disruptions and extra costs incurred in order to cope with disruptions. These descriptions can be made out by the users themselves, and in this way capture the experience of the people in the field and provide a realistic and well-grounded platform for computing the costs and possible savings. In this case, the main benefits from Flyline were found to be a routine cost reduction of $500,000 per annum, and saving on disruption costs of $750,000 or more each year.

A prototype can be built to take care of showing the users the scope, extension and interface layers of the system. By considering active objects (hypertexts) in association with the workflows the design can be carried to the point where the user interface is suitable for comment and amendment. The announcing message consists of a report listing the possible trips to be flown, with active areas in which bids may be composed. The scheduling contract cycle involves the transfer of the pilots' selections to a resolving program. This sorts the trips into those with no bids, those which may be satisfied by a straightforward application of the rules and conflicts requiring human intervention. The results form the substance of the subsequent announcing message.

Flyline can be implemented using X400 compatible store and forward technology, with interactive voice response, hypertext or IBM Common User Access interfaces.

On the other hand, the AMY workstation can be used to support the activities of flight crew management whether related to payment, work or organisation. At interface design level, one can envisage dividing the screen into an area for tools, an area related to tasks and an area for talking.

Personal tools and workspace. Standard devices and software for personal productivity can be represented by icons such as a laser-printer, a telephone, electronic mail, a scanner, a fax, recording devices and a set of software packages such as text and graphic editors, spreadsheets, etc. The bidline conversations are managed in this way. *Operational activity* is supported by an enhanced online information centre/library. Its purpose is to assist users to locate documents and software, reserve scarce resources (such as a video conference server) and deliver distance-learning materials. Services are provided by a mixture of automated aids and professional support navigated by an active organisational 'map'.

The simplest form of support for *ad hoc* interaction is sharing a document or computer application. For example, a form may be raised and passed through a more or less sophisticated process of revision to trigger action by its various recipients. Spontaneous interaction might be supported through the notions of a 'venue' and an 'outer office'. By activating the 'building' icon, the user moves into a public domain where he/she has placed her diary. Subsequent activations of this button from within the domain would lead down a customised 'corridor' to other outer offices.

More sophisticated audio/data conferencing can be activated on demand either by dragging names into the exchange (to create a new venue) or by re-invoking an existing conference (for example, by activating the 'telephone conference' button). An audio/data conference is a venue with its own tools and workspace, which may include specific presentation aids, telepointers, whiteboards, etc. It is also envisaged that small-scale desktop video conferences may be set up by prior reservation of a video mosaic transceiver.

Implications

In the kind of environment envisaged so far, the user is going to be working with computer-supported communication very intensively. He/she will be facing real problems arising from a part of the world that they wish to influence. The systems, because of their multiple impacts, should not be regarded as just more efficient ways of automating (streamlining) transactions, but as a new formative context (see ch. 1), for they can provide support for three kinds of work: representing the world, thinking about it and manipulating it. For example, Flyline will automate and streamline the existing routines of the bidline, improving the *efficiency* of the logistics department. But, once in use, the new network will embed new routines of work, which at the same time will decrease co-ordination costs and help create a new formative context. By new routines we mean activities not strictly related to the bidding process, but having impacts on the content of the task and socialisation, such as:

the provision of daily information from the company and access to pre-existing network services;

the improvement in communications between different fleet locations;

the establishment of bulletin boards where messages can be exchanged regarding operations, the fleet, special interests, etc.;

the access to systems in the crew management area for communication and problem solving.

More broadly, these useful routines can relieve the isolation of flight crew and lead to a new team-oriented context by (socialisation, learning and transformation effects):

eroding the current culture of isolation and individualism in crews: everybody can reach everyone else without intruding (reading and answering mail are always options that reside with the individual);

supporting informal and formal exchanges on problems and solutions related to operational, technical, in-flight and off-flight issues;

diffusing an attitude which encourages them to give and expect feedback, reflect on problems, and share valid information;

increasing trust based on improved communication between crew management, airline and the crew.

Flyline can improve the market mechanism of the bidding process, and at the same time it makes available routines for supporting the linkages within and across the teams that compose the crew area. This in turn should foster the adoption by the crew of a team-oriented worldview in tackling and solving operational, managerial, technical and personal problems.

Flyline must, then, be looked at for its contextual effects as a *strategic* information system for the management of the crucial human resource of the airline: the crew. The ultimate question that Flyline addresses is not just how to make the bidline more efficient, but what the airline wants to do with its most valuable workforce and how it is going about the problem of creating a more team-oriented organisation, mentality and culture. Flyline cannot be fully appreciated if considered in isolation from these broader issues.

The features we see attached to AMY are a necessary requirement for universal real-time access, multimedia, easy-to-use interfaces, teleconferencing, etc. Some of these have a self-evident instrumental value, such as the joint consultation of files between distant locations, the possibility opened up for distance learning or the technical expertise acquired in using workstations connected to a high-bandwidth network.

But to appreciate the strategic value of AMY one needs once again to look at its context-creating aspects. AMY provides its users (crew management) with very powerful tools to build as a team systems, prototypes, interfaces and applications in an advanced environment. This can be used to develop information and communication systems such as those based on structured e-mail, or other communicating applications. But it can also serve as a vehicle for trying out the new routines and procedures, roles and responsibilities that would accompany such systems. Crew managers will be able to operate not only as a decision-making and problem-solving team, but also as a design team. In this way technology becomes both a product of and a factor in socialisation in the workplace (Benson and Lloyd, 1983).

To summarise: if we consider the systems we have proposed, we see that they have an impact on the data and messages that are exchanged in an organisation. Second, they have an impact on jobs, what one can do and how one works; but the more subtle, contextual impact is on the way one looks at the world, at one's job, at relationships with colleagues and at how one can improve the organisation, or design the next application.

Finally, reflecting on the way the project has actually been carried out, groupware seems to be an application that is not only innovative in the services it provides, but in the way it is built; that is, groupware makes us think differently of what end-user development can be (see ch. 8). That is to say, by working closely with users such as the pilots, able to tinker with and develop information systems for their own use, a few interesting aspects have emerged. First, no matter how systems are conceived and introduced in a user setting, they are *open*; that is, users can officially or informally add new routines, avoid some and by-pass others. Second, the 'do-it-yourself' activities, or *bricolage*, that we find in many large organisations should not be regarded as the outcome of ineffective or chaotic systems development; rather, they should be valued as a proper manifestation of end-user computing, a true source of innovation in technology usage and organisational adaptation.

In the future, the more systems will be open, easy to use and offering powerful tools, the more *bricolage* will be widespread and become the *de facto* way of building new systems. What today is regarded by sceptics as 'mickey-mousing' will appear to have a strategic relevance for organisational learning about the new technology (see ch. 9).

As this project points out, the particular challenge for the management of data processing is to govern such a complex development process in a manner that sustains the coherence of global system architecture and its security, integrity and robustness.

12 Networks and markets in public administration

Introduction

The problem of how to apply computers in public administration, both central and local, is tackled in this chapter in a different way than is normally the case. The economic perspective and the notion of mediating technology are particularly useful for shedding new light on the debate about the opportunities and limitations of automating the public sector. This new perspective requires an enlargement of the field of analysis in various directions.

First, the notion of economic exchange as the fundamental way to look at business organisations and their information requirements must be integrated with that of *political exchange*, specific to public governing bodies. Second, in order to appreciate the limitations and the possibilities of applying information technology, both at state administration level and on the territory administered by the state, there is a need to analyse the ways in which any public authority interacts with the community and the activities over its territory. In approaching this analysis, we will use two of the models we have seen so far: the decision model and the transaction-cost model.

The first suggests a cybernetic, or control, approach to the design of computer-based systems in public administration. The second takes into account the complex relationships between the central or local authorities and other agencies or organisations operating on the territory. The latter model proposes to view public authorities not as given immutable organisations, but rather as those that perform certain activities, some of which can be delegated to other institutions such as the market or the firm, also through deregulation and privatisation, depending upon the availability of a new telecommunication and information infrastructure.

As a consequence, the issue of whether and how to automate the public administration is not so much solved as dissolved in the terms in which it is usually posed. The design of computer systems that can support public administration should be considered jointly with the issues of deregulation and outsourcing and the trade-off between centralised planning and market mechanisms.

The Italian case

What is the state of the art of automation in public administration and how can it be compared with the level of computerisation of other industries and sectors? In what follows we address these questions based on the italian case, where sufficient statistics are available to allow a first comparison of the levels of computerisation in different sectors. It is our assumption that such statistics will not differ significantly for the other industrialised countries.

The first measure of the level of computerisation, a very approximate one, is given by the ratio between the present-day value of existing installed hardware in a given industry and the percentage of people employed in that industry. In the Italian case, it turns out that local and central public administration have a level of computerisation which is roughly half that of banks, insurance companies and large retailers. If we turn to more sophisticated indicators, the gap widens. That is to say, instead of comparing the number of computers with the number of people employed, we should compare the ratios between the information workers (Porat, 1977) present in the various sectors, excluding agriculture, and the value of the hardware installed in the same sectors. In this way we obtain a measure of the penetration of computer technology that takes into account the information nature of the various activities performed in a given industry.

In other words, if an industry employs mainly manual workers, it can be expected that there will be a low usage of information technology and possibly a very high usage of production automation or robotics. This type of effect was not revealed by the first ratio we employed, whereas now we can avail ourselves of a more precise measure showing the extent to which the information activities are in fact automated. The latter measure highlights an even wider gap. The computerisation level is very high in the financial and banking sectors, around 8, low in manufacturing, 1.3, and very low in public administration, 0.6. Thus the gap between public administration and the financial and banking sectors can be measured in terms of 1 to 10.

One of the largest social-survey institutions in Italy, Censis (Censis, 1985), has also tried to compare the levels of computer usage in various sectors of economic activity. Specifically, it has built a complex statistical indicator that summarises both qualitative and quantitative aspects of the use of computers in different sectors of the Italian economy. According to the Censis report, the introduction of computers into public administration has been very dynamic in the last twenty years, so that the level of computerisation in the public sector can be valued as intermediate.

However, as far as the *use* of systems is concerned, the mainly automated areas in public administration are the traditional bread-and-butter procedures, that is, accounting routines and payrolls. The degree of automation is much lower in applications for decision support at managerial level. Finally, when comparing the level of computer culture and skills in using the applications available, the qualitative indicators of Censis give the public administration a very low ranking compared to other sectors.

Riddles and interpretations

The data and the indicators regarding the Italian case raise the following questions:

How is it that the computerisation level of public administration is so low, given the fact that administration is a bureaucracy based on routines and procedures which in principle should be relatively easy to automate?

Why do banks, insurance companies and large retailers have a computerisation level that is relatively so high?

Why do different sociological case studies show that the introduction of computers into public administration is characterised by many more conflicts and problems than on average is the case for banks or manufacturing firms (Galloudec-Genuys, 1980)?

Why is the computerisation of public administration so fragmented? It is not clear why certain areas in the public sector, like the postal bank, are highly automated, while others, like the Cadastre, have very little automation despite huge investments in computer technology.

To these riddles serious explanations and interpretations have been offered by various observers. What follows is a short list of the leading ones.

The conspiracy view

According to such an explanation, the poor state of computerisation in public administration is mainly due to a political will that wants to keep the public sector in a chronic state of disarray. The agents of the conspiracy may be the politicians, who are only interested in supporting their clients, or the bureaucrats, who wish to keep their power, or, finally, the total lack of a sound planning approach. Such an interpretation suggests a possible therapy: the bad politicians have to be replaced by the good ones in the control room, and the sloppy policies by the effective ones.

Before accepting this type of recommendation, however, it should be clarified why there is such a high density of bad agents in public administration as compared, for example, with the banking industry. Also, this explanation seems to depend too much on the supposed inclinations of the agents, and ignores what the constraints are that the public sector as a system imposes on their actions, beside their will, their thirst for power or their desire to maintain the status quo.

The cultural explanation

Computers are not used because there is a low level of competence in the data-processing personnel of the public sector. But is this just a description of a symptom or the diagnosis of the cause? The logic of the argument seems to be the following: there is a low level of computer usage because the computer culture is not rooted firmly enough. The therapy is self-evident. What is needed is a heavy dose of education and computer literacy, and of course, more machines. However, the question then is: why do all the uncultivated people meet in the public sector?

Personnel and pay

The issue of data-processing personnel is the consequence of the previous two interpretations. Lack of culture and planning are due to the fact that data-processing personnel are often underpaid in the public sector. This ensures the continuous loss of the best resources. In the past, at least for Italy, this has been the case. However, at both local and central level, there are now various ways to by-pass such an obstacle. More and more private or publicly owned firms are created that provide data-processing services to public administration from the outside, so that the constraints on pay levels can be largely eliminated.

The managerial explanation

This explanation is grounded in an analogy between the public administration as an organisation and the business firm. Public administration can be seen as a pyramid, where, starting from the bottom, one can identify bureaucratic processes, social provision processes and a planning, political process. In the bureaucratic process what is required is the automation of internal procedures that make the bureaucracy function more efficiently. At the higher level, public administration is seen as the provider of services to the community. According to such a mission, computers can be used to support the automatic delivery of some of these services, especially those linked to acounting and billing, and other services which are document-based. The third role of public administration is as an agency for planning external economic activities. Such planning is complex, highly political and, like any strategic activity, less prone to be supported by computers.

No wonder, then, that one can find in public administration a great deal of 'bureaucratic' computer applications, fewer service-oriented applications and very few strategic-planning applications. The deficiency of such reasoning is that it does not help us to understand why public adminstration in general is less automated than other organisations. The analogy with the pyramid model of private organisations in fact indicates that in any organisation one has lower-level decision-making processes that are heavily automated and top decision-making processes that are less automated because they are more complex and less programmable (Gorry and Scott-Morton, 1971).

This explanation can indicate and suggest the reasons why there is an uneven level of automation at the different hierarchical levels of the public sector or, for that matter, other private organisations, but cannot explain the relative gap between the public sector and the organisations operating in other industries.

The organisational perspective

This perspective is the opposite to the conspiracy view. Here, structural factors and mechanisms are at the centre of attention. Specifically, the reason why public administration is so little automated is due to the fact that, at least in the Italian case, its mission is to apply laws to produce acts independently of the specific problem or the environment in which public administration has to operate (Mortara, 1984). In other words, public administration is a closed organisation with an internal logic that, only in a very loosely coupled way, matches the needs and exigencies stemming from the surrounding environment. This explains why the public sector tends to expand by creating further routines which are not correlated to the functions that the environment requires.

The outcome is an organisation which is 'protobureaucratic', that is, far from the ideal bureaucracy as described by Weber (1947). In a protobureaucratic organisation phenomena such as high departmentalisation, fragmentation of procedures and high levels of rigidity tend to recur. It is easy to understand the difficulties of computerisation in such a context, in that computer-based information systems require a certain integration of various departments. It is our conclusion that this explanation is largely true, at least in the Italian case. Possibly, what is still left unresolved is why such application rules and procedures, which are totally insensitive to environmental stimuli, could emerge at all. Also this perspective cannot justify the fact that bad and good applications of information technology can coexist side by side in different departments.

At the end of this short list, one can envisage the requirements for an alternative explanation. In a nutshell, this should highlight those structural factors that cause the lower level of computerisation of the public sector in a comparative fashion. Otherwise, one runs the risk of focusing too much on the supposed uniqueness of the case of the public sector, disregarding the possibility of comparing different institutional alternatives to solve the same problem. These comparisons are very important, especially when we think about reforming the public sector through the redesigning of organisational and information systems. The alternative explanation should look at the public sector as an open system; a system that is open to the customers, to the citizens, to the political and economic markets. More specifically, one needs:

a comparative framework which is not limited to the public sector only: this requires the establishment of a common language in order to speak of similar problems in socio-economic organisations, which are usually treated separately;

a study of the interaction between public administration and its relevant environments;

an analysis of the information activities carried out by the public sector.

Models of administration and exchange

In order to compare the penetration of information technology in the various sectors, we should refer to the transaction-costs perspective (ch. 6). This would point out that in the banking and financial sectors the prevailing form of organisation is that of the *market*. Banks, for example, play an intermediary role in market transactions of goods and services (see ch. 10). In the manufacturing sector what characterises production is mostly a *hierarchical* organisation of work, whereby the basic transaction between the employer and employee is arranged through an employment contract. Markets are easier to automate, which would explain why certain sectors, in which market or quasi-market arrangements obtain, show a higher level of computerisation than others.

In the public sector the nature of the exchanges is more complex, however. For one thing, although the internal workings of public administration can be described as a bureaucracy, the scope of operation of the administration concerns an environment populated by organisations and individuals with which transactions are not purely economic. To begin with, the nature of the relationship can be described as loosely coupled, for example a local authority operates on a territory where there are citizens, as well as firms and associations. No one specific organisational form or type of contract seems to prevail (recall the notion of hypo-integrated system introduced in chapter 7). But the nature of the linkages is not only 'loosely coupled'; it is also 'integrated' by other elements that are specifically political. Indeed, sociologists and political scientists describe the relationship between the administration and the surrounding community as a *political exchange*.

While objects of economic exchange are goods, services and money, the object of political exchange can be laws, regulations, plans and provisions, and more subtle, but not less important, goods such as the acknowledgement of the identity of groups that operate in the community. In exchange for identity recognition, these groups offer to the administration legitimacy, consensus, support and order, essential to the smooth carrying out of the other exchanges, such as those of an economic nature. One can see the political exchange at work whenever an association, a union or a movement bargains with the administration for some provisions, laws or regulations in exchange for order and consensus: the lobbying phenomenon is an expression of the political exchange.

The complexity and the structure of the exchanges between the citizens and the administration may vary according to the basic relationship between the state and the community. As we have understood the different applications of the mediating technology by making reference to different types of governance of economic transactions, the impacts and the opportunities for computerisation in the public sector can only be appreciated by analysing the different kinds of political exchange.

Consider the four ideal types, applicable at least to Western democracies which are discussed in the following subsections.

The minimal state

This form of administration is perfectly permeable to the interests of the community as expressed by a free-market economy. It captures all the conflicting interests and qualities as emerging through the market. It merely institutionalises the rules of the game of the free market which generates the distribution of wealth and interests without interfering with the process or its final outcome. The minimal state guarantees public and private order through general norms such as the enforcement of private property. Note how the order which is maintained is not created by the state, but is one that private citizens have given to themselves.

The political exchange takes place once and for all at the outset. Politicians and public administrators guarantee order and security to society and its system of diverse interests and unequal goals. In exchange, they receive political goods such as acknowledgement and identification of society with the politicians and their role. Such acknowledgement is also given once and for all. This leads to the emergence from within the society of a political class which is autonomous. Indirectly, the boundary of the minimal state is defined by the market, that is, the network of economic exchanges that identify the very system of interests which is captured by the minimal state.

The pluralist state

With the increase in the demands and needs of different groups in society, and the turbulence and complexity of society in general, the public sector tries to cope by multiplying and diversifying the functions and departments of its organisation, in order to respond to the various sectorial interests. In this way the state becomes selectively permeable to the pressures of society, and especially of organised movements or lobbies. Internally, the administration is so diversified and departmentalised that each new function or office is relatively autonomous from the others, while it is in direct contact with outside opinion or pressure groups.

This generates the multiplying of departments and increases the bureaucratic rivalry between the various offices which compete for the resources available within the administration. The political exchange does not take place once and for all. On the contrary, it becomes frequent, explicit and *ad hoc*; that is, tailored to the negotiations between a given office and the relevant external pressure groups. The objects of exchange are special provisions or laws, that is sectorial, *ad hoc* privileges that the politicians are able to offer to the interest groups through the various administrative functions and offices. Usually, laws are designed to meet an expressed interest, to foster that interest or try to stop it according to circumstances.

The politicians, in return, obtain sectorial consensus and the possibility of programming the behaviour of that segment of society that has been the object of legislation. To let itself be programmed is what that societal sector offers to the politician. Such political good can represent a success factor for the politician in his/her bureaucratic competition against other offices and political parties. Indeed, the latter tend more and more to become administrative offices themselves. Finally, it is the network of sectorial interests that sets the boundary and the scope of the pluralist state.

The planning state

This model of state has a strong administrative and bureaucratic apparatus that is usually centralised, and it is characterised by the fact that it has a proactive attitude. In fact, this model state operates through intervention programmes aimed at solving market failures, taking care of equity beside efficiency, that is, through welfare policies aimed at improving the living conditions of those parts of society that have been damaged by the social costs of the market.

As for the minimal state, the provisions and laws generated by the redistributional state are of a general nature, that is, they concern large social strata and classes that are not organised. The provisions usually concern the distribution of planned benefits to outcasts and the poor, interventions for income redistribution and so on. Society offers the politicians its approval, consensus and collaboration with the general order. In other words, it offers a certain stability of the social processes, a stability that is an essential prerequisite to guaranteeing the efficacy of planning interventions. The limit of state action can be represented by the emergence of powerful pressure groups, of corporations or guilds that can make centralised interventions more difficult. If these pressure groups are powerful enough, then the so called social programmes turn into *ad hoc* provisions that do not address the general interest, but just specific pressures of powerful lobbies.

The totalitarian state

In this case the structure of society is identified with the state bureaucracy. The community becomes merely the lower layer of the hierarchical state structure. From political, the exchange becomes strictly bureaucratic. It is a continuous exchange and concerns, like the employment contract in the hierarchy, the moving up of individuals and groups through the social and state hierarchies. It deals with the exchange of favours within the bureaucracy, the forms of perfunctory or spontaneous co-operation and so on. The limit of the totalitarian state is given by the fragmented structure of private interests of the individual members, or functionaries of the apparatus.

Before considering what role computers can play in respect of the four models just sketched, a few general comments are in order.

In the political exchange at least one of the goods exchanged is consensus, the acknowledgement by one of the partners of the other. Recognising the other's identity is something taken for granted in any economic transaction, where identities, especially when exchanging commodities, do not really matter: in a perfect market there is the meeting of faceless buyers and faceless sellers (ch. 5). In the political exchange, by contrast, acknowledging a partner may be a complex process, and a very important part of the exchange itself.

Such a cycle unfolds in the following way: there is an emerging pressure group with an emerging identity; such a group exercises pressure on the apparatus, and the state reacts by creating an office, department or function that corresponds to that specific pressure. Consider the minimal state that operates in an environment defined by the free market, where there is no collective action. Whenever forms of collective action emerge that can let themselves be heard by the state apparatus and are able to give themselves an identity and let this identity be acknowledged by the state, this will induce in the state an adequate response. For example, consider the labour movement or the ecology movement: they have transformed themselves into unions or green parties and the states have responded historically in the following stages:

by first acknowledging their identities;

then by developing functions within the administration that could interface with the new identities, such as the minister for labour or the environment minister.

Note, finally, how in the four models just described the state plays a different role in mediating the intertwining of interests which are emerging in society. To the minimal state society delegates the maintenance of the roles of the free market, without giving it any power to modify such rules. The pluralist state mediates interests by diversifying its apparatus and its selective interventions. The planning state becomes the umpire that guides interests and intervenes in order to correct market distortions. Finally, the totalitarian states mediates as a hierarchy through the chain of command.

To be sure, these four models of state and administration are ideal types. Real administrations, for example a regional government, a local authority or even a ministry, can be made of a mixture of all of the four ideal models. Thus a local authority may have a preference for a planning policy, but does not have enough resources, or does not develop enough offices, structures and intervention plans to exercise an effective government action. Then, the local government will let outside interests develop, behaving *de facto* as a pluralist or even a minimal state.

Models of computerisation

We can now envisage different types of interactions between information technology and the public sector according to the various models seen so far. Such interaction is complex. On the one hand, the technology is an important resource within the public sector that can become a factor in the bureaucratic competition with the administration. Those who can control the technology and apply it for their purposes can gain an advantage in such a competition. On the other hand, it represents an important tool for creating more effective programmes and plans.

Thus, technology can support and streamline some of the exchanges between the apparatus and the environment. Specifically, it can allow a more effective data collection and feedback on the activities on the territory that have to be controlled and planned. It can support the running of sophisticated models to apply cost–benefit analysis, or more generally, the analysis of consequences of various interventions. Also, it can improve the delivery of existing services and represent the platform for the creation of new services for the community.

Finally, the technology can intervene directly in the processes of political exchange. In this area, there are only experimental applications. In some American cities and towns, the processes of expressing consensus and the definition of collective identities that are so important for political exchange take place directly, through voting online in real time through two-way cable television. Such systems allow the continuous measure of consensus on specific initiatives and interventions of the administration. The opportunities for having faster feedback from the community are thus improved and the administration could become, in its turn, more complex and flexible in diversifying its own structure and in delivering its sectorial responses, may be electronically, to multiple interest groups (Etzioni, 1972; Rodotà, 1982).

Let us now consider in more detail the impacts of computers for each of the four ideal models of state.

The minimal state: telematics as a market-support system

By definition the minimal state does not intervene in the market, but just guarantees its autonomous working. Information technology can become an important part of those rules, procedures, routines and infrastructure that the state provides to implement and support the market. Because mediating technology allows market transactions to be created and stream-lined, the minimal state can improve the functioning of the market. Systems like videotex indicate how a state can offer support to the invisible hand of the market. The scope and content of what runs on the infrastructure are defined by market forces: for example, information contained in databanks is not imposed by the state, but is itself a commodity that can be bought and sold in the electronic information markets.

In a way, then, political exchange is not touched by mediating techno-logy, because political exchange occurs once and for all, while economic transactions take place on the electronic market. On the other hand, computers and networks can be applied to transform those universal services provided by the state into electronic mass markets or personalised electronic private services (see ch. 5).

The pluralist state: information technology as a resource in bureaucratic competition

This second model includes most of the current applications of information technology at both local and central level. It can explain the fragmented application of data processing that one can observe in the Italian case, and not only in that case. If the logic that dominates this type of state is institutional openness to particular interests and a set of organisational responses that generates diversification of agencies and offices, the application of information technology will not contradict this logic; on the contrary, it will be embedded in it.

Data-processing applications will develop unevenly within the administration. Successful applications will be the result of the political exchange between a given department that wants to automate its procedures or the services it provides to citizens and organisations and the corresponding segment of society. If the political exchange does not go through in an effective way, applications will most probably fail. It is evident that the computerisation will result in a fragmented picture and a set of applications that cannot be used for pursuing general plans and strategies.

The planning state: socially oriented applications of information technology

In this model the planning state can use information technology to implement and support plans and policies that address market failures. In particular, it can support the welfare policy in established fields (through universal services) and open up new applications. For example, information technology can provide communication structures for groups, minorities or people who have few chances of participating, such as the handicapped or the elderly (customised, public services). It can also improve the functioning of the labour market by providing infrastructures, such as electronic parks, so that even people who are marginal to the labour market, for example young mothers, can, thanks to telework, participate in the (electronic) labour market.

Also, two-way systems can provide continuous feedback on the plans and legislation being approved by the government. Society does not need to gather in pressure groups, but can express its consensus or disapproval on an individual and collective basis thanks to the new infrastructure (Etzioni, 1972). Note, however, that frequent feedback and frequent evaluation of consensus can render such a structure less *stable* in its planning and intervention cycle than without the new technology.

The totalitarian state: Big Brother

Here computers represent the nightmare of Big Brother, who can operate all the procedures of the state bureaucracy that include the community. The computers support and reinforce the hierarchical chain of command and control throughout society. As a result, all members of society will depend on a sort of universal service organisation and will be monitored closely by an apparatus which is inaccessible and opaque.

However, it is possible that, as in any bureaucracy, political exchange will express itself through the informal exchange of favours, so that the automated bureaucracy may turn into an electronic jungle with various niches and transactions that stay out of reach of Big Brother. Here, as in the previous case, the multiplying of the micro individual exchanges will not allow the emergence of a collective identity.

A cybernetic approach to information-systems design

How can we go about the design of computer-based information systems in public administration? A systematic analysis of the matching of information technology and the different models of state just examined allows us to evaluate the feasibility of alternative design strategies.

First, let us consider a typical approach based on the decision-making perspective (see ch. 6). This perspective suggests looking at public administration as a *control system*. In such a cybernetic system the goals are fixed by the political bodies, for example the local council or the parliament. Policies and interventions depend on the goals to be achieved and the feedback that comes from the territory and the community. The implementation of policies takes place through the administrative apparatus, where competencies are usually split and bureaucratic barriers are ubiquitous. The processes to be controlled on the territory are varied and characterised by the loose coupling of individuals, institutions and informal groups.

According to the cybernetic approach, it is possible to control the socio-economic processes occurring on the territory on the basis of sufficiently wide knowledge of such phenomena. The public decision maker can through information technology achieve higher levels of rationality, so as to be able to implement policies on the basis of the feedback it receives and on the knowledge of the state of the system. Unfortunately, there are various examples of information systems designed according to this model that remain at the planning stage or just become failures, such as the Italian National Health Service information system or the new Land Registry.

In all such cases the main decision-making unit is in the central administration. The cybernetic model prescribes that this decision maker should receive the data gathered from all over the country, processed through the local branches of the central ministries. Often, the design and implementation of such centralised control systems are too costly, long and depend too much on the smooth co-operation of the local offices. But the performance of the local office is idiosyncratic, uneven and unreliable: hence, the whole system becomes a patchwork of automated procedures, and the goal of centralised control does not materialise in practice. A more prudent version of the cybernetic approach has thus emerged after repeated failures. It acknowledges the following preconditions for the success of any territorial system:

> One needs to integrate the scattered knowledge on the territorial processes, so that a first crucial problem is the centralisation of the scattered memory of the decision-making unit operating on the territory.

> One needs to design not only the system, but also the bargaining and participation processes through which the agents can be involved in the recomposition of the scattered memory and knowledge. The administration must be able to set up 'information contracts' by which new services or information are provided in exchange for such participation.

> It is recognised that public administration as an organisation is in itself fragmented, and that the various internal divisions and the overall departmental organisation may follow a logic and some objectives which are different from, or even at odds with, the loose structure connecting the relevant processes on the territory. So, for example, the functional subdivision between different units in public administration may not correspond to the unified exigencies of organisations on the territory such as the firms, associations or households. Overcoming the lack of congruence between the internal organisation of the apparatus and the loose 'organisation' of the various institutions operating on the territory may require the redesign of the co-ordination mechanisms within the public agency. In systems language, the internal variety of the public administration as an organisation must match or replicate the variety of the territory (Ashby, 1966).

While, in the less sophisticated version of the cybernetic approach, information systems had a centralised architecture designed to support and enforce vertical information flows, in the more advanced version information technology can have a role but only under certain circumstances, strictly dependent upon the possibility of modifying the organisational structure of the administration and setting up participatory processes for its computerisation.

Thus, the computer-based information systems will concern only a part of the information and data available; the informal part, the one most difficult to access, will stay out, and will be collected and analysed only occasionally. The architecture of the information system will not be centralised, but distributed or networked, so that the system will be able to better support scattered decision making units across existing departments. The applications will be updated thanks to 'information contracts' through which the users, both inside and outside the administration, provide data, while they receive value-added analyses or better services in exchange.

In Italy there are a few pilot examples of systems designed for public administration according to such a philosophy. They are to be found especially at the level of local authorities, regional or communal, industrial districts (Pyke, Beccatini and Sengenberger, 1990) or as the outcome of systems designed by associations, such as the videotex service provided by the Association of Communes, Ancitel, or consortia, like the videotex for the Prato textile district (Mathis, 1988).

The limits of the cybernetic approach

The limitations of the earlier version of the cybernetic approach are by now clear. First, a centralised, all-knowing planning authority does not obtain: the administrative apparatus and the territory to be governed form a hypo-integrated system (ch. 7). Second, the approach makes no provision for taking into account the incentives required to get the data from individuals and organisations that operate outside the bureaucratic apparatus. Third, the fragmented internal structure of the administration usually cannot observe and intervene in the socio-economic processes of the territory and the community in a consistent way that matches the level and nature of the interdependencies among such processes.

Recall now the four models of state described above and note where this version of the cybernetic approach could be applied, at least ideally. It is evident that the approach plays no role in the minimal state, while it may have one in the totalitarian state. In the other two forms of administration it will be ineffective. That is to say, in the pluralist model it will deliver a series of failures, like fragmented computerisation, sky-rocketing costs and gaps between the needs of the citizens, outside organisations and the administration itself.

To be sure, the approach has more chances to integrate itself with the planning state, especially if it is able to establish a series of information contracts with the users. However, even this more advanced way of introducing information technology into the public sector, that we have connoted as the more sophisticated cybernetic approach, is subject to some limitations that are embedded both in the model of the planning administration and in the approach itself.

Its basic flaw boils down to the fact that it avoids a comparative analysis and is not contingent upon the decision-making performance of different socio-economic institutions. In other words, before embarking on any computerisation effort in the public sector, the action of the administration must be evaluated in relation to the actions of other institutions that already operate on the territory.

The designer should ask himself/herself the following preliminary question: for a given problem, is it necessary to automate the administration in order to make it more effective in solving that problem, or is it better (in efficiency and equity terms) to delegate the solution of that problem to institutions which lie outside the boundaries of the administration? Is it better to set up a new universal service or put in place the infrastructure for an electronic market or many customised markets that can take care of themselves?

It may well be that trying to automate the extant administration at all costs for executing that specific task, without taking into account other institutional alternatives, produces meaningless, or simply too costly, results in relative terms. At the extreme, one could envisage the possibility of applying information technology so that the outside institutions, and not the public administration, can better solve the problem. In this way, the public administration could limit itself to providing an infrastructure, or outline the plans for an infrastructure, and leave the development of the applications to the outside institutions.

But what are these other institutions? First of all, there are teams, markets and hierarchical firms, and these have already been examined in the first chapters of this volume. But on the territory one can also find other relevant institutions, such as informal relations, political and juridical institutions (Sowell, 1980). Their performance has to be briefly examined in order to complete the picture and allow us to set out a comparative analysis and design.

Informal relations

These institutions are flexible and especially not as costly; they are based on trust and on a common stock of agreements between participants. The cost is low because there are hidden investments made by society as a whole in the past, in terms of familiarity with certain traditions, sharing of common values and so on. They are flexible because they can easily be attuned to circumstances and tailored to emerging needs; they are not categorical and adaptation is always possible. Often, informal relations are criticised by computer specialists as lacking in transparency, but they seem to ignore the fact that informal relations are not just nice additions to the major social institutions. Not only do they include important decision-making processes, like those which occur in the family and in informal groups, but they also generate that background social capital without which the other institutions would not be able to work at all. For example, language is something which is of value in any business transaction (Winograd and Flores, 1986), but at the same time is an outcome of informal social processes. Ethics is another crucial complement of the background social capital without which the cost of functioning of even the simplest economic or social institution would be astronomical.

Political organisations

Political organisations include local authorities and the central state. These institutions provide a series of stable rights and have the resources to enforce them in order to protect certain personal areas of people's lives, areas that are in a way put 'outside the scope of market forces'. The political organisations have the following decision-making problems:

The constant effort of identifying which decisions should be attributed to economic organisations like the market or to informal organisations, and which should fall within the scope of public administration.

The need for feedback and adaptation. Public and political institutions are rigid and more isolated than economic ones. Political power is subject to a different feedback from that of economic power. It is not just entry or exit, but it is voice, protest and vote (Hirschman, 1970). This sort of feedback is slower and less effective if not in the extreme case of revolution, and even then history seems to show that effective adaptation is also required from those new political institutions that emerge from radical reforms. In particular, any public administrative apparatus is isolated because it cannot receive directly feedback from the market and the voice of the electorate, if not through the mediation of political representatives. On the other hand, what is required of political and legal institutions is not speed of response but the liability for legal acts. Hence, the decisions of the public authority can only intervene from the outside every now and then, and indirectly, on most economic transactions.

The juridical institutions

The juridical institutions are necessary to fill the gaps of the political institutions, for example, when interpreting laws and regulations; they also contribute to render certain procedures more rigid in order to avoid too much flexibility, for example in matters that may involve ethics. The decisions made by the juridical institutions are categorical and universal.

They address a universal public, and for this reason they are exactly the opposite of informal relations, which depend upon circumstances, the partners involved and may not be consequential.

Table 12.1 summarises the characteristics of the typical decision-making processes that take place in the various institutions examined so far, including the firm and the market.

The cybernetic approach takes for granted the role of public administration, but the comparison of how public administration performs under certain decision-making circumstances shows that it can be totally inadequate for solving problems, with automation or *without*. Specifically:

The costs necessary to reach consensus on certain decisions are largely ignored; it may be that market competition allows for faster generation, implementation and diffusion of solutions.

Planning by the public administration is based on indicators of complex socio-economic phenomena. However, the simplification induced by controlling a system through the use of indicators is often neglected. All indicators are not neutral and can generate unexpected outcomes. Their sheer existence can trigger new behaviours that without the indicator would not take place in the first place. This may affect deeply the effectiveness of any policy based on an indicator. Again, the decentralised decision-making processes that occur in the market, or the more opaque ones that obtain through informal relations, may be quicker to implement and more effective.

The use of political and juridical institutions to affect the economy incurs rigidity and slowness. At the same time, alternative arrangements outside the scope of such non-market institutions tend to be neglected.

Exploring new design alternatives

In conclusion, we can now formulate some design choices that take into account the models of state based on the idea of political exchange, and the interplay of the various socio-economic institutions discussed so far. Specifically, we can set out a strategy for automation of the public sector, considering the various models of administration, and envisage how information technology could support the shift from one model to another.

The minimal state. If the perfect market is not a state of nature and the economics of *laissez faire* is the outcome of a deliberate action of the state, it is also true that the state can limit its own scope of intervention to the provision of public goods, such as defence, leaving to the market and the interplay of individual interests the execution of economic transactions related to goods and services. The application of information technology in such a context should be addressed in general to the improvement of the working of markets, to the reduction of

Table 12.1 *Decision-making processes in the main socio-economic institutions*

Institution	Response time	Cost	Adaptability	Knowledge required	Separability	Degree of proceduralisation	Sequentiality
Informal relations	short/long	low	high	informal, idiosyncratic	low	low	medium/high
Market	short	low	high	standardised	low	low	low
Firm	medium	medium	partial	procedural	medium	medium	medium
Team	short	medium/low	high	informal	low	low	medium/high
Political organisations	long	high	low	consensus and persuasion	high	high	high
Legal institution	very long	very high	very low	formal and highly articulated	very high	very high	very high

market failures so as to limit further the intervention of the state. The mediating technology would represent an infrastructure, a collective good which is made available by the state to increase the transparency of markets. For example, an application would play the same role as printing money, namely to decrease transaction costs. Most universal services would be deeply reformed through the establishment of private mass electronic markets and personalised markets (see ch. 5).

The pluralist state. As mentioned above, this is a more frequent occurrence where the public administration has lost its role of distant, or non-selective entity towards the pressures coming from the market and from society. The pluralist state, instead, has a discriminating attitude and addresses legislative activity in order to meet specific interests and pressures. As a consequence, the market functioning may be altered, while the state broadens its scope of intervention as a supplier of services and favours, often in competition with or as substitution for the market. However, such a quantitative extension goes along with the qualitative degradation of the service provided to the entire community because of the limitation of resources (degraded universal services). Information technology can hardly modify such a situation. Its introduction and application is threatened by two factors: one is the proto-bureaucratisation of the internal structures of the apparatus; the other is the fragmentation of the pressures of the various groups. What will emerge will be an automation 'in bits' of a universal service. This reflects the pasted-up nature of the administration and of the knowledge the agents apply within the bureaucratic structure and in the economy (Hayek, 1945).

Starting from the pluralist state and its automation 'in bits', what are the design alternatives that can be available and realistic? From such a departure point, it is possible either to go back to a minimal-state situation supported by the mediating technology, or to move towards the planning state. The two alternatives have different costs and benefits. Moving towards the minimal state can take place, first of all, through effective and widespread deregulation and privatisation policies, especially aimed at those sectors where the market proves to be a viable alternative.

Those services which are collective goods will always be provided by the state, but may be under a different form. For example, one possibility is that the state acts as a collective mediator, that is, as an agency that operates on the market in competition with private structures. The state takes upon itself a role of intermediary entrepreneur able to identify unfulfilled needs and combine goods and services bought on the market from private suppliers in order to enact new markets for collective services, always in competition with other institutions. As an intermediary entrepreneur, the state will not be sheltered from feedback regarding its performance in satisfying people's needs.

On the contrary, it will have to stay in touch with the evolution of such needs, if it wants to survive on the market for those services it provides. Information technology can act here as a mediating technology to support the collective mediator, for example by rapidly gathering dispersed needs, so that standardised service can be tailored *ad hoc* through flexible coordination (Stone, 1980); for example, the mediating technology could support public reservation systems for multiple private rides, as an alternative to public transportation, which can be more flexible and be provided at market price. This design tack, then, envisages the introduction of computers in a socio-economic context, where the scope for the market has been broadened, the role of the public administration has been reduced and changed so as to make it able to operate directly on the market. Computer applications shift accordingly from planning and control procedures to network-based market-support systems (see ch. 5).

The second alternative consists in moving towards the planning state. The difficulties of such a move have already been listed above. It requires a detailed forecast of the general laws that the state can propose; their implementation, then, needs a high degree of consensus and sense of justice. Also, public administration must be able to overcome the limits posed by bounded rationality (see ch. 1), trying to develop and implement socio-economic programmes almost in real time. The controllability of the socio-economic environment, which is the basis of an effective planning policy, seems to depend, however, more upon a high level of justice than on the level of welfare.

In other words, the welfare state as a regulating system of the economy requires a high degree of trust and justice so that the collective goods that are generated by planning interventions do not become objects of free riding by individuals or interest groups. The other major issue is the fragmentation of social knowledge that is a threat to any central planning endeavour. On both of these issues, justice and fragmentation of knowledge, the mediating technology may not have a significant direct impact.

In sum, whilst under the present circumstances in Western societies, the minimal state supported by the mediating technologies and roles, may have chances to take off as a new way to automate, and change, public administration, the adoption of a planning state where computers are put to the service of planning activity seems to be more difficult to achieve. Table 12.2 summarises the problems that are faced by the various design alternatives compared with the present situation in public administration.

Table 12.2 IT strategies for the public administration

Actual model of state	Model of state that drives the introduction of IT		
	Minimal state	Pluralist state	Planning state
Minimal state	computerised minimal state	computerisation in bits	computers cannot support adequately universal services
Pluralist state	deregulation, middlemen and electronic markets	departmentalised computerisation	proliferation of computer based applications
Planning state	deregulation, middlemen and electronic markets	partial deregulation and computerisation	computerised welfare state

Conclusion

The developments outlined in the Introduction concerning technology and industrial organisation will result in the empowerment of the end user, to the point where he/she will be able to design complex socio-technical systems to cope with new and challenging tasks. Such socio-technical systems include decentralised organisations spanning different industries and the boundaries between the public and private sectors. Federations of small firms, alliances between competitors, and consortia are just a few examples of how these organisations may look. Their information systems will be highly distributed, allowing them to share images, beside text, data and voice. The continuous re-engineering of socio-technical systems will be allowed by the enhanced self-programming capacity of people and systems. As a consequence, management will be more and more engaged in a sort of high-tech, powerful form of tinkering with the capabilities, technologies and organisational mechanisms at hand. Such tinkering, or *bricolage*, given the power of the tools available, will acquire a broader scope, so that in designing the socio-technical systems of the future, tactical and strategic considerations will intermingle, as suggested in chapter 9.

In this book we have provided two important elements for improving and supporting such high-tech *bricolage*. First, we have analysed in detail the structure and function of two important components of the Lego that will constitute the organisation of the future: teams and markets. We have discussed them as ideal models that can be found in many arrangements very popular today in the management literature, ranging from the Japanese models of operations and quality control to the functioning of the price system in the economy. We have shown their applicability as generic control mechanisms (Ouchi, 1979) that can both complement and replace the traditional hierarchy.

Furthermore, we have shown the logic embedded in their respective information systems, suggesting that the re-engineering of an organisation to solve a given problem or execute a complex task should amount to combining these three fundamental forms, the hierarchy, the market and the team.

The design includes elements of tinkering, that is, prototyping, but also a serious analysis of what are the prevailing mechanisms adopted to solve today that task, their transaction costs and possible, more efficient alternatives. The design of any kind of information system should be carried out on the basis of such an organisational analysis: the role of information technology should be tested both conceptually and practically (Newman, 1980) as a means of decreasing the relevant transaction costs in a given organisational context and/or as a means of making the existing organisational mix shift to a new, more efficient one.

Seeing organisations as networks of transactions helps us understand also the contractual nature of this *bricolage* exercise, the need to involve the user, and more generally to set up a web of contracts able to foster the technological and organisational process of change.

We have emphasised, however, that no matter how carefully systems and organisations are designed, they possess an open and indeterminate nature. Users can always re-invent the systems we offer them by applying their ingenuity and autonomy: local, situated developments are bound to unfold further once the new systems are in place. Why, then, is the focus of this book on a specific theory of organisations based on the New Institutional Economics (Williamson, 1975)?

As John Seely Brown has recently suggested, the development and introduction of new technologies are influenced by a dialectics, or, as mentioned in the Introduction, a dance, between *bricolage* and backbone, fluctuations and plans: one conditions and at the same time enhances and supports the other, if deployed flexibly (Brown, 1991).

For us the backbone is provided by the transaction-costs approach, a robust theory of organisations and of the ways people in business organisations use, produce and communicate data, information and knowledge. The design of information systems, whether carried out according to structured methodologies, participative approaches or prototyping, must rely on such a backbone, otherwise it may easily fail. We submit that most of the current systems-development approaches, especially those concerned with the analysis of users' requirements, are based on very schematic, if not poor and outdated, theories of organisation. In fact, the problem with many structured design methodologies is that they do not contain any 'backbone theory' of organisations. Their concern with data flows often hides reliance on models of organisations based on the presumption of unlimited rationality of the agents. Excessive passion for decision support, expert and executive information systems often leads them to neglect the collective and interdependent nature of organisational decision making, and the role of information and knowledge in influencing such inter-dependence.

The transaction-costs approach helps the designer or user to understand the functioning of fundamental organisational forms and the logic of their relevant information systems, and provides him/her with the rules and criteria according to which these mechanisms can be recombined and supported by an advanced technological infrastructure. The models are powerful enough to help the designers and users to avoid the most common mistakes and illusions when applying new powerful technologies.

In Part II we have seen the possibilities of application of the transaction-costs approach to various phases of the system life cycle, and we have tested the usefulness of the economic concepts in tackling under a new light issues such as information-requirements analysis, centralising or decentralising information systems, the economic evaluation and design of strategic information systems. To be sure, the exploration has not been exhaustive. The field is still very much open to research and further contributions on the same, or new areas (Ciborra, 1987c). A promising venue today seems to be the development of tools that contain more intelligence in organisation design, by embedding rudimentary concepts and rules of transaction-costs economics. Such tools could also support the specification and the joint design of organisational structures and information systems for strategic applications. Finally, the approach seems to be flexible enough to accommodate the development of new organisations and information systems in those nations that are undergoing transition to a market economy, while inevitably retaining both team-like and bureaucratic elements of the past such as solidarity and universal services.

References

Ackoff, R. L. 1967. Management misinformation systems. *Management Science* 14 (4), 147–56.

Adair, J. 1986. *Effective Teambuilding*. Aldershot: Gower.

Akerlof, G. 1970. The market for lemons: quality uncertainty and the market mechanism. *Quarterly Journal of Economics* 89, 488–500.

Alchian, A. A., and H. Demsetz 1972. Production, information costs and economic organization. *American Economic Review* 62, 5 (December), 777–95.

Allen, T. J. 1977. *Managing the Flow of Technology*. Cambridge, Mass.: MIT Press.

Ansa, 1989. *The Ansa Reference Manual*. Cambridge: Architecture Projects Management.

Antonelli, C. 1981. Transborder data flows and international business – a pilot study. OECD report DSTI/ICCP/81.16, (June). Paris: OECD.

(ed.) 1988. *New Information Technology and Industrial Change: the Italian Case*. Dordrecht: Kluwer.

Aoki, M. 1988. *Information Incentives, and Bargaining in the Japanese Economy*. Cambridge: Cambridge University Press.

Argyris, C. 1982. *Reasoning, Learning, and Action*. San Francisco: Jossey-Bass.

1985. *Strategy, Change and Defensive Routines*. Boston, Mass.: Pitman.

Argyris, C., and D. Schön 1978. *Organizational Learning*. Reading, Mass.: Addison-Wesley.

Argyris, C., R. Putnam and D. Smith 1985. *Action Science*. San Francisco: Jossey-Bass.

Arrow, K. J. 1974. *The Limits of Organization*. New York: W. W. Norton.

Ashby, W. R. 1966. *Design for a Brain*. London: Science Paperbacks.

Bain, J. S. 1968. *Industrial Organization*, 2nd edn. New York: Wiley.

Bakos, J. Y., and M. E. Treacy 1986. Information technology and corporate strategy: a research perspective. *MIS Quarterly* (June), 107–19.

Baligh, H. H., and L. E. Richartz 1967. *Vertical Market Structures*. Boston, Mass.: Allyn and Bacon.

Barney, J. B. 1985. Types of competition and the theory of strategy: toward an integrative framework. Manuscript, UCLA (spring).

1986. Organizational culture: can it be a source of sustained competitive advantage? *Academy of Management Review* 11 (3), 656–65.

Barth, F. 1981. *Process and Form in Social Life*. London: Routledge and Kegan Paul.

Bateson, G. 1972. *Steps to an Ecology of Mind*. New York: Ballantine.

Beath, C. M. 1987. Managing the user relationship in information systems development projects: a transaction governance approach. *Proceedings ICIS Conference, Pittsburgh, Pa.* (December), 415–26.

Beath, C. and B. Ives 1986. Competitive information systems in support of pricing. *MIS Quarterly* 110, 1 (March), 85–96.

Beeby, W. D. 1983. The heart of integration: a sound data base. *IEEE Spectrum* 20 (5), 44–8.

Benjamin, R. I. 1982. Information technology in the 1990s: a long range planning scenario. *MIS quarterly* 6 (June), 11–31.

1992. Critical IT issues: the next ten years. *Sloan Management Review* (summer), 7–19.

Benson, I. and J. Lloyd 1983. *New Technology and Industrial Change: Labour and the Scientific–Technical Revolution*. London: Kogan Page, New York: Nichols.

Benson, I., C. Ciborra and S. Proffitt 1990. Some social and economic consequences of groupware for flight crew. *Proceedings CSCW '90* (October) 119–29. New York: ACM.

Best, M. 1990. *The New Competition–Institutions of Industrial Restructuring*. Cambridge, Mass.: Harvard University Press.

Bikson, T. K., J. D. Goodchilds, L. Huddy, J. D. Eveland and S. Schneider 1991. *Networked Information Technology and the Transition to Retirement*. Santa Monica, Calif.: RAND.

Bion, W. 1961. *Experiences in Groups and Other Papers*. London: Tavistock.

Bittner, E. 1965. The concept of organisation. *Social Research* 32 (3), 239–55.

Bostrom, R. P. and J. S. Heinen 1977. MIS problems and failures: a sociotechnical perspective. *MIS Quarterly* (December), 11–28.

Brandt, G., B. Kunding, V. Papadimitriou and J. Thomae 1978. *Computer und Arbeitsprozess*. Frankfurt: Campus.

Bravermann, H. 1974. *Labor and Monopoly Capital*. New York: Monthly Review Press.

Briefs, U., C. Ciborra and L. Schneider (eds.) 1984. *Systems Design for, with and by the Users*. Amsterdam: North-Holland.

Bright, J. R. 1958. *Automation and Management*. Boston, Mass.: Harvard University Press.

Brooks, F. P. 1982. *The Mythical Man – Month*. Reading, Mass.: Addison-Wesley.

Brooks, H. 1981. Science, technology and society in the 1980s. In *Science and Technology Policy for the 80s*. Paris: OECD.

Brousseau, E. 1991. Les Contracts dans une économie d'échange et de production. PhD thesis, University Paris-Nord.

Brown, J. S. 1991. Research that reinvents the corporation. *Harvard Business Review* (January–February), 102–11.

Brown, J. S. and P. Duguid 1991. Organizational learning and communities-of-practice: toward a unified view of working, learning and innovation. *Organization Science*, 2, 1 (February), 40–57.

Brynjolfsson, E., T. W. Malone, V. Gurbaxani and A. Kambil 1989. Does information technology lead to smaller firms? Manuscript, MIT, Center for Coordination Science.

Bucci, G. and D. N. Streeter 1979. A methodology for the design of distributed information systems. *Communications of the ACM* 22, 233–45.

Burnstine, D. 1980. The theory behind BIAIT. *Proceedings of the Annual Conference of ACM*. Nashville, Tenn. New York: ACM.

Cash, J. I. and B. Konsynski 1985. IS redraws competitive boundaries. *Harvard Business Review* 63, 2 (March–April), 134–42.

Censis 1985. *Gestione dell'informazione e nuova informatica nella pubblica amministrazione*. Milan: Franco Angeli.

Ceri, S. and G. Pelagatti 1984. *Distributed Databases: Principles and Systems*. New York: McGraw-Hill.

Chamberlin, E. H. 1933. *The Theory of Monopolistic Competition*. Cambridge, Mass.: Harvard University Press.

Chandler, A.D. 1978. *The Visible Hand*. Cambridge, Mass.: Harvard University Press.

Chen, P. P. 1977. The entity-relationship model – a basis for the enterprise view of data. *AFIPS Conference Proceedings* 46, 77–84.

Ciborra, C. U. 1981. Information systems and transactions architecture. *International Journal of Policy Analysis and Information Systems* 5 (4), 305–24.

1983. Markets, bureaucracies and groups in the information society. *Information Economics and Policy* 1, 145–60.

1987a. Reframing the role of computers in organizations – the transaction costs approach. *Office, Technology and People* 3, 17–38.

1987b. Management information systems: a contractual view. In R. Galliers (ed.) *Information Analysis*. Reading, Mass.: Addison-Wesley.

1987c. Research agenda for a transaction costs approach to information systems. In R. J. Boland and R. A. Hirschheim (eds.) *Critical Issues in Information Systems Research*. New York: Wiley.

1991. Alliances as learning experiments: cooperation, competition and change in high-tech industries. In L. Mytelka (ed.) *Strategic Partnerships and the World Economy*. London: Pinter.

1992. Technological change in the workplace. In B. Oscarsson and J. E. Thurman (eds.) *On Business and Work: Towards New Frontiers*. Geneva: ILO.

Ciborra, C. U., P. Migliarese and P. Romano 1984. A methodological inquiry into organizational noise in socio-technical systems. *Human Relations* 37 (8), 565–88.

Ciborra, C. U. and G. F. Lanzara, 1989. Change and formative contexts in information systems development. In H. K. Klein and K. Kumar (eds.) *Systems Development for Human Progress*, Amsterdam: North Holland. 21–40.

1990. Designing dynamic artifacts: computer systems as formative contexts. In P.

Gagliardi (ed.), *Symbols and Artifacts: Views of the Corporate Landscape,* Berlin: De Gruyter.

Ciborra C. U. and Olson, M. H. 1989. Encountering electronic work groups. *Office, Automation and People* 4 (4) 285–98.

Ciborra, C. U. and C. Roveda 1981. Impact of information technology upon organizational structures. In *Microelectronics, Productivity and Employment.* Paris: OECD–ICCP.

Ciborra, C. U. and L. Schneider 1992. Transforming the routines and contexts of management, work and technology. In P. S. Adler (ed.) *The Future of Work.* Oxford: Oxford University Press.

Clemons, E. K. 1986. Information systems for sustainable competitive advantage. *Information and Management* (November), 131–6.

1991. Evaluation of strategic investments in information technology. *Communications of the ACM* 34, 1 (January), 23–36.

Clemons, E. K. and M. Row 1988. McKesson Drug Company: a case study of Economost – a strategic information system. *Journal of Management Information Systems* 5, 1 (Summer), 36–50.

Coase, R. 1937. The nature of the firm. *Economica* (November), 387–405

1960. The problem of social cost. *Journal of Law and Economics* 15 (1), 1–44.

Cohen, P. R. and C. R. Perrault 1979. Elements of a plan-based theory of speech acts. *Cognitive Science* 3, 177–212.

Copeland, D. G. and J. L. McKenney 1988. Airline reservation systems: lessons from history. *MIS Quarterly* 12, 3 (September): 353–70.

Couger, J. D., M. A. Colter and R. W. Knapp 1982. *Advanced System Development/ Feasibility Techniques.* New York: Wiley.

Crozier, M. 1983. Implications for the organization. In H. J. Otway and M. Peltu (eds.) *New Office Technology.* London: Frances Pinter.

Cyert, R. M. and J. G. March 1963. *A Behavioural Theory of the Firm.* Englewood Cliffs, N.J.: Prentice Hall.

Dahlam, C. J. 1979. The problem of externality. *Journal of Law and Economics* 22, 141–62.

Dahlbom, B. and L. Mathiassen 1991. *Struggling with Quality: the Philosophy of Developing Computer Systems.* Report 4, Department of Computer Sciences, University of Gœteborg.

Davenport, R. A. 1979. Data analysis – experience with a formal methodology. In P. A. Samet *EURO IFIP 79 (Proceedings of the European Conference on Applied Information Technology of the International Federation for Information Processing) London, 25–8 September, 1979,* Amsterdam: North Holland.

Davis, G. B. 1982. Strategies for information requirements determination. *IBM Systems Journal* 21 (6), 4–30.

Davis, G. B. and M. C. Munro 1977. Determining management information needs: a comparison of methods. *MIS Quarterly* (June), 55–66.

De Cindio F., G. De Michelis, C. Simone, R. Vassallo and A. Zaboni 1986. *CHAOS as Coordination Technology. Proceedings of the First Conference of Computer Supported Group Work. December 1986.* New York: ACM.

De Michelis, G. 1989. Le tecnologie dell'informazione e della comunicazione a supporto degli accordi di cooperazione tra imprese. In *Tecnologie dell'Informazione e Accordi tra Imprese*. Milano: Edizioni Comunità.

De Sanctis, G. and B. R. Gallupe 1985. Group decision support systems: a new frontier. *Data Base* Winter, 3–10.

1987. A foundation for the study of group decision support systems. *Management Science* 33, 5 (May), 589–609.

Demsetz, H. 1967. Towards a theory of property rights. *American Economic Review* 57 (2), 347–59.

Demski, J. S. 1980. *Information Analysis*, 2nd edn. Reading, Mass.: Addison-Wesley.

Douglas, M. 1986. *How Institutions Think*. Syracuse: Syracuse University Press.

Egan, B. L. 1991. *Information Superhighways: the Economics of an Advanced Public Communication Networks*. Boston, Mass.: Artech House.

Ellis, C. A., S. J. Gibbs and G. L. Rein 1991. Groupware: some issues and experiences. *Communications of the ACM* 34, 1 (January), 39–58.

Elster, J. 1979. *Ulysses and the Syrens*. Cambridge: Cambridge University Press.

Emery, F. E. 1972. Characteristics of socio-technical systems. In L. E. Davis and J. C. Taylor (eds.) *Design of Jobs*. Harmondsworth: Penguin.

1978. *The Fifth Kondradrieff Wave*. Canberra: Centre for Continuing Education, ANU.

Emery, F. E. and E. L. Trist, 1960. Socio-technical systems. In C. Churchman and M. Verhulst (eds.) *Management Sciences, Models and Technique*. London: Pergamon.

Emery, J. C. 1969. *Organizational Planning and Control Systems Theory and Technology*. New York: Macmillan.

1977. Managerial and economic issues in distributes computing. In B. Gilchrist (ed.) *Informationn Processing 77*. Amsterdam: North-Holland.

Etzioni, A. 1972. Minerva: an electronic town hall. *Policy Sciences* 3, 457–74.

Evans, J. 1982. Negotiating technological change. ETUI, Brussels.

Feeny, D. and B. Ives 1990. In search of sustainability, *Journal of Management Information Systems*, 7, 1 (Summer), 27–46.

Feldman, M. S. and J. G. March 1981. Information in organizations as signal and symbol. *Administrative Science Quarterly* 26, 2 (June), 171–86.

Festinger, L. 1957. *A Theory of Cognitive Dissonance*. New York: Harper and Row.

Fiol, C. M. and M. A. Lyles 1985. Organizational learning. *Academy of Management Review* 10 (4), 803–13.

Flores, F. and J. J. Ludlow 1981. Doing and speaking in the office. In G. Fish and R. Sprague (eds.) *DSS: Issues and Challenges*. London: Pergamon Press.

Francis, A. 1986. *New Technology at Work*. Oxford: Clarendon Press.

Gagliardi, P. (ed.) 1990. *Symbols and Artifacts: Views of the Corporate Landscape*. Berlin: de Gruyter.

Galbraith, J. R. 1977. *Organization Design*. Reading, Mass.: Addison-Wesley.

Galeghen, J., R. E. Kraut and C. Egido (ed.) 1990. *Intellectual Teamwork: the Social and Technological Foundations of Cooperative Work*. New York: Lawrence Erlbaum.

Galloudec-Genuys, F. 1980. *Une Informatique pour les administrés?* Paris: La Documentation Française.

Gasser, L. 1986. The integration of computing and routine work. *ACM Transactions on Office Information Systems* 4, 3 (July): 205–25.

Gershuny, J. 1978. *After Industrial Society? The Emerging Self-Service Economy.* London: Mcmillan.

Gordon, P. 1989. *La Place du marché.* Paris: La Documentation Française.

Gorry, G. A. and Scott-Morton, M. S. 1971. A framework for management information systems. *Sloan Management Review* 13 (1), 55–70.

Greif, I. (ed.) 1988. *Computer Supported Cooperative Work: a Book of Readings.* San Mateo, Calif.: Morgan Kaufmann.

Greiner, R. and G. Metes 1992. *Enterprise Networking – Working Together Apart.* Boston, Mass.: Digital Press.

Gulick, L. and L. Urwick (eds.) 1937. *Papers on the Science of Administration.* New York: Institute of Public Administration.

Gurbaxani, V. and S. Whang 1991. The impact of information systems on organizations and markets. *Communications of the ACM* 34, 1 (January): 59–73.

Hackman J. R. 1986. Group level issues in the design and training of cockpit crews. In I. W. Orlady and I. I. Clayton Foushee (eds.) *Cockpit Resource Management Training.* NASA Conference Publication.

Hahm, W. and T. K. Bikson 1988. Retirees using e-mail and networked computers. *International Journal of Technology and Aging* 2 (2), 113–23.

Hartley, K. and C. Tisdell 1981. *Micro-Economic Policy.* New York: John Wiley.

Hayek, F. A. 1945. The use of knowledge in society. *American Economic Review* (September), 519–30.

Hedberg, B. and Jonsson, S. 1978. Designing semi-confusing information systems for organizations in changing environments. *Accounting, Organizations and Society* 3 (1), 47–64.

Heiner, R. 1983. The origin of predictable behavior. *American Economic Review* 73, 560–95.

Henderson, J. C. and N. Venkatraman 1989. Strategic alignment: a process model for integrating information technology and business strategies. *Sloan-MIT Wp* 30, 86–9.

Herbst, P. G. 1962. *Autonomous Group Functioning* London: Tavistock.

1976. *Alternatives to Hierarchies.* Leiden: Martinus Nijhoff.

Hess, J. D. 1983. *The Economics of Organization.* Amsterdam: North-Holland.

Hewitt, C. and P. De Jong 1984. Open systems. In M. L. Brodie, J. Mylopulos and J. W. Schmidt (eds.) *On Conceptual Modeling,* New York: Springer.

Hirschleifer, J. 1980. *Price Theory and Applications,* 2nd edn. Englewood Cliffs, N.J.: Prentice-Hall.

Hirschman, A. O. 1970. *Exit, Voice, and Loyalty.* Cambridge, Mass.: Harvard University Press.

Hopper, M. D. 1990. Rattling SABRE – new ways to compete on information. *Harvard Business Review* 68, 3 (May–June), 118–25.

Huber, G. P. 1984. The nature and design of post-industrial organizations. *Management Science* 30 (8), 928–51.

Itami, H. 1987. *Mobilizing Invisible Assets.* Cambridge, Mass.: Harvard University Press.

Ives, B. and G. Learmonth 1984. The information system as a competitive weapon. *Communications of the ACM* 27, 123 (December), 1193–201.

Ives, B. and R. O. Mason 1989. Can information technology revitalize your customer service? Manuscript, Southern Methodist University, Dallas.

Jackson, B. B. 1985. *Winning and Keeping Industrial Customers.* Lexington, Mass.: Lexington Books.

Janis, I. L. 1972. *Victims of Groupthink.* Boston, Mass.: Houghton Mifflin.

Jensen, M. C. and W. H. Meckling 1973. Theory of the firm: managerial behavior, agency costs and ownership structure. *Journal of Financial Economics* 3 (October), 305–60.

Johansen, R. 1988. *Groupware – Computer Support for Business Teams.* New York: The Free Press.

Johnston, H. R. and M. R. Vitale 1988. Creating competitive advantage with interorganizational information systems. *MIS Quarterly* (June), 153–65.

Jonscher, C. 1980. A theory of economic organization. PhD thesis, Department of Economics, Harvard University, Cambridge, Mass.

Kahnemann, D. and A. Tversky 1973. On the psychology of prediction. *Psychological Review* 80 (4), 237–51.

Keen, P. G. W. 1981. Information systems and organizational change. *Communications of the ACM* 24 (1), 24–33.

1991. *Shaping the Future – Business Design Through Information Technology.* Boston, Mass.: Harvard Business School Press.

Keen, P. G. W. and M. S. Scott Morton 1978. *Decision Support Systems: an Organizational Perspective.* Reading, Mass.: Addison-Wesley.

Kelly, J. E. 1982. *Scientific Management, Job Redesign and Work Performance.* London: Academic Press.

Knight, F. H. 1921. *Risk, Uncertainty and Profit.* Boston, Mass.: Houghton Mifflin.

Kreps, D. M. 1990. *A Course in Microeconomic Theory.* New York: Harvester Wheatsheaf.

Kriebel, C. H. and J. H. Moore 1980. Economics and management information systems. In E. R. McLean (ed.) *Proceedings of the 1st Conference on Information Systems,* 19–31 New York: ACM.

Lanzara, G. F. and L. Mathiassen 1985. Mapping situations within a systems development project. *Information and Management* 8, 3–20.

Lee, R. M. 1980. Candid: a logical calculus for describing financial contracts. PhD dissertation, The Wharton School, University of Pennsylvania.

Lemoine, P. 1980. Informatisation and economic development. OECD report, DSTI/ICCP/80.17. Paris: OECD.

Levitt, B. and J. G. March 1988. Organizational learning. *Annual Review of Sociology* 14, 319–40.

Lewin, K. 1936. *Principles of Topological Psychology.* New York: McGraw-Hill. 1947. Frontiers in group dynamics. *Human Relations* 1, 5–41.

McFarlan, W. F. 1984. Information technology changes the way you compete. *Harvard Business Review* 62, 3 (May–June), 98–103.

McFarlan, W. F. and J. L. McKenney 1983. *Corporate Information Systems Management.* Homewood, Ill.: Richard D. Irwin.

McKenney, J. L. and W. F. McFarlan 1982. The information archipelago – maps and bridges. *Harvard Business Review* 60, 5 (September–October): 109–19.

Malone, T. W., R. I. Benjamin and J. Yates 1987. Electronic markets and electronic hierarchies. *Communications of the ACM* 30, 484–97.

Malone, T. W. and K. Crowston 1990. What is coordination theory and how can it help design cooperative work systems? In *Proceedings of the Third Conference on Computer-Supported Cooperative Work*, Los Angeles, October 1990, New York: ACM.

March, J. G. and H. A. Simon 1958. *Organizations.* New York: Wiley.

Marchand, M. 1987. *Les Paradis informationels.* Paris: Masson.

Markus, L. and D. Robey 1988. Information technology and organizational change: casual structure in theory and research. *Management Science* 34, 5 (May), 583–98.

Markus, M. L. 1983. Power, politics and MIS implementation. *Communications of the ACM* 26 (6), 430–44.

Marschak, J. and R. Radner 1972. *Economic Theory of Teams.* New Haven, Conn.: Yale University Press.

Masuch, M. 1985. Vicious circles in organizations. *Administrative Science Quarterly* 30 (March), 14–33.

Mathis, A. 1988. Enea: progetto telematica per l'area tessile di Prato. *Media 2000*, 49 (January), 86–95.

Mayo, E. 1933. *The Human Problems of an Industrial Civilization.* New York: Macmillan.

Medina-Mora R., T. Winograd, R. Flores and F. Flores. The Action workflow approach to workflow management technology, *Proceedings CSCW '92* (November). New York: ACM. 281–8.

Meissner, M. 1969. *Technology and the Worker: Technical Demands and Social Processes in Industry.* San Francisco: Chandler.

Minsky, M. 1975. A framework for representing knowledge. In P. H. Winston (ed.) *The Psychology of Computer Vision.* New York: McGraw-Hill.

Mintzberg, H. 1990. The design school: reconsidering the basic premises of strategic management. *Strategic Management Journal* 11, 171–95.

Mortara, V. 1984. Prime impressioni sul rapporto Formez relativo all'organizzazione ed il funzionamento delle amministrazioni centrali dello stato. *Il Nuovo Governo Locale* 2 (2), 21–38.

Mumford, E. A. 1979. *Participative Approach to Computer Systems Design.* London: Associated Business Press.

1983. Successful systems design. In H. J. Otway and M. Peltu (eds.) *New Office Technology.* London: Frances Pinter.

Nelson, R. R. and S. G. Winter 1982. *An Evolutionary Theory of Economic Change.* Cambridge, Mass.: Harvard University Press.

Newman, W. 1980. Office models and office systems design. In N. Naffah (ed.)

Integrated Office Systems – Burotics. Amsterdam: North-Holland.

Nisbett, R. and L. Ross 1980. *Human Inference: Strategies and Shortcomings of Social Judgement.* Englewood Cliffs, N.J.: Prentice Hall.

Nolan, R. L. and M. MacFarlan 1974. Effective edp project management. In R. Nolan (ed.) *Managing the Data Resource Function.* St Paul, Minn.: West Publishing.

Nonaka, I. 1988. Toward middle–up–down management: accelerating information creation. *Sloan Management Review* 29, 3 (Spring), 9–18.

1991. The knowledge creating corporation. *Harvard Business Review* 69, 6 (November–December), 96–104.

Nonaka, I. and T. Yamanouchi 1989. Managing innovation as a self-renewing process. *Journal of Business Venturing* 4, 299–315.

Nora, S. and A. Minc 1980. *L'Informatisation de la société.* Paris: La Documentation Française, 1978; American translation, Cambridge, Mass.: MIT Press.

Norman, D. A. 1983. Some observations on mental models. In D. Gentner and A. L. Stevens (eds.) *Mental Models.* Hillsdale, N.J.: Lawrence Erlbaum.

Nygaard, K. 1983. Participation in system development: the task ahead. In U. Briefs, C. Ciborra and L. Schneider (eds.) *Systems Design for, with and by the Users.* Amsterdam: North Holland.

Nygaard, K. and O. T. Bergo 1975. The trade unions, new users of research. *Personnel Review* 4 (2), 32–7.

Okun, A. 1981. *Prices and Quantities.* Oxford: Basil Blackwell.

Olson, M. 1965. *The Logic of Collective Action.* Cambridge, Mass.: Harvard University Press.

Olson, M. H. 1981. Remote office work: implications for individuals and organization (CRIS working paper no. 25). Graduate School of Business Administration, New York University.

1983. Remote office work: changing work patterns in space and time. *Communications of the ACM* 26 (3), 182–7.

Ouchi, W. G. 1979. A conceptual framework for the design of organizational control mechanisms. *Management Science* 25, 833–48.

1980. Markets, bureaucracies and clans. *Administrative Science Quarterly* 25 (March), 120–42.

1981. *Theory Z.* Reading, Mass.: Addison-Wesley.

Pava, C. 1982. Microelectronics and the design of organization. Working paper, Division of Research, Graduate School of Business Administration, Harvard University, Cambridge, Mass.

Peebles, R. and E. Manning 1979. System architecture for distributed data management. In Wesley W. Chu and Peter P. Chen (eds.) *Centralised and Distributed Data Base Systems.* New York: IEEE.

Phlips, L. 1988. *The Economics of Imperfect Information.* Cambridge: Cambridge University Press.

Piaget, J. 1974. *Understanding Causality.* New York: Norton.

Piore, M. and C. F. Sabel 1984. *The Second Industrial Divide.* New York: Basic Books.

Polany, M. 1966. *The Tacit Dimension.* Garden City, N.Y.: Doubleday.

Porat, M. 1977. The information economy: definition and measurement. OT special publication 77–12 (1), US Department of Commerce, Washington, D.C.

1978. Communication policy in an information society. In G. O. Robinson (ed.) *Communications for Tomorrow–Policy Perspectives for the 80s*. New York: Praeger.

Porter, M. E. 1980. *Competitive Strategy*. New York: The Free Press.

Porter, M. E. and V. E. Millar 1985. How information gives you competitive advantage. *Harvard Business Review* 63, 4 (July–August), 149–60.

Prahalad, C. K. and G. Hamel 1990. The core competence of the corporation. *Harvard Business Review* 68, 3 (May–June), 79–93.

Prigogine, I. and I. Stenger 1984. *Order out of Chaos*. New York: Bantam.

Pyke, F., G. Becattini and W. Sengenberger 1990. *Industrial Districts and Inter-firm Co-operation in Italy*., Geneva: ILO.

Radner, R. 1989. Teams. In J. Eatwell, M. Millgate and P. Newman (eds.) *Allocation, Information and Markets*. London: Macmillan.

Ramaprasad, A. 1987. Cognitive process as a basis for MIS and DSS design. *Management Science* 33 (2), 139–48.

Rice, A. K. 1958. *Productivity and Social Organisation*. London: Tavistock.

Rice, R. E. 1980. The impacts of computer-mediated organizational and interpersonal communication. In M. E. Williams (ed.) *Annual Review of Information Science and Technology* 1 (5), 221–49.

Rice, R. E. and E. M. Rogers 1980. Reinvention in the innovation process. *Knowledge* 1, 4 (June), 488–514.

Richman, T. 1987. Mrs. Fields' secret ingredient. *Inc. Magazine* (October), 65–72.

Ricketts, M. 1987. *The Economics of Business Enterprise*. New York: Harvester Wheatsheaf.

Rockart, J. F. 1979. Chief executives define their own data needs. *Harvard Business Review* 57, 2 (May–June), 81–93.

Rodotà, S. 1982. Tecnologie dell'informazione e frontiere del sistema socio-politico. *Politica del Diritto* 13, 1 (March), 25–39.

Rosenberg, N. 1982. *Inside the Black Box: Technology and Economics*. Cambridge: Cambridge University Press.

Rubin, P. H. 1990. *Managing Business Transactions*. New York: Free Press.

Salomon, J. J. 1981. *Prométhée empetré*. Paris: Pergamon Press.

Schank, R. and R. P. Abelson 1977. *Scripts, Plans, Goals and Understanding: an Inquiry into Human Knowledge Structures*. Hillsdale, N.J.: Lawrence Erlbaum.

Schelling, T. C. 1980. *The Strategy of Conflict*, 2nd edn. Cambridge, Mass.: Harvard University Press.

Schneider, L. and C. U. Ciborra. 1983. Technology bargaining in Norway. In U. Briefs, C. U. Ciborra and L. Schneider (eds.) *Systems Design By the Users, With the Users, For the Users*. Amsterdam: North-Holland.

Schneider, V., J. M. Charon, I. Miles, G. Thomas and T. Vedel 1990. The dynamics of videotex development in Britain, France and Germany: a cross-national comparison. Paper presented at the Eighth International Conference of The International Telecommunications Society, Venice, March 1990.

Schön, D. A. 1979. *The Reflective Practioner*. New York: Basic Books.

Schotter, A. 1981. *The Economic Theory of Social Institutions.* Cambridge: Cambridge University Press.

Schumpeter, J. A. 1950. *Capitalism, Socialism, and Democracy* 3rd edn., New York: Harper and Row.

Schutz, A. 1964. *Collected Papers: Studies in Social Theory,* ed. Arvid Brodersen. The Hague: Martinus Nijhoff.

Schutz, A. and T. Luckmann 1973. *The Structures of the Life World.* Evanston, Ill.: Northwestern University Press.

Scott Morton, M. S. 1991. *The Corporation of the 1990s – Information Technology and Organizational Transformation.* Oxford: Oxford University Press.

Searle, J. R. 1969. *Speech Acts: an Essay in the Philosophy of Language.* Cambridge: Cambridge University Press.

Senge, P. 1990. *The Fifth Discipline,* New York: Doubleday Currency.

Sibley, E. H. 1977. The impact of database technology on business systems. In B. Gilchrist (ed.) *Information Processing 77.* Amsterdam: North-Holland.

Simon, H. A. 1976. *Administrative Behavior.* New York: The Free Press.

1977. *The New Science of Management Decision.* Englewood Cliffs, N.J.: Prentice Hall.

1981. *The Sciences of the Artificial.* Cambridge, Mass.: MIT Press.

Smith, A. 1922. *The Wealth of Nations.* London: J. M. Dent.

Sowell, T. 1980. *Knowledge and Decisions.* New York: Basic Books.

Sprague, E. H. 1980. A framework for the development of decision support systems. *MIS Quarterly* 4 (4), 1–24.

Sproull, L. and S. Kiesler 1986. Reducing social context cues: electronic mail in organizational communication. *Management Science* 32 (11): 1492–512.

1991. *Connections: New Ways of Working in the Networked Organization.* Cambridge, Mass.: MIT Press.

Stefik, M., G. Foster, D. G. Bobrow, K. Kahn, S. Lanning and L. Suchman 1987. Beyond the chalkboard: computer support for collaboration and problem solving in meetings. *Communications of the ACM* 30, 1 (January), 32–47.

Steiner, T. D. and D. B. Teixeira 1990. *Technology in Banking.* Homewood, Ill.: Dow Jones-Irwin.

Sternberg, R. J. and R. K. Wagner (eds.) 1986. *Practical Intelligence* Cambridge: Cambridge University Press.

Stigler, G. J. 1961. The economics of information. *Journal of Political Economy* 69, 213–85.

Stone, P. J. 1980. Social evolution and a computer science challenge. *Scientia* 25, 125–46.

Strassmann, P. A. 1985. *Information Payoff – the Transformation of Work in the Electronic Age.* New York: The Free Press.

1990. *The Business Value of Computers – an Executive's Guide.* New Canaan, Ct.: The Information Economics Press.

Strauss, A. 1978. *Negotiations: Varieties, Contexts, Processes and Social Order.* San Francisco: Jossey Bass.

Streeter, D. N. 1973. Centralization or dispersion of computing facilities. *IBM Systems Journal* 12, 283–301.

Suchman, L. A. 1987. *Plans and Situated Actions: the Problem of Human–Machine Communication.* Cambridge: Cambridge University Press.

Suchman, L. A. and E. Wynn, 1984. Procedures and problems in the office. *Office, Technology and People* 2 (2), 133–54.

Sussman, G. 1976. *Autonomy at Work a Socio-technical Analysis of Participative Management.* New York: Praeger.

Takeuchi, H. and I. Nonaka 1986. The new new product development game. *Harvard Business Review* 64, 1 (January–February), 137–46.

Taylor, F. W. 1911. *The Principles of Scientific Management.* New York: Harper.

Thompson, J. D. 1967. *Organizations in Action.* New York: McGraw Hill.

Trist, E. L. 1981. The evolution of socio-technical systems. Occasional Paper, 2 (June). Ontario Quality of Working Life Center.

Trist, E. L. and K. W. Bamforth 1951. Some social and psychological consequences of the longwall method of coal getting. *Human Relations* 1 (4), 13–38.

Trist, E. L., G. W. Higgin, H. Murray and A. B. Pollock 1963. *Organizational Choice.* London: Tavistock.

Turoff, M. and S. R. Hiltz 1982. Computer support for group versus individual decisions. *IEEE Trans. Commun.* 30 (2), 82–91.

Tversky, A. and D. Kahneman 1974. Judgment under uncertainty: heuristics and biases. *Science* 185, 1124–31.

1981. The framing of decisions and the psychology of choice. *Science* 211 (January), 453–8.

Ullman-Margalit, E. 1978. *The Emergence of Norms.* Oxford: Oxford University Press.

Unger, R. M. 1987. *False Necessity.* Cambridge: Cambridge University Press.

Venkatraman, N. and J. E. Short 1990. Strategies for electronic integration: from order-entry to value-added partnerships at Baxter. Manuscript, Sloan School, MIT.

Vepsäläinen, A. 1990. The impact of information technology on corporate strategy. *Proceedings of the Nordic GUIDE,* Rovaniemi (April).

Vepsäläinen, A. and M. Mäkelin 1987. Service-oriented systems and the economics of organizational transactions. *Proceedings of the 10th IRIS Conference,* Vaskivesi (August).

Vitale, M. 1986. The growing risks of information systems success. *MIS Quarterly* 10, 4 (December), 327–34.

Walton, R. E. 1989. *Up and Running – Integrating Information Technology and the Organization.* Boston, Mass.: Harvard Business School Press.

Weber, M. 1947. *The Theory of Social and Economic Organization.* London: William Hodge.

Weick, K. E. 1976. Educational organizations as loosely coupled systems. *Administrative Science Quarterly* 21 (March), 1–19.

1979. *The Social Psychology of Organizing,* 2nd edn. New York: Random House.

Whisler, T. L. 1970. *The Impacts of Computers on Organizations.* New York: Praeger.

Williamson, O. E. 1975. *Markets and Hierarchies: Analysis and Antitrust Implications.* New York: Free Press.

1981. The economics of organization: the transaction costs approach. *American Journal of Sociology* 87 (3), 548–77.

1985. *The Economic Institutions of Capitalism.* New York: Free Press.

Winograd, T. 1986. A language action perspective on the design of cooperative work. *CSCW Conference Proceedings*, Austin, Tex. (December).

Winograd, T. and F. Flores 1986. *Understanding Computers and Cognition: a New Foundation for Design.* Norwood, N.J.: Ablex.

Wiseman, C. 1988. *Strategic Information Systems.* Homewood, Ill.: Irwin.

Woodward, J. 1965. *Industrial Organisation: Theory and Practice.* London: Oxford University Press.

Zimmermann, H. 1980. OSI reference model – the ISO model of architecture for open systems interconnection. *IEEE Transactions on Communications* 28, 4 (April), 425–32.

Zuboff, S. 1988. *In the Age of the Smart Machine.* New York: Basic Books.

Author index

243

Subject index

247